DATA SCIENCE

Using Artificial Intelligence and Machine Learning

DATA SCIENCE

Using Artificial Intelligence and Machine Learning

Dr. Gujjeti Nagaraju

NAMYA PRESS.com

Published by

Namya Press

India: 213, Vardan House, 7/28 Ansari Road Darya Ganj - Delhi India 110002
USA: 10685-B Hazelhurst Dr. # 31013 Houston, Texas USA - 77043
Email: namyapress@gmail.com
Website: https://namyapress.com

Edition	:	First Published in 2024 (Namya Press)
Title	:	Data Science Using Artificial Intelligence and Machine Learning
Author	:	Dr. Gujjeti Nagaraju
ISBN	:	978-93-5545849-0
Copyright	:	© Dr. Gujjeti Nagaraju. 2024 All Rights Reserved

Acknowledgement

Writing a book of this magnitude requires the collaboration and support of many individuals and organizations, without whom this project would not have been possible.

First and foremost, we extend our deepest gratitude to our families for their unwavering support and understanding throughout the countless hours spent researching, writing, and revising this book. Their encouragement has been a constant source of motivation.

We are indebted to our colleagues and mentors whose insights and expertise have enriched the content of this book. Their willingness to share knowledge and engage in discussions has been invaluable.

A special thanks to the reviewers whose constructive feedback and suggestions have significantly improved the clarity and depth of the material presented here.

We would like to acknowledge the publishers and editorial team for their professionalism and guidance throughout the publication process. Their commitment to quality has been instrumental in bringing this project to fruition.

Finally, to the readers of this book, we hope that you find it informative, engaging, and useful in your journey through the fascinating world of data science, artificial intelligence, and machine learning.

Thank you all for being a part of this endeavor.

—Dr. Gujjeti Nagaraju

Preface

In the age of data abundance, our ability to harness information has become paramount. Data science, fueled by artificial intelligence and machine learning, stands at the forefront of this technological revolution. This book is a comprehensive guide designed to equip you with the knowledge and skills needed to navigate this exciting field.

Understanding the Landscape

Data science has evolved from being a niche discipline to a cornerstone of modern business and research. Today, organizations across industries rely on data scientists to extract insights, make informed decisions, and drive innovation. Artificial intelligence and machine learning techniques lie at the heart of these advancements, enabling computers to learn from data and make predictions or decisions.

A Practical Approach

This book takes a hands-on approach to learning. Whether you are a novice or a seasoned data professional, you will find practical examples, case studies, and exercises that will deepen your understanding and sharpen your skills. From foundational concepts to advanced algorithms, each chapter is crafted to build upon the previous one, ensuring a logical progression through the material.

—Dr. Gujjeti Nagaraju

Contents

1

Introduction to Data Science

1.1 OVERVIEW OF DATA SCIENCE

Data science is an interdisciplinary area that extracts knowledge and insights from both structured and unstructured data using scientific procedures, systems, algorithms, and methodologies. It integrates several fields, including computer science, statistics, and domain knowledge, to analyze data and produce useful insights.

Components of Data Science

The subject of data science is multifaceted and contains various essential elements that work together to facilitate the process of deriving valuable insights from data. Here's a closer look at each element:

1. Data collecting

The first stage in thc data science process is data collecting. It entails obtaining information from a range of sources, including external data providers, web scraping, sensors, databases, and surveys. Since they have an immediate effect on the stages of analysis that follow, the quality and applicability of the data acquired are crucial. This stage frequently necessitates a high level of topic expertise to guarantee the data is suitable for the given issue.

2. Data Cleaning

Errors, missing values, and inconsistent data are common features of unprocessed data. In order to get the data ready for analysis, these problems must be fixed. This procedure is called data cleaning, or data pretreatment. Commonly used methods include addressing missing data, eliminating duplicates, fixing data types, and normalizing data distributions. Since clean data improves the quality and dependability of analytical results, effective data cleaning is essential.

3. Data Analysis

Examining, converting, and modeling data in order to find relevant information, make inferences, and aid in decision-making is the process of data analysis. This entails exploratory data analysis (EDA), hypothesis testing, and statistical analysis. EDA summarizes the key features of the data and looks for patterns, anomalies, or trends using quantitative and visual methods. This stage directs the choice of suitable modeling tools and aids in comprehending the fundamental structure of the data.

4. Data Visualization

The graphical depiction of information and conclusions is known as data visualization. The use of visual aids like heatmaps, charts, graphs, and dashboards makes complex data easier to interpret and digest. It is simpler to spot patterns, trends, and connections with effective visualization than it may be with unprocessed data. For this, programs like Matplotlib, Seaborn, Tableau, and Power BI are frequently utilized.

5. Machine Learning

A key element of data science is machine learning (ML), which is teaching algorithms to learn from data and make judgments or predictions without having to be explicitly programmed for a given purpose. ML is separated into:

- **Supervised Learning:** Regression and classification tasks, for example, involve training a model on labeled data with known outcomes.
- **Unsupervised Learning:** Uses unlabeled data to train a model in order to find hidden groupings or patterns (e.g., association and clustering tasks).
- **Reinforcement Learning:** This method involves rewarding desired actions and penalizing undesired ones in order to teach a model to make a series of decisions.

6. Artificial Intelligence (AI)

AI includes more advanced methods than machine learning (ML) that let computers carry out jobs that need human intelligence.

Artificial Intelligence (AI) techniques like computer vision and Natural Language Processing (NLP) improve the capacity to analyze and make use of unstructured data in data science. For instance, computer vision permits the interpretation of visual data such as photographs and videos, while natural language processing (NLP) enables machines to comprehend and produce human language.

Through the integration of these elements, data science enables an all-encompassing methodology for resolving intricate issues, empowering institutions to make data-informed choices and identify novel prospects. Because all the parts work together, from data gathering to AI implementation, the process is seamless and efficient in producing insights that can be put into practice.

The Role of AI and ML in Data Science

Data science's potential is greatly enhanced by the application of machine learning (ML) and artificial intelligence (AI). The basis for automating and improving data processing and analysis is artificial intelligence (AI), which is the creation of systems that are capable of carrying out tasks that ordinarily need human intelligence. Machine Learning, a subset of AI, falls under this wide category and is concerned with creating algorithms that let computers use data to learn from and make judgments. We can go beyond conventional statistical analysis and into predictive and prescriptive analytics by combining AI and ML with data science.

Intricate patterns and linkages in huge datasets that are frequently undetectable to human analysts can be found by machine learning models. With amazing accuracy, these models may be taught to carry out particular tasks including anomaly detection, regression, grouping, and classification. Labeled datasets are necessary for supervised learning algorithms like neural networks, support vector machines, and linear regression to learn from and generate correct predictions or classifications of incoming data.

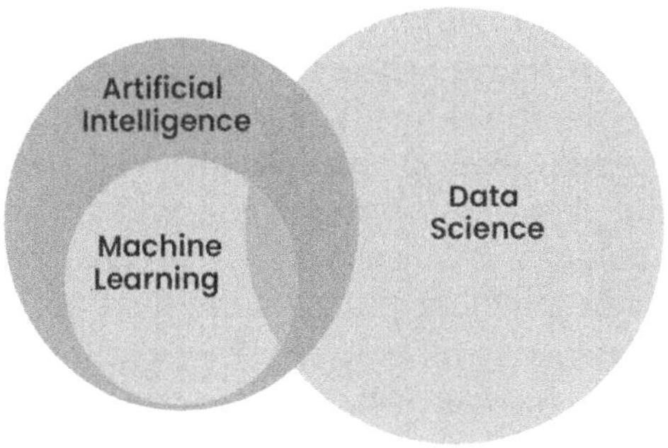

Unsupervised learning methods are used to find hidden patterns or groups within data; these algorithms include principal component analysis and k-means clustering. They do not require labeled data. Another area of machine learning is reinforcement learning, which is especially useful in dynamic contexts where a model must continuously adapt and improve. Reinforcement learning trains models using a system of rewards and punishments.

By enabling the study of unstructured data, AI techniques like Computer Vision and Natural Language Processing (NLP) further broaden the scope of Data Science. Text data from social media, consumer reviews, and other sources can be analyzed thanks to natural language processing (NLP), which makes it feasible to generate and interpret human language. Conversely, computer vision makes it possible to extract valuable information from image and video data, which is helpful in fields like automated surveillance and medical imaging. Using intricate rules and data analysis, expert systemsa conventional AI techniqueprovide intelligent suggestions and decisions that mimic the ability of a human expert to make decisions.

In addition to improving data analysis's efficiency and accuracy, the incorporation of AI and ML into data science creates new opportunities for creativity and learning. By utilizing these technologies, businesses may create predictive models that inform strategic decision-making, automate repetitive operations, and extract more information from their data. Data science will definitely benefit greatly from AI and ML technologies as they develop further, opening up new areas of research and use for the discipline.

Data Science Workflow

The Data Science workflow is a methodical way to addressing data-driven issues and includes a number of essential phases to guarantee the precision and efficacy of the conclusions drawn. Every stage contributes to the process as a whole, building on the one before it to produce a thorough and reliable model.

1. **Problem Definition:** Clearly identifying and defining the business problem that has to be solved is the first stage. In order to establish goals, specify success criteria, and comprehend the environment in which the solution will be used, cooperation with stakeholders is necessary. A precise problem definition aids in providing a clear path for the next actions.
2. **Data Collection:** This step involves gathering pertinent data from multiple sources related to the issue. This can involve

using external APIs, online scraping, internal databases, or buying datasets from other companies. The significance and caliber of the gathered data are vital since they influence the results of the analysis that follows and the functionality of the model.

3. **Data Preprocessing:** After the information is gathered, it needs to be cleaned and made ready for examination. This include dealing with missing numbers, eliminating duplicates, fixing mistakes, and formatting the data appropriately. In order to improve model performance, feature engineeringwhich entails generating new features from preexisting datais also carried out at this point.

4. **Exploratory Data Analysis (EDA):** In this crucial stage, data scientists look for patterns, connections, and abnormalities in the data. To do this, statistical methods and data visualizations like box plots, scatter plots, and histograms are used to extract insights from the data. EDA guides the selection of modeling approaches and aids in comprehending the underlying structure of the data.
5. **Model Building:** Using the preprocessed data, a variety of machine learning methods are performed to create prediction models in this stage. This include choosing the right algorithms, adjusting hyperparameters, and using the training dataset to train the models. In order to make sure the models are not overfitting and can effectively generalize to new data, methods like crossvalidation are employed.
6. **Model Evaluation:** A different test dataset is used to assess the models' performance after they have been built. The models' efficacy is evaluated using measures like ROCAUC, F1score, accuracy, precision, recall, and F1score. In order to finetune and enhance model performance, this stage may entail iterating over the modelbuilding procedure.
7. **Deployment:** A model is put into a production environment after it has been designed and proven to work well. Developing user interfaces for end users to engage with the model or integrating it into alreadyexisting systems are some examples of deployment strategies. Realtime prediction APIs can also be developed. At this point, it is critical to ensure the model's scalability and stability.
8. **Monitoring and Maintenance:** The last phase entails keeping an eye on how well the model is performing in the realworld setting to make sure it stays accurate and applicable. This entails monitoring the model's predictions, updating it with fresh data as it becomes available, and modifying it to take into consideration evolving circumstances or data drift. Frequent upkeep guarantees that the model will remain valuable for a long time.

Each of these processes is iterative and frequently necessitates going back and improving earlier actions in light of fresh information and input. Data scientists may methodically address complex challenges and create reliable, datadriven solutions by adhering to an organized workflow.

Applications of Data Science

Numerous industries have undergone revolutionary changes because to data science, which uses insights from data to provide creative answers to challenging issues. Here are a few thorough uses in different domains:

Healthcare

Data science plays a key role in drug discovery, customized medicine, and predictive analytics in the healthcare industry. By examining past medical data, predictive analytics can predict illness outbreaks, patient readmissions, and even possible epidemics. By customizing therapies to each patient's needs, personalized medicine can improve results and minimize unwanted effects. Machine learning algorithms that identify promising drug candidates speed up the process of finding new drugs and reduce the time and expense of bringing them to market.

Finance

Data science is used by the finance sector for risk management, algorithmic trading, and fraud detection. Fraud detection systems use transaction pattern analysis to spot irregularities and instantly report possible fraud. In order to execute trades at the best moments, optimize returns, and reduce risks, algorithmic trading employs sophisticated algorithms. Risk management is evaluating the possible hazards associated with loans and investments in order to assist financial organizations in making wise decisions and minimizing losses.

Retail

Data science improves recommendation systems, demand forecasting, and customer segmentation in the retail industry. In order to implement focused marketing techniques, customer segmentation entails breaking up the client base into discrete groups according to their preferences, demographics, and purchase patterns. Demand forecasting helps merchants successfully manage inventory and lower the likelihood of stockouts or overstock situations by projecting future product demand. In order to improve customer happiness and revenue, recommendation systems use customer data to offer things that customers are likely to buy.

Manufacturing

Data science is used by the manufacturing sector for supply chain optimization, quality assurance, and predictive maintenance.

By analyzing equipment data, predictive maintenance models can identify potential problems before they arise, saving money on repairs and downtime. Data analytics is used by quality control systems to track production procedures and spot flaws early on, guaranteeing highquality output. Analyzing data from several supply chain stages is known as supply chain optimization, and its goals are to increase delivery times, lower costs, and increase efficiency.

Marketing

Data science is utilized in marketing for customer lifetime value projection, campaign performance, and sentiment analysis. Sentiment analysis assesses consumer reviews and social media posts to determine how the general public feels about particular businesses and items. An analysis of marketing campaign performance is used to determine the success of campaigns, which aids in strategy optimization and ROI maximization. Forecasting client lifetime value enables more effective resource allocation and customer retention tactics by estimating the total revenue a business may anticipate from a customer over the course of their relationship.

Because data science can handle and evaluate massive amounts of data, it helps businesses make wise decisions, streamline processes, and add value. Enterprises can achieve a competitive advantage in their respective markets by utilizing AI and ML in conjunction with sophisticated analytical tools.

Example Case Study: Predicting Customer Churn

Problem description: A telecom company is experiencing excessive churn, or the loss of customers. The pace at which clients discontinue doing business with a company is referred to as churn. Because keeping current customers is frequently more costeffective than obtaining new ones, reducing churn is essential. The organization seeks to identify which clients are most likely to defect so that they may apply focused retention tactics.

Data Collection: Compiling thorough client data is the initial stage. This data includes billing details (e.g., monthly charges, payment history), customer service interactions (e.g., number of complaints, support tickets), service usage patterns (e.g., call logs, internet usage), and demographic data (e.g., age, gender, location). Additionally essential for developing predictive models is historical churn data, which shows which customers have already departed.

- **Data Preprocessing:** Unprocessed data frequently has missing values, outliers, and inconsistencies; it is rarely flawless. To address these problems, cleaning the data is a part of data preprocessing. Missing values are filled in using strategies like imputation, and anomalies are found and dealt with with the aid of outlier detection techniques. To maintain uniformity, data is also standardized or normalized, particularly when working with features that have varied scales.
- **Exploratory Data Analysis (EDA):** To comprehend the linkages and underlying structure of the data, EDA is a crucial step. In order to find patterns and connections, analysts employ a variety of statistical methods and visualization strategies. For example, bar charts can display the relationship between categories features and churn rates, whereas histograms can display the distribution of numerical features. The relationship between service utilization and churn may be shown using scatter plots. This stage aids in the engineering and feature choices that are essential for developing models.
- **Model Building:** To efficiently assess model performance, the preprocessed data is divided into training and testing sets. A variety of machine learning algorithms, including gradient boosting machines, decision trees, logistic regression, and random forests, can be used to forecast churn. Every method has advantages and disadvantages. For instance, logistic regression can be easily understood, while random forests and gradient boosting machines frequently deliver greater accuracy. Hyperparameter adjustment is done in this step to maximize model performance.
- **Model Evaluation:** A variety of measures are used to assess the models once they have been trained. While precision, recall, and the F1score offer a more accurate assessment for unbalanced datasets like churn prediction, accuracy assesses the model's overall soundness. Recall quantifies the number of actual churners that were successfully recognized, whereas precision shows the proportion of predicted churn cases that were churners. The harmonic mean of recall and precision yields the F1score, which strikes a compromise between the two.
- **Deployment:** The optimal model is subsequently introduced into the operational setting. To provide realtime prediction, this entails connecting the model with the business's current systems. The algorithm has the ability to identify clients that pose a high risk for targeted marketing campaigns or customer

service interventions. In order to guarantee that the model's predictions hold true throughout time, constant observation is necessary. To adjust to shifting consumer behavior, this entails monitoring the model's performance and updating it with fresh information.

The telecom business can improve retention rates by proactively addressing issues that lead to consumer discontent by anticipating customer churn. This improves consumer loyalty while also making a substantial financial contribution to the business. This case study demonstrates the effectiveness of data science, supported by AI and ML methods, in resolving actual business issues.

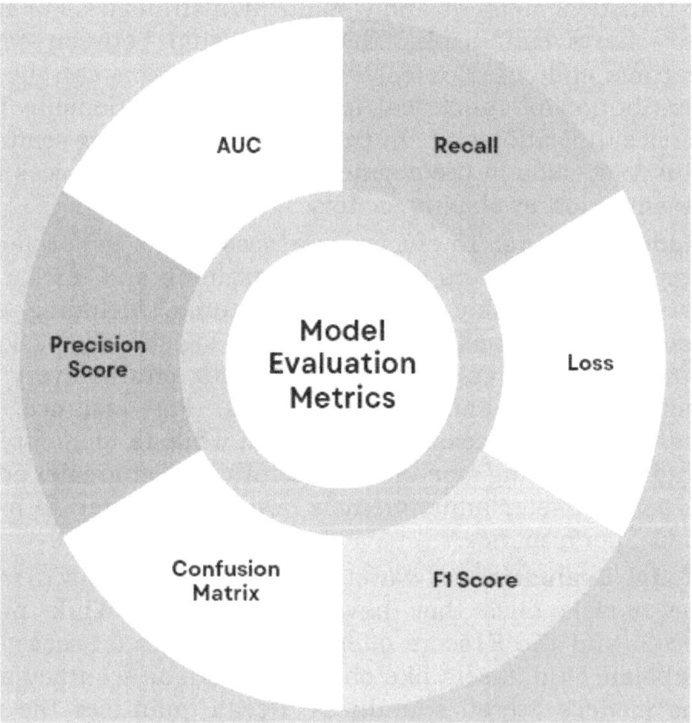

Conclusion

Datadriven decisionmaking, made possible by AI and MLenhanced data science, is revolutionizing numerous industries. Organizations can acquire a competitive edge, identify hidden patterns, and forecast future trends by utilizing sophisticated analytical approaches. Realizing the full potential of Data Science requires an understanding of its methodology and applications.

1.2 KEY CONCEPTS AND TERMINOLOGIES

It is essential to grasp the basic terms and concepts in the quickly developing fields of Data Science, Artificial Intelligence (AI), and Machine Learning (ML). An extensive review of the essential words and ideas that serve as the cornerstone of these fields is given in this chapter.

1. Data Science

The multidisciplinary subject of data science uses a range of scientific techniques, algorithms, and systems to mine data for information and insights that may be put to use. To analyze both organized and unstructured data, it combines methods from information theory, computer science, statistics, and domain experience. Finding patterns in data, generating predictions, and assisting in decisionmaking are the objectives of data science.

Key Components of Data Science

1. **Information Gathering:** The first stage of the data science process is collecting data from many sources, including sensors, databases, web scraping, and surveys. Both structured and unstructured datasuch as text, photos, and videoscan be arranged in rows and columns.
2. **Cleaning Data:** This stage, which is also known as data preparation, is essential since raw data frequently has errors, missing values, and noise. To get the data ready for analysis, methods like imputation, normalization, and outlier detection are used.
3. **Data Analysis:** Statistical and computational techniques are used at this point to examine and comprehend the data. Finding patterns, connections, and anomalies in the data is made easier with the use of methods like exploratory data analysis (EDA), inferential statistics, and descriptive statistics.
4. **Modeling Data:** This entails utilizing machine learning algorithms to create descriptive or predictive models. Techniques like regression, classification, clustering, or deep learning may be applied, depending on the issue. The type of data and the particular goals of the study serve as a guidance for the model selection.
5. **Data Visualization:** Charts, graphs, and dashboards are examples of visualization tools that help convey data insights effectively. Through the use of visualization, stakeholders

can more easily understand trends, outliers, and patterns in complex data.

6. **Interpretation and DecisionMaking:** Making educated decisions requires evaluating the analysis's findings in the last stage. This could involve formulating policies, making smart economic decisions, or making scientific discoveries. One of the most important abilities for data scientists is the capacity to convert technical discoveries into practical insights.

RealWorld Applications

Data Science is pivotal in numerous industries:

- **Healthcare:** Forecasting patient results, customizing care, and streamlining hospitalworkflows.
- **Finance:** Algorithmic trading, risk management, and fraud detection.
- **Retail:** Personalized marketing, consumer segmentation, and inventory management.
- **Transportation:** Autonomous driving, demand prediction, and route optimization.
- **Social Media:** Analysis of user behavior, recommendation engines, and sentiment.

Future Trends

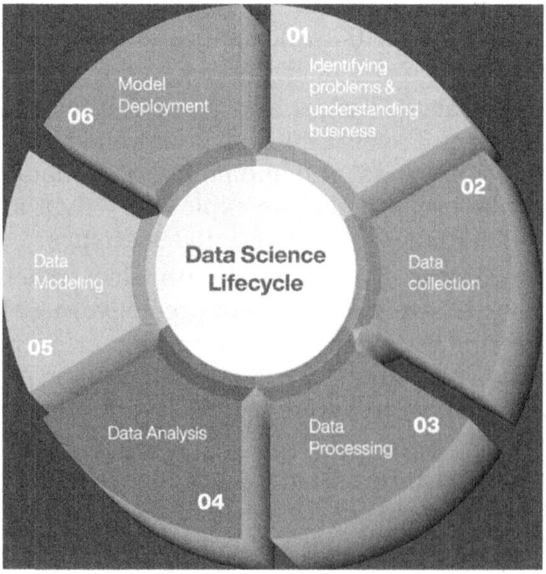

Data science is a constantly changing area, with new capabilities being driven by advances in AI and ML. The future of data science is being shaped by trends like automated machine learning (AutoML), the emergence of big data technologies, and the growing significance of ethical considerations in AI.

2. Artificial Intelligence (AI)

Definition

The term artificial intelligence (AI) describes a machine's capacity to mimic intelligent human behavior. Artificial intelligence (AI) systems are made to carry out tasks like speech recognition, visual perception, language translation, and decisionmaking that normally need human intelligence. Developing autonomous systems that can learn from their experiences and function better is the ultimate goal of artificial intelligence.

Key Concepts in AI

- **Learning:** Using statistical models and algorithms, AI systems are able to learn from data. This education may be reinforced, unsupervised, or monitored.
- **Reasoning:** Artificial intelligence (AI) uses reasoning to solve issues. This can involve organizing, arranging, and problemsolving.
- **Perception:** AI systems are capable of deciphering sensory input to comprehend theirsurroundings. This covers auditory perception (speech and sound identification), visualperception (computer vision), and other senses.
- **Natural Language Processing (NLP):** AI makes it possible for machines to comprehend and react to spoken language. Semantics (meaning) and syntax (structure) are both involved in this.

AI Techniques and Methods

AI employs a variety of techniques to achieve intelligent behavior:

- **Machine Learning (ML):** A branch of artificial intelligence, ML is the development of algorithms that let machines learn from and make judgments or predictions based on data.
- **Intelligent Systems:** These are modeled after the structure of the human brain and are madeup of layers of networked

nodes, or neurons, that analyze information so they can recognizepatterns and draw conclusions from them.

- **Deep Learning:** An area of machine learning that analyzes data with intricate structures byemploying multilayered neural networks. It works very well for speech and picturerecognition.
- **Expert Systems:** Artificial intelligence programs that simulate human experts' decision-making processes. They tackle certain problems by using a set of rules and knowledge bases.
- **Robotics:** Combining artificial intelligence (AI) with mechanical devices to carry out activities requiring movement, perception, and manipulation.

Applications of AI

AI is transforming various industries and aspects of daily life:

- **Healthcare:** Robotic surgery, tailored medicine, and diagnostic imaging are all made possible by AI.
- **Finance:** AI aids in algorithmic trading, fraud detection, and customized financial guidance.
- **Transportation:** AI powers driverless cars, enhancing safety and route optimization.
- **Customer Service:** AIpowered chatbots and virtual assistants improve customer experience and offer roundtheclock assistance.
- **Entertainment:** AI makes music, builds virtual worlds in video games, and suggests content on streaming services.

Ethical and Societal Implications

The swift progression of artificial intelligence raises important moral and cultural questions:

- **Bias and Fairness:** If biases are not adequately addressed, AI systems have the potential to reinforce or even magnify preexisting ones.
- **Privacy:** Data security and personal privacy are issues that are brought up by the usage of AI in data analysis.
- **Job Displacement:** AIpowered automation may cause some job categories to disappear, requiring reskilling and a workforce transition.
- **Accountability:** In highstakes situations like the criminal justice or healthcare systems, it might be difficult to assign blame for judgments made by AI systems.

Future of AI

AI has a bright future ahead of it. There will likely be constant progress in the following areas:

- **General AI:** Developing systems with generalized cognitive capabilities to do a variety of jobs.
- **Integration with IoT:** The Internet of Things (IoT) and artificial intelligence (AI) together will make environments and gadgets smarter.
- **HumanAI Collaboration:** Improving the way in which AI systems and people collaborate to get better results.
- **Ethical AI:** Creating guidelines and procedures to guarantee the equitable and responsible application of AI technology.
- **Image suggestion:** Infographic comparing Narrow AI, General AI, and Superintelligent AI.

3. Machine Learning (ML)

A crucial branch of artificial intelligence (AI) called machine learning (ML) focuses on creating systems that can process and interpret data to learn from and make judgments. With machine learning (ML), a system can learn patterns and generate predictions on its own, in contrast to traditional programming, where all rules and logic must be explicitly coded by a programmer. This learning is accomplished by algorithms that, by identifying patterns in data, progressively enhance their performance on a given task.

Types of Machine Learning

- **Supervised Learning:** A labeled dataset is used to train the model in supervised learning, meaning that every training example has an output label associated with it. The model's ability to translate inputs into the appropriate output is the main goal. Classification (e.g., spam detection, image recognition) and regression (e.g., stock market trends, house price prediction) are common supervised learning tasks.
- **Unsupervised Learning:** In unsupervised learning, a model is trained using unlabeled response data. The model looks for underlying patterns or structures in the data. Clustering (e.g., customer segmentation, grouping similar documents) and dimensionality reduction (e.g., principal component analysis for lowering the amount of features while keeping variance) are common unsupervised learning techniques.

- **Learning Reinforcement:** Reinforcement learning (RL), which takes its cues from behavioral psychology, is a process where an agent gains decisionmaking skills by acting and getting feedback from its surroundings in the form of rewards or penalties. Applications where an agent must make a succession of decisions, such robotics, automated trading, and game play (like AlphaGo and Chess AI), frequently use this kind of learning.

Key Algorithms

- **Linear Regression:** Continuous values can be predicted using Linear Regression. It uses a linear equation to model the relationship between a dependent variable and one or more independent variables.
- **Decision Trees:** a model resembling a tree that is applied to regression and classification tasks. By tracing the branches of the tree from the root to the leaf nodes, it divides the data into subsets according to the value of the input features.
- **Neural Networks:** Consisting of multiple interconnected node layers (neurons). During training, the weight of each link is changed. Neural networks are very good at complicated tasks like voice and image recognition.
- **Support vector machines (SVM):** Classification and regression are performed using SVMs. SVM searches the feature space for the hyperplane that best divides data points of various classes.
- **KMeans Clustering:** Based on feature similarity, this unsupervised technique divides data into K different clusters.

Applications of Machine Learning

ML has a wide array of applications across various domains:

- **Healthcare:** Medical image analysis, tailored treatment regimens, and disease prediction.
- **Finance:** Algorithmic trading, risk assessment, and fraud detection.
- **Marketing:** Sentiment analysis, recommendation engines, and customer segmentation.
- **Transportation:** Route optimization, traffic prediction, and autonomous driving.
- **Manufacturing:** Process optimization, quality assurance, and predictive maintenance.

Challenges in Machine Learning

Despite its powerful capabilities, ML faces several challenges:

- **Data Quantity and Quality:** Sufficient, pertinent, and highquality data are essential for training successful models.
- **Unfitting and Overfitting:** Models need to be able to adapt well to fresh data. When a model learns the training data too well, it becomes overfit and starts to capture noise instead of the underlying pattern. When a model is too basic to accurately represent the structure of the data, underfitting happens.
- **Model Interpretability:** It might be hard to grasp how decisions are made when dealing with complex models, such as deep neural networks.
- **Computational Resources:** ML model training necessitates a substantial amount of computational power and resources, particularly for deep learning models.

Future of Machine Learning

With continued research focused on enhancing model efficiency, interpretability, and the capacity to learn from fewer data points (fewshot learning), machine learning (ML) has even more potential for the future. It's also anticipated that integration with other technologies, like quantum computing and sophisticated data privacy techniques, will push the limits of machine learning.

Practitioners can more successfully negotiate the challenges of creating, implementing, and sustaining ML systems to solve problems in the real world by being aware of these specific ML facets.

4. Deep Learning

Definition

The goal of deep learning, a specific branch of machine learning, is to train artificial neural networks to make sense of enormous volumes of data. Deep learning models continue to get better as the amount of data increases, in contrast to typical machine learning algorithms that reach a performance plateau when given additional data. Because these models dynamically acquire hierarchical features from input, they are very effective at complex pattern and representation tasks, like speech and image recognition.

Neural Networks

Neural networks, which draw inspiration from the structure and functions of the human brain, provide the foundation of deep learning. Layers of connected nodes, or "neurons," make up a neural network, and each connection has a weight. These layers fall under the following general categories:

- **Input Layer:** The first layer to receive inputs of raw data.
- **Hidden levels:** Complicated calculations and transformations are carried out via intermediate levels. In deep learning, the term "deep" refers to the presence of numerous hidden layers.
- **Output Layer:** The last layer that generates the categorization or prediction made by the model.

Deep Learning Architectures

Numerous sophisticated structures have been created to manage various jobs and data types:

- **Convolutional Neural Networks (CNNs):** CNNs utilize convolutional filters to capture spatial hierarchies in data and are mostly used for image and video analysis.
- **RNNs (Recurrent Neural Networks):** RNNs are made to handle sequential data, such as time series or natural language. They remember prior inputs thanks to directed cycles formed by their connections.
- **Long Short-Term Memory Networks (LSTMs):** An RNN type that efficiently captures longterm dependencies, hence overcoming the drawbacks of conventional RNNs.
- **Generative Adversarial Networks (GANs):** Made up of a discriminator and a generator neural network, which compete with one another to produce realisticlooking synthetic data.

Training Deep Networks

Backpropagation is the procedure used to change the weights of connections in deep neural networks during training. In order to minimize the loss, the weights are adjusted based on the gradient of the loss function, which computes the difference between the expected and actual outputs for each weight. Optimization techniques that are frequently utilized include gradient descent and its derivatives (such as stochastic gradient descent and Adam optimizer).

Activation Functions

The network gains nonlinearity via activation functions, which helps it recognize intricate patterns. Typical activation functions consist of:

- **ReLU (Rectified Linear Unit):** Introduces nonlinearity by producing zero if the input is negative and the input directly if it is positive.
- **Sigmoid:** Effective for binary classification, this function compresses input values to a range between 0 and 1.
- **Tanh (Hyperbolic Tangent):** Often utilized in buried layers, this function is comparable to Sigmoid but produces values between 1 and 1.

Applications

Deep learning has revolutionized numerous fields by achieving stateoftheart results in:

- **Computer Vision:** Facial recognition, object identification, and image classification.
- **Natural Language Processing (NLP):** Chatbots, sentiment analysis, and machine translation.
- **Speech Recognition:** Voiceactivated assistants that translate spoken words into text.
- **Healthcare:** Customized treatment regimens, medical image analysis, and predictive diagnoses.

Challenges

Deep learning is successful, but it has drawbacks as well.

- **Data Requirements:** To train efficiently, a significant amount of labeled data is needed.
- **Computational Resources:** Requires a lot of memory and processing power, frequently requiring specialist hardware like GPUs.
- **Interpretability:** Because models are frequently viewed as "black boxes," it can be challenging to comprehend how they arrive at conclusions.
- **Overfitting:** Propensity to perform well when training on data that hasn't been seen, but poorly when it hasn't been adequately regularized.

Deep learning keeps expanding the realm of what artificial intelligence and machine learning can accomplish, spurring innovation in a variety of fields and applications. In the era of big data and artificial intelligence, its capacity to autonomously learn from complex data makes it a key technological advancement.

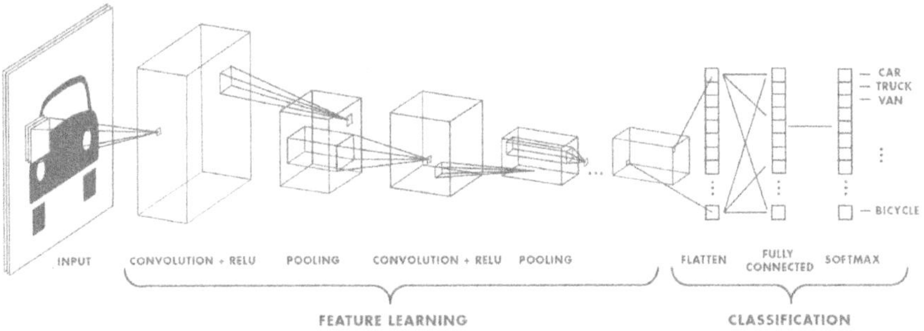

Convolutional Neural Network (CNN)

5. Key Terminologies

Data Types

Structured and unstructured data fall into two broad groups in the field of data science. Structured data is wellorganized and can be found in databases with ease. It contains data types that arrange nicely into rows and columns, such as dates, numbers, and strings. SQL databases and Excel spreadsheets are two examples. On the other hand, unstructured datahas no set format, which makes analysis more difficult. It includes social media posts, photos, videos, and text among other data kinds. Advanced computer vision and natural language processing (NLP) techniques are frequently needed for the analysis of unstructured data.

Model Evaluation Metrics

Many assessment criteria are used to evaluate the effectiveness of machine learning models. Accuracy quantifies the percentage of accurate forecasts among all forecasts. Although helpful, it may be deceptive in datasets that are not balanced. Precision is a useful metric in situations where false positives might be expensive because it shows the percentage of actual positive outcomes among all positive forecasts. Recall calculates the percentage of real positive findings that are actually positive, which is significant when it comes to missing positive situations.

By computing their harmonic mean, the F1 Score strikes a compromise between recall and precision, yielding a solitary measure that takes into consideration both false positives and false negatives. The model's overall ability to distinguish between positive and negative classes across a range of threshold settings is measured by the ROCAUC (Receiver Operating Characteristic Area Under Curve), where the AUC indicates the degree of separability.

Overfitting and Underfitting

Finding the right balance between model complexity and performance is crucial in machine learning. When a model learns the training data too well, it becomes overfitted and starts to capture noise in addition to the underlying patterns. As a result, there is low generalization to new, unseen data but excellent accuracy on training data. On the other hand, underfitting occurs when a model performs poorly on both training and testing datasets because it is overly simplistic and fails to identify the underlying trends in the data. Methods like regularization, trimming, and crossvalidation are used to address these problems and enhance model generalization.

Feature Engineering

In order to enhance model performance, feature engineering entails adding new features or changing ones that already exist. In the pipeline of data preparation, it is an essential stage. The encoding categorical variables technique transforms categorical data into numerical format (e.g., onehot encoding); feature scaling standardizes features to have zero mean and unit variance; and normalization adjusts numerical features to a standard range. A model's prediction ability can be greatly increased by effective feature engineering by feeding it with more relevant and instructive inputs.

Neural Networks and Deep Learning

Neural networks, which are composed of layers of connected nodes or neurons, are the fundamental building blocks of deep learning. Every neuron incorporates nonlinearity into the model by applying a activation function (such ReLU, Sigmoid, or Tanh) to its input, which allows the model to capture intricate patterns. Training a neural network includes gradient descent and backpropagation to modify the weights of connections. Multiple hidden layer deep neural networks have transformed domains including autonomous driving, natural language processing, and picture identification by obtaining previously unheardof accuracy in challenging tasks.

Data Preprocessing Techniques

Preprocessing data is necessary before supplying it to machine learning models. Normalization scales data to a standard range, typically between 0 and 1, to facilitate convergence during training. Encoding converts categorical data into numerical format, making it appropriate for algorithms that require numerical input. Data cleaning removes missing values, duplicates, and inconsistencies to assure data quality.Feature scaling ensures that features have similar scales by standardizing them, which helps to make model training more successful and efficient. Improving the resilience and performance of the model requires these preprocessing steps.

Bias and Variance

Constructing robust machine learning models requires an understanding of and ability to manage variance and bias. Bias is the error that arises when a simplified model is used to approximate a realworld problem. Excessive bias might make the model perform poorly by underfitting the data. Conversely, Variance describes how sensitive the model is to changes in the training set. When there is a high variance in the data, the model may overfit and capture noise in addition to the underlying patterns. A key idea in machine learning is the biasvariance tradeoff, where the objective is to strike a balance that minimizes overall error.

The foundation of knowledge in data science, AI, and ML is formed by these essential terms, which help practitioners efficiently traverse and utilize these technologies to address challenging challenges.

Conclusion

Anyone working in data science, artificial intelligence, or machine learning has to understand these fundamental ideas and jargon. With this fundamental understanding, practitioners can successfully deploy the right techniques and resources to handle complicated datadriven problems.

1.3 DATA SCIENCE LIFECYCLE

The Data Science Lifecycle is a methodical approach to problemsolving with data. It consists of a number of steps that direct the process from gathering data to producing useful insights. The lifecycle of Data Science utilizing Artificial Intelligence (AI) and Machine Learning (ML) comprises multiple crucial stages, all of which are essential for the effective culmination of the project. Let's take a closer look at each of these phases, supported with pictures, charts, and graphs to provide a thorough comprehension.

1. Problem Definition

The core of each data science project is the problem specification stage. It lays out the business problem or research question that needs to be answered in detail, setting the stage for the rest of the lifecycle. Engaging with stakeholders to fully understand their needs and objectives is part of this phase. These corporate objectives must be converted into precise, quantifiable, and doable data science goals.

In order to understand the context and subtleties of the problem, domain experts and data scientists work together during this phase. They specify the success measures and key performance indicators (KPIs) that will be used to assess the project's results. Furthermore, it's critical to comprehend the restrictions and constraints, such as those related to time, computational resources, and data availability.

Determining the project's scope is another aspect of this phase. A clearly defined scope keeps the project focused and manageable while also assisting in controlling expectations. For example, the scope might involve evaluating customer activity data, finding trends that lead to churn, and constructing predictive models to forecast future churn if the goal is to increase customer retention rates.

Moreover, a crucial part of defining a topic is developing hypotheses. Wellinformed predictions or assumptions that can be verified by facts are called hypotheses. One theory could be, for instance, that clients who get in touch with customer support a lot are more prone to leave. The following stages of data gathering and analysis are guided by these hypotheses.

2. Data Collection

In order to address the problem defined in the first phase, pertinent data is acquired from several sources during the foundational stage of the Data Science Lifecycledata gathering. The success of the stages that follow in the lifecycle is greatly influenced by the quality and quantity of data that is gathered, which makes this step crucial. Depending on the type of data and its source, a variety of methods and instruments may be used during the data collection process.

Techniques and Tools for Data Collection

1. **Databases:** Relational databases such as PostgreSQL, MySQL, and NoSQL databases like MongoDB are frequently used to

store structured data. Usually, in order to retrieve this data, one must write SQL queries to extract pertinent data.

2. **Application Programming Interfaces, (APIs):** A lot of services offer APIs that let users access data programmatically. For example, financial firms may offer APIs to access stock prices or economic indicators, while social media sites such as Facebook and Twitter offer APIs to gather data on user interactions.
3. **Web Scraping:** Information can be extracted from websites using web scraping technologies such as Beautiful Soup, Scrapy, or Selenium when the data is available there but not in a structured fashion. This technique is especially helpful for gathering a lot of information from many websites.
4. **Manual Entry:** When working with tiny datasets or when automated approaches are impractical, data entry may occasionally be necessary. Although laborintensive, this method may be necessary for some kinds of qualitative data.
5. **Sensors and Logs:** These are essential components for timeseries data. For instance, IoT devices continuously provide streams of data from sensors that track the functioning of machinery, the environment, or user interactions. Likewise, server logs offer comprehensive documentation of actions taken within an online environment.

Challenges in Data Collection

Getting data can be difficult for a number of reasons, such as:

- **Data Quality:** It is crucial to guarantee the data's correctness, dependability, and completeness. Data of poor quality can result in inaccurate analyses and conclusions.
- **Volume and range:** Robust data management systems are necessary to handle huge volumes of data and a wide range of data types (structured, semistructured, and unstructured).
- **Data Privacy and Security:** Strict compliance with privacy laws (such as GDPR) and the deployment of security measures are required when gathering sensitive data in order to guard against breaches and unauthorized access.
- **Data Integration:** Because multiple sources' formats, structures, and semantics differ, combining data from them might be difficult. Careful preparation and the application of the right technologies are necessary for successful data integration.

Importance of Data Collection

In the data science lifecycle, the data collecting phase establishes the foundation for all other phases. Reliable information provides the foundation for analysis, modeling, and prediction when highquality data is collected, which produces more accurate and useful insights. Through the utilization of methodical techniques for gathering data and resolving possible obstacles, data scientists can establish a strong basis for their analytical pursuits.

Sources of Data

Source	Type of Data	Example
Databases	Structured Data	SQL databases
APIs	SemiStructured Data	RESTful APIs
Web Scraping	Unstructured Data	HTML content from websites
Sensors/Logs	TimeSeries Data	IoT sensor data, server logs

3. Data Preparation

A crucial and frequently time-consuming stage of the data science lifecycle is data preparation. This phase comprises a number of crucial procedures designed to convert unstructured data into an organized, clean format appropriate for modeling and analysis.

Data Cleaning

The initial stage of data preparation is data cleaning. It entails locating and fixing mistakes and discrepancies in the data to guarantee accuracy and dependability. Managing missing numbers, fixing mistakes, and getting rid of duplicates are typical chores. A number of techniques can be used to deal with missing values, including imputation, which substitutes values such as the mean, median, or an algorithmically derived value for the missing data.

Data Transformation

Data transformation is the process of transforming data into a format that makes analysis easier. In order to make numerical features easier for machine learning algorithms to process, this may entail normalizing or scaling them so that they lie within a same range. While standardization changes data to have a mean of zero and a standard deviation of one, normalization frequently adjusts the data to a range of 0 to 1.

Feature Engineering

The process of adding new features or altering current ones in order to enhance the functionality of machine learning models is known as feature engineering. This could involve extracting textual features for text analysis using methods like TFIDF (Term FrequencyInverse Document Frequency) or creating new variables from existing data, like an age variable from a date of birth.

Data Integration

Since data is frequently gathered from several sources, data integration is required. To build a single dataset, this method aggregates data from many databases or data silos. In order to ensure consistency and address problems, it frequently entails matching and merging records from many sources.

Data Reduction

Techniques for data reduction are used to condense the dataset while preserving important information. To do this, dimensionality reduction techniques like Principal Component Analysis (PCA) may be used to minimize the amount of features while preserving the most crucial data. In order to make the dataset smaller, easier to handle, and process more quickly, it might also incorporate data sampling techniques.

Data Encoding

Encoding is frequently required to transform categorical data into a numerical format so that machine learning algorithms can handle it. In order to ensure that machine learning algorithms can correctly read category variables, techniques like onehot encoding convert them into a series of binary variables.

Data Preparation Workflow

A typical data preparation workflow might look like this:

1. **Data Collection:** Gather raw data from various sources.
2. **Data Cleaning:** Handle missing values, correct errors, and remove duplicates.
3. **Data Transformation:** Normalize and scale numerical features.
4. **Feature Engineering:** Create and modify features to improve model performance.

5. **Data Integration:** Combine data from different sources into a single dataset.
6. **Data Reduction:** Apply dimensionality reduction and sampling techniques.
7. **Data Encoding:** Convert categorical data into numerical format.

Data scientists make sure that the next phases of the data science lifecycle, such as exploratory data analysis and modeling, may be carried out successfully by carefully preparing the data. Better insights, more accurate models, and ultimately more dependable and useful outcomes are all derived from wellprepared data.

4. Exploratory Data Analysis (EDA)

An important stage in the data science lifecycle, exploratory data analysis (EDA) lays the groundwork for later processes. To determine trends, find anomalies, and comprehend the data's underlying structure, it entails analyzing and displaying the data. EDA summarizes the key features of the data, frequently using visual aids, to assist data scientists in making sense of it. Descriptive statistics that shed light on the data's central tendency and dispersion are produced throughout this procedure, including mean, median, and standard deviation.

Since they can highlight patterns, connections, and anomalies that summary data alone might miss, visualizations are essential to EDA. Histograms, which display the distribution of a single variable, box plots, which highlight outliers and summarize the main features of the distribution, scatter plots, which show the relationship between two variables, and heatmaps, which can show correlations between several variables, are examples of common visual aids.

EDA also entails data preparation and cleaning, which includes addressing missing values, eliminating duplication, and resolving discrepancies. Data scientists can make sure the data is correct and prepared for additional analysis by using these procedures. EDA also involves hypothesis testing, which allows one to evaluate preliminary theories about the data using statistical techniques, so directing the course of the analysis and modeling.

In general, EDA is an iterative process that gives data scientists a greater understanding of the data and empowers them to choose models and algorithms wisely for later stages of the data science lifecycle. It is a synthesis of analytical methods and intuition, where important discoveries and insights can be obtained through inventive data visualization and summarization.

5. Data Modeling

In order to find patterns, correlations, and insights in the produced data, statistical models and machine learning algorithms are deployed during the crucial data modeling phase of the data science lifecycle. The intention is to develop models that, given the data, can yield useful descriptions or precise forecasts.

Types of Data Modeling

1. **Supervised Learning:** Using labeled data, where the output or target variable is known, models are trained using this method. Typical algorithms consist of:
   - **Linear Regression:** This method is used to forecast a continuous result, such sales income or home values.
   - **Trees of Decision:** These provide interpretable models that divide data into branches according to feature values and are utilized for both regression and classification tasks.
   - **Support Vector Machines (SVM):** SVMs are useful for classification jobs because they identify the best hyperplane to divide the data into distinct classes.
2. **Unsupervised Learning:** In this scenario, the models operate on unlabeled data with the goal of locating innate structures in the absence of predetermined labels. Important algorithms consist of:
   - **Grouping by KMeans:** This technique, which is frequently used in market basket analysis and client segmentation, clusters data items according to their commonalities.
   - **Principal Component Analysis (PCA):** A dimensionality reduction method that preserves as much variance as feasible by transforming data into a set of orthogonal components.
3. **Learning Under SemiSupervision:** integrates labeled and unlabeled data to increase the accuracy of learning. When there is a dearth of labeled data but an abundance of unlabeled data, this strategy is especially helpful.
4. **Learning by Reinforcement:** In this kind of learning, an agent makes choices in order to maximize the total number of rewards in the environment. It is extensively utilized in industries such as autonomous driving, gaming, and robotics.

Model Building Process

- **Feature Engineering and Selection:** Extracting pertinent features from unprocessed data. A well-engineered feature can greatly improve the performance of the model.
- **Training and Validation:** To train the model and evaluate its performance, the data is divided into training and validation sets.
- **Hyperparameter Tuning:** Modifying algorithmic parameters to enhance model efficacy. Methods like random and grid searches are frequently employed.

Practical Considerations

- **Overfitting vs. Underfitting:** An overly complex model is one that catches noise in the data, whereas an underfit model is one that is too basic and misses underlying patterns. Crossvalidation and regularization methods like Lasso and Ridge regression aid in striking the correct balance.
- **Model Interpretability:** While some modelslike neural networksare more sophisticated but capable of efficiently handling enormous amounts of unstructured data, others, like decision trees and linear regression, are simpler to understand.
- **Scalability:** It is essential to make sure the model can manage huge datasets and function effectively in a production setting. This can be facilitated by methods such as parallel processing and the use of distributed computing frameworks (like Apache Spark).

Combining science and art, data modeling necessitates a thorough comprehension of both the data and the algorithms. Data scientists may fully utilize their data by carefully choosing and fine-tuning models, leading to insights and choices that significantly advance both research and business.

Machine Learning Algorithms

Algorithm	Type	Example Use Case
Linear Regression	Supervised Learning	Predicting house prices
Decision Trees	Supervised Learning	Customer segmentation
KMeans Clustering	Unsupervised Learning	Market basket analysis
Neural Networks	Deep Learning	Image and speech recognition

6. Model Evaluation

The effectiveness and dependability of the machine learning models are ascertained during the model evaluation step of the data science lifecycle. It entails a thorough evaluation of a model's predictive performance on brandnew, untested data. This stage guarantees that the model performs effectively when applied to realworld data in addition to being accurate when trained on training data.

Key Concepts and Metrics

1. **Accuracy:** This indicates what percentage of all forecasts were accurate. Even while accuracy is a straightforward and understandable measure, it is not always reliable, particularly when datasets are unbalanced and one class predominates over the others.
2. **Precision and Recall:** These measures come in handy especially when dealing with classification issues. The percentage of accurate positive predictions among all positive predictions the model makes is called precision, or positive predictive value. The percentage of genuine positive predictions among all actual positive cases in the dataset is measured by recall, which is sometimes referred to as sensitivity or true positive rate. Although high recall and precision are preferred, there is frequently a tradeoff between the two.
3. **F1 Score:** The F1 score is a single metric that strikes a balance between recall and precision. It is calculated as the harmonic mean of both variables. When you need to strike the ideal balance between recall and precision, it is really helpful.
4. **ROCAUC (Receiver Operating Characteristic Area Under the Curve):** At different threshold settings, the true positive rate is plotted versus the false positive rate on the ROC curve. An overall performance measure across all categorization criteria is provided by the area under this curve, or AUC. A model that performs better is indicated by a higher AUC.
5. **Confusion Matrix:** This table displays the true positives, true negatives, false positives, and false negatives in order to provide an overview of the performance of a classification model. It offers a thorough rundown of the predictive power of the model.

Practical Considerations

To guarantee the robustness of the evaluation outcomes, it is crucial to employ strategies like crossvalidation during the model evaluation process. In crossvalidation, the dataset is divided into several folds, and the model is iteratively trained and validated on each fold. Understanding the model's performance variability and preventing problems like overfittinga situation in which the model performs well on training data but badly on unknown dataare made easier with this.

When choosing evaluation measures, it's also critical to take the project's specific objectives and the business context into account. For example, in the context of medical diagnosis, memory may be more crucial than accuracy in order to identify as many positive cases as feasible. On the other hand, in a spam detection system, accuracy could take precedence in order to reduce the number of false positives.

Common Evaluation Metrics

Metric	Description
Accuracy	Proportion of correct predictions
Precision	True positives divided by all positive predictions
Recall	True positives divided by all actual positives
F1 Score	Harmonic mean of precision and recall
ROCAUC	Area under the Receiver Operating Characteristic curve

7. Model Deployment

A crucial phase in the data science lifecycle, model deployment is where intensive data analysis and model building come together to become practical applications. When a model is deployed, the emphasis moves from test settings to realworld systems where the model's judgments and predictions might affect business outcomes and operational procedures.

A number of crucial factors must be taken into account during the model deployment process to guarantee its dependability and efficacy. First of all, it demands that the learned model be incorporated into the application infrastructure or target system. Depending on deployment objectives and limits, this integration can take many different forms, such as delivering as a web service that can be accessed via APIs or directly embedding into software applications or Internet of things devices.

Second, it's critical to guarantee the deployed model's performance and scalability. The system needs to be able to manage different loads and data quantities in an effective manner without sacrificing prediction accuracy or speed. Methods like orchestration (like Kubernetes) and containerization (like Docker) are frequently used to handle these intricacies and guarantee errorfree operations in production settings.

In order to ensure that the deployed model acts as anticipated across a range of situations and inputs, model deployment also entails extensive testing and validation. This validation process involves ensuring that any updates or retraining of the model are smoothly integrated into the production workflow, monitoring for drift in the input data distributions over time, and checking for consistency in the outputs.

Last but not least, model deployment is a continuous process that needs constant upkeep and observation rather than a onetime occurrence. Tracking metrics and key performance indicators (KPIs) allows you to evaluate the model's efficacy, dependability, and accuracy under realworld scenarios. Retraining the model with new data on a regular basis might be one of the maintenance tasks, allowing it to adjust to evolving patterns or behaviors in its operating environment.

To put it briefly, model deployment helps businesses make largescale, datadriven decisions by bridging the gap between theoretical model development and practical applications. Data scientists may make sure that their modeling and analytic efforts result in real business value and longterm competitive advantage by following best practices in deployment.

8. Model Monitoring and Maintenance

A crucial part of the data science lifecycle is model maintenance and monitoring, particularly once a model has been implemented in a realworld setting. It is crucial to keep an eye on a model's performance after it begins to make predictions based on actual data in order to make sure it continues to be accurate and dependable over time.

Monitoring Performance

Monitoring a model entails keeping track of several performance indicators to evaluate the model's effectiveness in practical situations. For classification models, these measures include accuracy, precision, recall, and F1 score; for regression models, they include mean squared error (MSE). These metrics are frequently shown using monitoring tools like Prometheus, Grafana, and custom dashboards, which may also be used to set up alerts for when performance falls below predetermined levels.

Data Drift Detection

Identifying and controlling data drift is one of the fundamental issues with model maintenance. If data drift is left unchecked, it might result in a decline in the performance of the model due to changes in the distribution of the input data over time. Data drift can be detected via monitoring tools by comparing the distributions of data now and during model training. Retraining the model with updated data or modifying the model to fit the new data distribution are two possible strategies to reduce data drift.

Model Retraining

Retraining the model on a regular basis could be required to keep it accurate. In order to keep the model current and capable of producing accurate predictions, it must be updated with fresh data. Depending on how quickly data changes and how important model accuracy is to business operations, retraining periods can fluctuate.

Automated Pipelines

Model maintenance can be streamlined by putting in place automated pipelines for distribution and retraining. Automated pipelines guarantee that the model is constantly receiving fresh data, that retraining occurs when performance metrics deteriorate, and that updated models are smoothly implemented into the production environment.

Versioning and Documentation

Effective model maintenance requires careful version control as well as performance documentation of the models. Versioning makes ensuring that modifications to the model or its inputs may be monitored and, if needed, undone. Collaboration and troubleshooting are made easier by the documentation, which offers insights into the behavior, assumptions, and dependencies of the model.

Feedback Loop and Stakeholder Communication

Keeping lines of communication open with stakeholders and creating a feedback loop are essential to figuring out how successfully the model achieves corporate goals. Feedback from stakeholders can shed light on possible problems with the performance of the model that automated monitoring could miss.

Monitoring Tools

Tool	Functionality
Prometheus	Monitoring and alerting toolkit
Grafana	Data visualization and monitoring
ELK Stack	Log management and analysis
MLFlow	Endtoend machine learning lifecycle management

Conclusion

A thorough structure known as the Data Science Lifecycle guarantees a methodical approach to addressing datadriven issues. Data scientists can obtain important insights and arrive at wise conclusions by utilizing AI and ML algorithms. Every stage of the lifecyclefrom problem description to model monitoringis essential to accomplishing the project's main goal in data science.

1.4 DATA SCIENCE VS. TRADITIONAL DATA ANALYSIS

The domains of Traditional Data Analysis and Data Science have become essential in today's world of datadriven decision making. Although gaining insights from data is the goal of both fields, their approaches, resources, and results are very different. This chapter examines these distinctions, highlighting how machine learning (ML) and artificial intelligence (AI) have shaped contemporary data science.

Traditional Data Analysis

For many years, the foundation of datadriven decisionmaking has been traditional data analysis. It entails using statistical methods to data summarization and interpretation in order to produce insights that guide strategic business choices. The comprehension of historical events and their causes is the main objective of classical data analysis. This is accomplished using a variety of techniques, including descriptive statistics, which use measures of variability (standard deviation, variance) and central tendency (mean, median, mode) to summarize data. By employing methods like confidence intervals, regression analysis, and hypothesis testing to make assumptions or predictions about a population based on a sample of data, inferential statistics go beyond this.

The capacity of traditional data analysis to offer a succinct and straightforward explanation of historical data is one of its main advantages. In this process, data visualization tools like pie charts, bar charts, and histograms are essential since they make complex data easily comprehensible. Trends, patterns, and outliers that might not be immediately obvious from raw data alone might be found with the aid of these visualizations.

Furthermore, statistical programs like SAS and SPSS, Microsoft Excel, and SQL databases are also essential components of traditional data analysis. The structured data that these technologies are intended to handle is data that has been prearranged, usually into rows and columns. These technologies help analysts make sure the data is reliable and appropriate for producing insights by doing tasks including data transformation, data cleaning, and statistical analysis.

Conventional data analysis is not without its limitations, though. Large and unstructured datasets, which are more prevalent in the digital age, are a major source of difficulties for it. Furthermore, traditional approaches are typically retroactive, emphasizing the analysis of historical data rather than the capacity to forecast future patterns or behaviors. Due to this constraint, data science has evolved to employ increasingly sophisticated methods that combine artificial intelligence (AI) and machine learning (ML) to close these gaps and produce more proactive and predictive insights.

Traditional Data Analysis Workflow

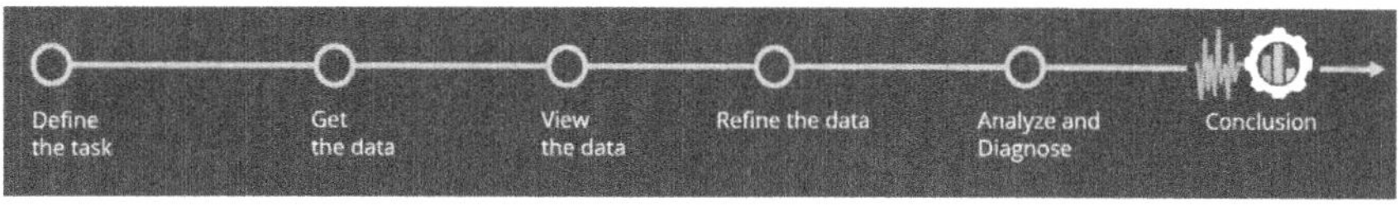

Table 1: Traditional Data Analysis Tools and Techniques

Technique	Description	Tools
Descriptive Statistics	Summarizing data using measures like mean and standard deviation	Excel, SPSS
Inferential Statistics	Drawing conclusions from data samples	R, SAS
Data Visualization	Representing data graphically	Tableau, Excel

Data Science

Data science is a broad field that interacts with computer science, statistics, and domainspecific knowledge, among other fields. It entails using a combination of sophisticated computer algorithms and analytical procedures in a methodical manner to extract meaningful knowledge and insights from data. Data gathering, data cleaning, data exploration, and data modeling are the fundamentals of data science. These processes frequently produce actionable insights that inform strategy development and decisionmaking.

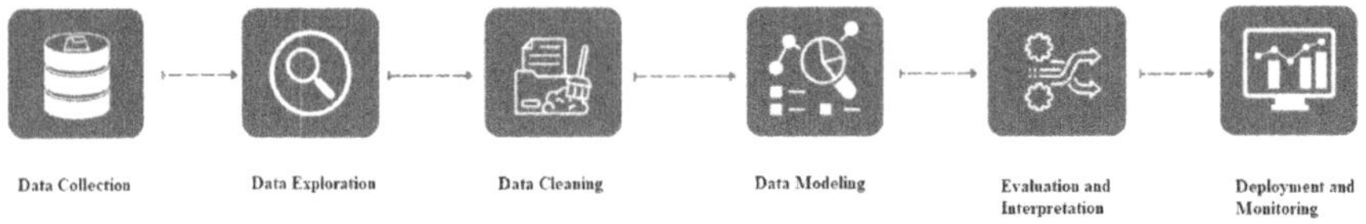

Key Components of Data Science

1. **Data Collection:** In this preliminary stage, unstructured (text, photos, videos) or organized (spreadsheets, databases) data are gathered from multiple sources. The volume, velocity, and variety of data available for analysis have expanded tremendously with the introduction of IoT and digitalization.
2. **Data Cleaning:** Thorough cleaning procedures are necessary since raw data is frequently noisy and unreliable. This process ensures the quality and dependability of the data by addressing missing numbers, eliminating duplicates, and fixing errors.
3. **Data Exploration:** Also referred to as exploratory data analysis (EDA), this stage entails applying statistical graphics and visualization tools to summarize the key features of the data. It facilitates the discovery of correlations, patterns, and anomalies in the data.
4. **Data Modeling:** The core of data science is the application of statistical and machine learning models to identify meaningful patterns and provide predictions. Regression analysis, classification, clustering, and deep learning are among the techniques; each is appropriate for a certain set of issues and data structures.
5. **Evaluation and Interpretation:** Metrics including as accuracy, precision, recall, and F1 score are used to assess the performance of models. In order to convert technical discoveries into useful commercial insights, these models must be interpreted.
6. **Deployment and Monitoring:** The last phase entails putting the model into a production setting so that it can offer predictions and insights in real time. Ongoing observation guarantees the model's accuracy and applicability over time.

Role of AI and ML in Data Science

Within data science, AI and ML are revolutionary technologies. Without explicit programming, machine learning, a subset of artificial intelligence, allows systems to learn from data and gradually improve their performance. The development of predictive models that can predict future trends, automate decisionmaking procedures, and reveal hidden patterns in complicated datasets is made possible by this capacity to generalize from data.

Table 2: Data Science Tools and Techniques

Technique	Description	Tools
Data Mining	Extracting useful information from large datasets	RapidMiner, Weka
Machine Learning	Building models that improve over time with more data	TensorFlow, Scikitlearn
Big Data Analytics	Processing and analyzing vast amounts of data	Hadoop, Spark
Predictive Analytics	Predicting future events based on historical data	IBM Watson, SAS

Comparing Data Science and Traditional Data Analysis

Although they are related, the domains of traditional data analysis and data science provide different methods for drawing conclusions from data. Conventional data analysis is based mostly on historical data and is essentially based on statistical methods for trend identification, hypothesis testing, and descriptive insights. This method frequently uses statistical tools, including data visualization, inferential statistics, and descriptive statistics, to summarize and analyze data in order to provide a clear understanding of historical trends and behaviors. These operations are normally carried out by traditional data analysts using programs like Excel, SPSS, and SAS, which are adequate for structured datasets of a limited scale.

On the other hand, data science is a more expansive and dynamic field of study that uses machine learning (ML) and artificial intelligence (AI) to evaluate data that is both structured and unstructured. In addition to comprehending historical data, data science also seeks to automate decisionmaking processes and forecast future trends. Advanced approaches like data mining, predictive analytics, and big data analytics are used in this discipline to handle large datasets that are too enormous for conventional methods to handle. Big data management and analysis are made easier by the frameworks and technologies used in data science, like TensorFlow, R, Python, and Hadoop.

The breadth and applications of these subjects are among the most notable distinctions. The main goals of traditional data analysis are to explain what has happened through descriptive and inferential methods. Data science, on the other hand, is prescriptive and predictive; its goal is to predict future events and recommend the best course of action. Machine learning (ML) algorithms underpin this predictive potential. These algorithms learn from data patterns and become more effective over time, delivering timely and useful insights.

Moreover, Data Science's capacity to manage unstructured data, including text, photos, and videos, creates new opportunities for gleaning insightful information from a variety of sources. In today's datarich environment, where the volume, variety, and velocity of data are constantly rising, this skill is crucial. Because of this, Data Science works especially well in highdimensional, complicated data contexts where other statistical techniques might not be as effective.

Datadriven decisionmaking still relies heavily on traditional data analysis, but data sciencewith its AI and ML capabilitiesgoes far beyond, providing prescriptive and predictive insights that spur innovation and tactical advantages. The incorporation of cuttingedge technologies into data science offers a more thorough and proactive approach, revolutionizing the way businesses interpret and use data.

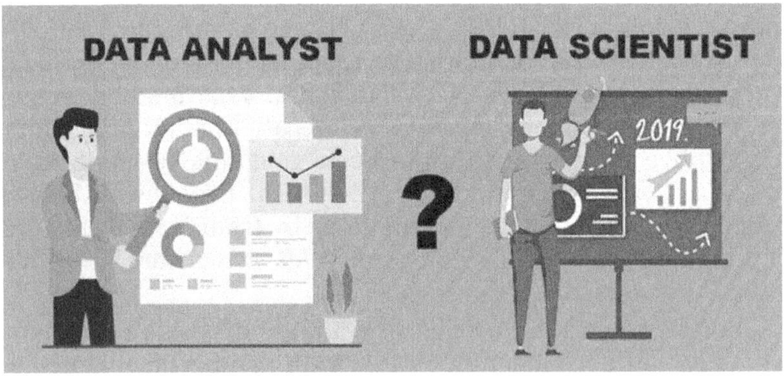

Table 3: Comparison of Traditional Data Analysis and Data Science

Aspect	Traditional Data Analysis	Data Science
Focus	Historical Data Analysis	Predictive and Prescriptive Analytics
Data Types	Structured	Structured and Unstructured

Aspect	Traditional Data Analysis	Data Science
Techniques	Statistical Methods	AI, ML, Data Mining
Tools	Excel, SPSS, SAS	Python, R, Hadoop, TensorFlow
Outcome	Descriptive and Inferential Insights	Predictive Models and Automated Decisions

Conclusion

Data use has undergone a paradigm shift with the transition from traditional data analysis to data science. Traditional approaches are still useful because they are dependable and simple, but data science, which is fueled by AI and ML, provides strong tools for influencing and predicting future events. Using data science gives firms the ability to use massive volumes of data to their advantage and make faster, better informed, and more intelligent decisions.

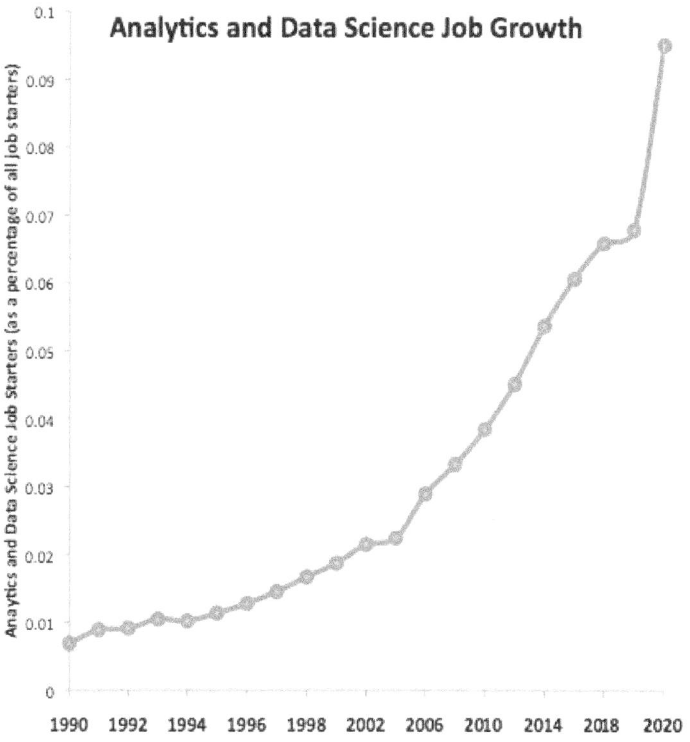

1.5 ROLE OF AI AND ML IN DATA SCIENCE

In the interdisciplinary discipline of data science, knowledge and insights are extracted from both organized and unstructured data using scientific procedures, systems, algorithms, and methods. Artificial Intelligence (AI) and Machine Learning (ML), two potent technologies that have completely changed how we evaluate data, generate predictions, and automate decisionmaking processes, are at the core of contemporary data science.

Understanding AI and ML

Artificial Intelligence (AI)

The goal of the large field of artificial intelligence (AI) is to build machines that are able to carry out tasks that would typically need human intelligence. Learning, reasoning, solving problems, comprehending natural language, and perceiving are some of these tasks. Narrow AI and General AI are the two categories into which AI may be divided. Weak AI, or narrow AI, is created to accomplish a single task, such internet searches or facial recognition. Though such systems are still theoretical and undeveloped, general artificial intelligence, also known as strong artificial intelligence, attempts to imitate human cognitive abilities and can accomplish any intellectual job that a human can.

Artificial Intelligence (AI) technologies cover a wide range of subfields, such as computer vision, which enables systems to interpret and understand visual information from the outside world, natural language processing (NLP), which allows machines to understand and respond to human language, and expert systems, which mimic the decisionmaking process of human experts using rules and logic. Robotics is another area of AI where intelligent agents may communicate with the outside world. Algorithms, contemporary hardware's processing capacity, and the availability of big datasets for the purpose of training these intelligent systems are what propel AI's progress.

Machine Learning (ML)

A crucial area of artificial intelligence called machine learning (ML) focuses on creating algorithms that let computers analyze data and draw conclusions. As ML systems are exposed to more data, they gradually become more proficient at a task. In this procedure, a model is trained using a dataset, its performance is validated using untested data, and iterative improvements are made to the model. ML is divided into various categories:

1. **Supervised Learning:** This involves labeled dataset training, where every training example has an output label associated with it. Support vector machines, decision trees, logistic regression, and linear regression are examples of common algorithms. Regression and classification tasks are examples of supervised learning.
2. **Unsupervised Learning:** Utilizes data that is not labeled. To identify trends and connections in the data is the aim. Unsupervised learning techniques such as clustering (Kmeans, hierarchical clustering) and association (Apriori algorithm) are frequently employed in market basket analysis and consumer segmentation.
3. **Semisupervised Learning:** A hybrid technique in which a substantial amount of unlabeled data and a minor amount of labeled data are used to train the algorithm. When classifying data is costly or timeconsuming, this is helpful.
4. **Reinforcement Learning:** Involves using rewards for desired actions and penalties for unwanted ones to train an agent to make a series of decisions. Applications include autonomous driving, robotics, and gaming.
5. **Deep Learning:** A branch of machine learning that models complicated patterns in data using multilayered neural networks (deep neural networks). Natural language processing, autonomous systems, image and audio recognition, and other fields have advanced significantly as a result of deep learning.

The Interplay between AI, ML, and Data Science

In order to analyze and interpret complicated data, data science combines a variety of tools, techniques, and ideas from computer science, statistics, and domain expertise. AI and ML are key components of this process. The entire workflowfrom gathering, cleaning, and preparing data to creating, assessing, and deploying modelsis covered by data science.

AI offers the sophisticated methods and theoretical framework for developing intelligentsystems in this interaction. Machine learning provides useful techniques for creating and improving prediction models. These AI and ML methods are used by data scientists to draw conclusions from data that may be put to use in a variety of industries, including marketing, finance, healthcare, and transportation.

AI vs. Data Science vs. Machine Learning

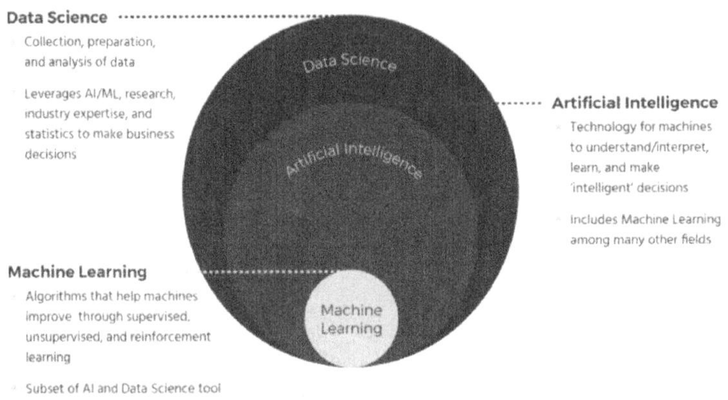

Data scientists can create better models, enhance data analysis procedures, and ultimately make better decisions by being knowledgeable about the nuances of AI and ML. The collaboration of various fields continues to push the limits of what can be done with data, opening the door to the development of more intelligent and adaptable systems that can solve some of the most difficult issues facing modern civilization.

Key Components of Data Science Using AI and ML

In data science initiatives, an organized process is commonly used to convert unstructured data into meaningful insights. Every step of this workflow is improved by AI and ML, increasing its effectiveness and efficiency. Here, we go more deeply into the essential elements at play:

Data Collection and Preprocessing

Every data science project begins with data collection, which is the process of gathering information from a variety of sources including databases, websites that are scraped, Internet of Things devices, and more. The caliber of this preliminary data greatly influences the caliber of the ensuing study. To deal with data noise, missing values, and inconsistencies, preprocessing is a crucial step. Data cleaning procedures including finding and fixing anomalies, normalizing data to bring all attributes to a similar scale, and feature selection to find the most pertinent data points may all be automated with the help of AI and ML. By seamlessly merging data from disparate sources, these technologies also aid in data integration by guaranteeing an extensive dataset for analysis.

Exploratory Data Analysis (EDA)

To find patterns, anomalies, and links in the data, exploratory data analysis (EDA) summarizes the key features of the data both graphically and statistically. Histograms, scatter plots, and heatmaps are examples of visualizations that may be automatically created by AIdriven algorithms and are useful for rapidly spotting important patterns and anomalies. Furthermore, sophisticated AI methods are able to automatically discover anomalies, or data points that substantially differ from the predicted trends. This enhances the correctness of the first insights obtained while expediting the EDA process.

Feature Engineering

Feature engineering involves generating new features from unprocessed data in order to improve the way machine learning models reflect the underlying issue. Variables must be transformed, interaction terms must be made, and new variables must be extracted from old ones. Artificial intelligence (AI) methods, like deep learning, may automatically produce highlevel characteristics from unprocessed data, particularly in complex data types like text and images. By selecting the most predictive traits, this automation helps to eliminate the need for the manual labor and specialized knowledge that are often needed for this stage.

Model Building and Evaluation

The foundation of data science is the creation of prediction models. To fit models to data, machine learning (ML) offers a wide range of algorithms, from straightforward linear regression to intricate deep learning networks. To evaluate these models' performance, model evaluation is essential. Metrics including accuracy, precision, recall, F1score, and area under the ROC curve (AUCROC) are used. By automating hyperparameter tuningoptimizing the parameters that regulate the algorithm's learning processartificial intelligence (AI) can improve this procedure. Methods like Bayesian optimization, random search, and grid search assist in identifying the optimal model configurations. AI can also help with model selection by analyzing several models and choosing the one that best fits the goals of the project.

Deployment and Monitoring

A model must be developed and tested before being implemented in a realworld setting where it can offer predictions or insights in real time. The model must be integrated into a system during deployment in order for it to be capable of handling input and output of data in real time. AIpowered solutions make it easier to continuously monitor the performance of models in use, identifying instances of "model drift," or the gradual deterioration of models as a result of modifications in data distribution. Models are automatically updated and retrained to maintain their accuracy and dependability over time.

Applications of AI and ML in Data Science

Because AI and ML make it possible to make decisions based on data, increase productivity, and reveal insightful information, they have a revolutionary effect on a variety of businesses. Here are a few specific examples of how AI and ML are being used in various industries:

Healthcare

AI and ML are essential to the healthcare industry's transformation in patient care and medical research. Largescale patient data can be analyzed by ML algorithms to forecast disease outbreaks, customize treatment regimens, and enhance diagnostic precision. For example, by evaluating past medical records and lifestyle information, machine learning algorithms can forecast the risk of diseases like diabetes or cardiac issues. AIpowered imaging devices also improve the precision of identifying anomalies in MRIs and Xrays, which promotes early diagnosis and better patient outcomes. Artificial intelligence (AI) is being used in healthcare in a way that includes robotic surgeries, in which surgeons are assisted by AIdriven robots in carrying out accurate, minimally invasive procedures.

Finance

AI and ML are used by the finance sector for a variety of purposes, including algorithmic trading and fraud detection. By analyzing transaction patterns, machine learning algorithms can spot anomalous activity that could point to fraud, boosting financial system security and confidence. To improve credit scoring accuracy in risk management, machine learning (ML) models evaluate credit risks by examining the financial records and credit behaviors of borrowers. AI is essential to algorithmic trading as well since it analyzes market trends and executes trades at the best moments to maximize profits. Additionally, chatbots driven by AI offer consumers tailored financial advice, enhancing the entire customer experience.

Marketing

Because AI and ML enable targeted advertising and individualized client interactions, they greatly enhance marketing techniques. Marketing professionals can efficiently adapt their efforts by identifying unique client groups through customer segmentation, which is achieved by ML algorithms analyzing consumer behavior and demographics. Businesses can proactively address issues by using sentiment analysis, powered by natural language processing (NLP), to better comprehend customer opinions and feedback from social media and reviews. Another effective tool is predictive analytics, which makes predictions about future consumer behavior based on past data. It helps with campaign planning, inventory control, and client retention tactics. Recommendation systems are further improved by AI, which offers consumers tailored content or product recommendations based on their interests and usage patterns.

Transportation

AI and ML are used in the transportation industry to develop driverless cars, improve safety, and streamline logistics. Selfdriving cars are already a reality thanks to autonomous vehicles, which use AI for realtime decisionmaking, navigation, and obstacle recognition. By optimizing routes for delivery and transportation services, machine learning algorithms lower fuel costs and expedite delivery times. By analyzing data from sensors on infrastructure and cars, predictive maintenance, fueled by machine learning, can identify possible problems before they arise, reducing maintenance expenses and downtime. Additionally, by modifying signal timings in response to current traffic circumstances, AIdriven traffic management systems enhance traffic flow in metropolitan areas.

Retail

AI and ML improve a number of areas of supply chain management and the shopping experience in retail. Personalized product recommendations are given to customers by AIdriven recommendation systems, which boosts revenue and client happiness. In order to optimize inventory levels and guarantee that popular items are constantly in stock while minimizing overstock of less popular items, machine learning algorithms examine sales data. Chatbots with AI capabilities help consumers identify items and get answers to their questions, enhancing customer support. Machine learning models are used in supply chain management to anticipate demand trends and improve logistics, which lowers costs and boosts productivity.

Manufacturing

Manufacturing is being revolutionized by AI and ML in three ways: process optimization, quality control, and predictive maintenance. Machine learning systems evaluate sensor data to forecast equipment problems, facilitating prompt repair and cutting downtime. Artificial intelligence (AI)driven quality control systems examine goods while they are being assembled, detecting flaws more precisely than human inspectors. Machine learning models examine production data to find bottlenecks and suggest fixes in the process of process optimization, which raises overall productivity and efficiency.

These examples show how AI and ML have enormous potential to change data science in a variety of industries. Businesses may increase operational efficiency, make smarter decisions, and provide their clients better goods and services by utilizing these technologies. The impact of AI and ML on data science and industry will only increase as these technologies develop, opening up new avenues for innovation and growth.

Challenges and Future Directions

Challenges

1. **Data Availability and Quality:** Ensuring the availability and quality of data is a major difficulty when using AI and ML in data research. Robust models require highquality data to be trained, yet data frequently originates from several sources with differing degrees of completeness and accuracy. A comprehensive, noisy, or biased set of data can seriously hinder machine learning models' performance. As a result, rigorous preparation, integration, and data cleansing are needed, all of which might take a lot of time and resources.
2. **Algorithm Bias:** Bias in machine learning algorithms originates from either intrinsic biases in the algorithms or biased data. Unfair or biased results may result from this, particularly in delicate fields like hiring, lending, and law enforcement. A crucial task is identifying and reducing bias, which calls for a close analysis of the models and the data. While methods like fairnessaware algorithms and bias detection are being developed, the problem still exists.

3. **Interpretability:** A lot of sophisticated machine learning models, especially deep learning models, are "black boxes," providing little information about the decisionmaking process. This lack of interpretability can be troublesome, particularly in fields where it's critical to comprehend the reasoning behind decisions, like banking and healthcare. While efforts are being made to create more interpretable models and methodologiessuch as modelagnostic approaches to prediction explanationit is still difficult to strike a balance between model complexity and interpretability.
4. **Scalability:** It gets harder to scale machine learning models to accommodate big datasets as data volumes increase exponentially. Strong infrastructure is needed for this, as well as strong computational capabilities and effective algorithms that can handle enormous volumes of data in a fair amount of time. Scalability problems are frequently addressed using distributed systems and cloud computing, but effectively managing these systems introduces another level of complexity.

Future Directions

1. **Explainable AI:** The development of Explainable AI (XAI) is one of the potential future directions. The goal of XAI is to develop models that not only function well but also offer concise, intelligible justifications for their judgments and forecasts. Gaining credibility and acceptability in crucial applications like as financial forecasting and medical diagnosis calls on this in particular. The goal of this field's research is to create techniques that help improve the transparency and interpretability of complicated models.
2. **Automated Machine Learning (AutoML):** aims to automate the entire process of using machine learning (ML) to solve realworld issues, including feature selection, data preprocessing, model selection, and hyperparameter tuning. This lessens the requirement for indepth knowledge and enables nonexperts to create efficient models. AutoML has the potential to democratize machine learning (ML), opening up the field to a wider audience and hastening the adoption of ML solutions in a range of sectors.
3. **Ethical AI:** It's critical to make sure AI systems function ethically as they become more commonplace. Creating and putting into practice rules and regulations that guarantee AI systems are just, responsible, and open is known as ethical AI. This entails

dealing with concerns like prejudice, privacy, and the effects of AI on society. It is probable that ethical considerations will receive greater attention in the future of AI, along with enhanced governmental control and the creation of best practices and standards.

4. **Integration of IoT and AI:** Intelligent, networked systems could be created through the convergence of AI and the Internet of Things (IoT). The integration of artificial intelligence (AI) with Internet of Things (IoT) devices can facilitate realtime data analysis and decisionmaking at the edge, improving system responsiveness and efficiency in domains including healthcare, industrial automation, and smart cities. Improvements in energy management, personalized services, and predictive maintenance will be fueled by this connection.

Conclusion

In data science, artificial intelligence (AI) and machine learning (ML) have become essential tools for analysis, prediction, and decisionmaking. They foster innovation. As these technologies advance, they will further change a number of industries and increase the effectiveness and influence of data science. Data scientists can fully utilize AI and ML to solve difficult problems and extract value from data by comprehending their functions and uses.

1.6 APPLICATIONS OF DATA SCIENCE

The discipline of data science has gained prominence as a crucial area that integrates machine learning (ML), artificial intelligence (AI), and statistical analysis to derive significant insights and forecasts from large datasets. This chapter examines the numerous uses of AI and ML in data science across a range of sectors.

1. Healthcare

The combination of data science, AI, and ML in the healthcare sector is fostering groundbreaking breakthroughs and enhancing patient outcomes. One prominent application of AI is predictive analytics, which forecasts patient admissions and readmissions by analyzing large datasets, including electronic health records (EHRs). This makes it possible for hospitals to improve patient care, cut down on wait times, and distribute resources more effectively.

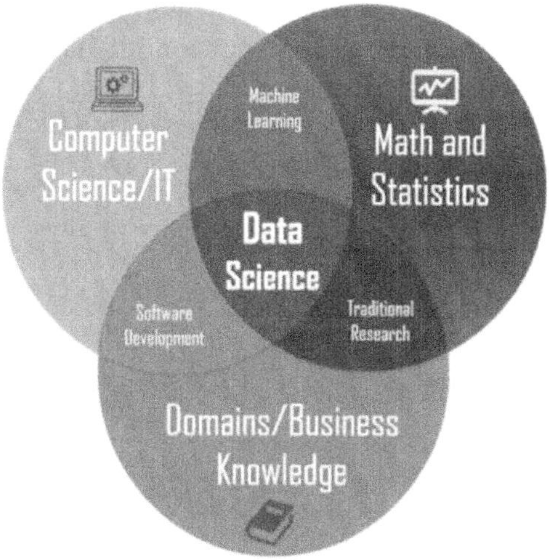

Personalized healthcare is another revolutionary use case. Healthcare providers can create individualized treatment programs by using ML models to examine lifestyle data, treatment histories, and genetic information. This strategy works especially well in cancer, where patients' survival rates can be greatly increased by receiving treatments that are specifically designed to match the genetic makeup of their tumor.

AI is having a significant influence in the field of medical imaging. Thousands of medical photos are used to train deep learning models to identify patterns that point to various conditions, including infections, tumors, and fractures. Early diagnosis and treatment are made easier by the fact that these models can frequently identify abnormalities faster and with greater accuracy than human radiologists.

Furthermore, chatbots powered by AI and virtual health assistants are getting more and more popular. By evaluating data from wearable devices, these systems can even monitor chronic illnesses and give patients quick medical advice and appointment scheduling capabilities. This lightens the load on medical staff while simultaneously improving patient participation.

Example: Predictive Analytics in Healthcare

Take into consideration a predictive model that predicts patient admissions as an example. The algorithm forecasts future admission rates with excellent accuracy by using seasonal patterns, past admission data, and outside variables like flu epidemics. With the help of this information, hospitals can plan ahead and make sure that they have enough staff members and resources on hand. The accuracy of the prediction model is demonstrated by the example below, which plots the expected versus actual patient admissions over time.

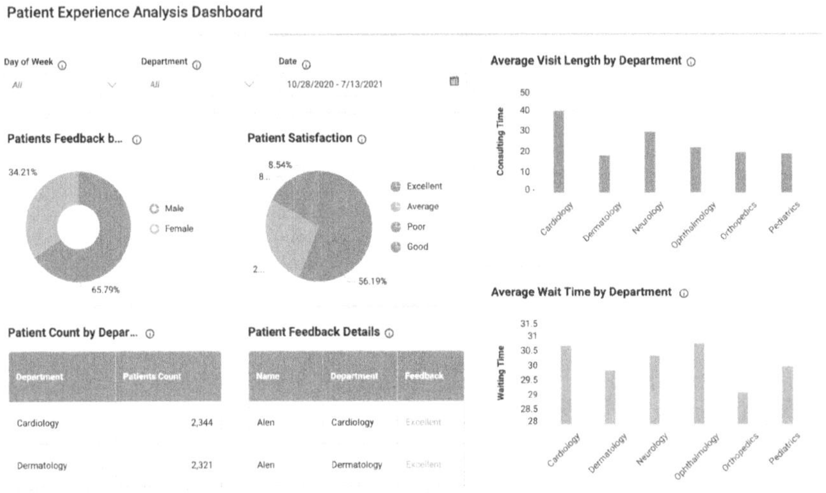

Example: Medical Imaging

AI systems analyze Xray, MRI, and CT scan pictures to find abnormalities in medical imaging. An AI model trained on thousands of mammograms, for example, can identify early indicators of breast cancer that a human eye might miss. Better patient outcomes and early treatments may result from the use of such technology.

Table 4: Comparison of Traditional vs. AI enhanced Diagnostics

Feature	Traditional Diagnostics	AIenhanced Diagnostics
Accuracy	Moderate	High
Time Consumption	High	Low
Cost	High	Moderate
Personalization	Low	High

Example: Virtual Health Assistants

AIpowered virtual health aides are capable of a wide range of tasks. They can advise on lifestyle choices, encourage patients to take their medications, and triage symptoms. To better manage their diabetes, a patient might, for instance, utilize a virtual assistant to monitor their blood sugar levels and get food recommendations.

2. Finance

Applications

The finance industry has undergone a substantial transformation thanks to data science, which uses AI and ML to improve productivity, accuracy, and security in a variety of financial operations. These are a few thorough applications:

- **Fraud Detection:** To identify and stop fraudulent activity, financial institutions use advanced machine learning algorithms. These algorithms use realtime analysis of massive volumes of transaction data to spot odd patterns and behaviors that could be signs of fraud. For example, the system may flag a credit card transaction as suspicious if it happens in a foreign country soon after a transaction in the user's own country. More sophisticated anomaly detection methods, such neural networks and clustering, allow for the quicker and more precise identification of fraudulent activity, lowering losses and enhancing security.
- **Algorithmic Trading:** By examining market data and patterns, AIdriven algorithmic trading systems execute trades at the best times. These computers outperform human traders by using intricate algorithms to predict market fluctuations and make snap decisions. These algorithms ensure higher returns on investments by utilizing techniques like reinforcement learning and time series analysis, which allow them to adapt to changing market conditions. As a branch of algorithmic trading, highfrequency trading (HFT) uses artificial intelligence (AI) to perform thousands of deals per second and profit from even the smallest price differences.
- **Credit Scoring:** Conventional credit scoring algorithms focus on a small number of data factors, like income and credit history. On the other hand, in order to evaluate creditworthiness, AIenhanced models take into account a wider variety of data, such as social media activity, online behavior, and transaction history. More accurate credit scores can result from ML algorithms' ability to spot minute patterns and correlations that traditional models would overlook. This enables lenders to make more educated choices, lower their default rates, and provide loans to more clientsincluding those with questionable credit histories.
- **Portfolio Management:** By offering individualized investment plans based on a person's financial goals, risk tolerance,

and market conditions, AI and ML are transforming portfolio management. Roboadvisors are AIpowered automated platforms that provide affordable, effective, and personalized investing advice. These platforms make sure that portfolios are balanced and in line with investors' goals by using predictive analytics to foresee market developments and optimize asset allocation.

- **Risk Management:** To improve risk management procedures, financial institutions use ML and AI. Predictive models evaluate the risk connected to different investments, loans, and financial instruments. These models can forecast possible dangers and offer insights into mitigating methods by examining past data and market trends. By taking a proactive stance, institutions can more successfully control their exposure to operational, credit, and market risks.

Example: Fraud Detection

A heatmap in fraud detection can show how frequently an algorithm picks up on transaction abnormalities. Analysts can concentrate their investigations on highrisk locations by using this image, which shows places with higher concentrations of suspicious activity. Typically, the heatmap would display clusters of fraudulent transactions, pointing out trends that need more investigation.

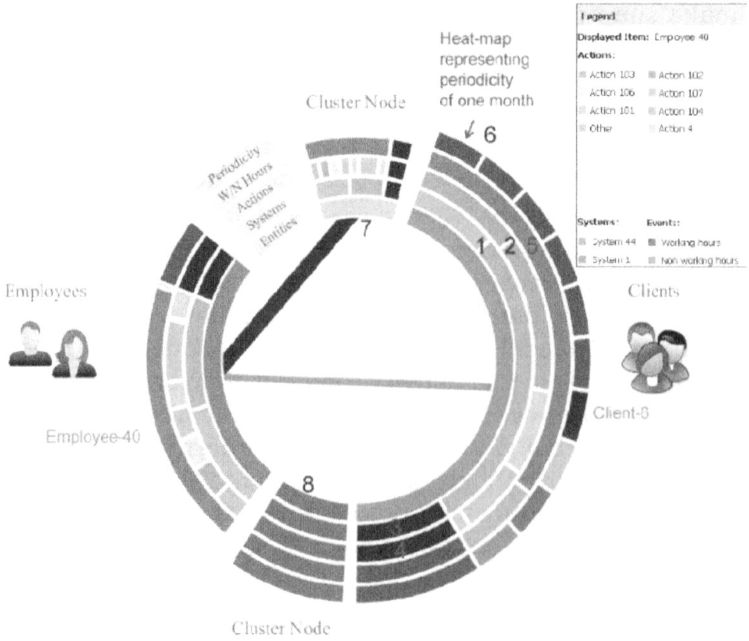

Graph: Performance of AI in Credit Scoring

The increase in predicted accuracy may be seen in a line graph that plots the accuracy of AIenhanced models against traditional credit scoring methods over time. With the use of AI, the accuracy of the graph may grow significantly, demonstrating how AI models improve creditworthiness and lower default rates.

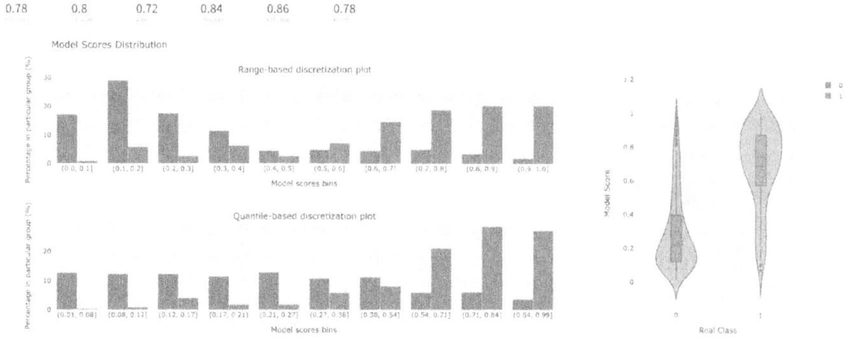

In general, stronger, more effective, and more secure financial operations have resulted from the integration of AI and ML in finance. Financial institutions can now manage risk, optimize investments, and enhance client experiences with the help of these cuttingedge technologies, which are propelling the sector toward a more datadriven future.

3. Retail

Applications

Through the use of AI and ML, data science has improved several business processes, including inventory management and consumer engagement, greatly changing the retail sector. Retailers may now make datadriven decisions that increase productivity and consumer happiness because they have access to sophisticated algorithms that evaluate massive volumes of data.

- **Client Segmentation:** Based on demographics, purchasing patterns, and other pertinent variables, merchants can use machine learning to divide their client base into discrete segments. By allowing for tailored marketing methods, this segmentation makes sure that promotional efforts are focused on the correct demographic. To increase engagement and sales within a certain consumer segment, a shop could, for example, identify that client segment and focus their marketing campaigns on sustainable goods.

- **Recommendation Systems:** AIpowered recommendation systems look through a customer's browsing and purchase history to make recommendations for items that they are likely to buy. Because they customize each customer's online buying experience, these technologies are essential for improving the overall shopping experience. For instance, a client who regularly purchases sporting goods may be given recommendations for the newest fitness monitors or running shoes, which promotes sales while simultaneously fostering greater customer pleasure and loyalty.
- **Inventory Management:** Optimizing inventory levels is greatly aided by predictive analytics. Machine learning models are used to estimate demand for different items through the analysis of sales data, seasonality tendencies, and other factors. This insight lowers the possibility of overstocking or stockouts by assisting shops in maintaining ideal stock levels. Predictive models, for example, can guarantee that highdemand items are sufficiently stocked over the holiday season, boosting sales potential and avoiding lost revenue from outofstock situations.
- **Price Optimization:** AI is used by retailers to establish the best possible price for their goods. In order to recommend the optimum prices that maximize profit margins and sales, machine learning algorithms examine consumer sensitivity to price changes, market demand, and competitor pricing. With the use of artificial intelligence (AI), retailers may use dynamic pricing methods to safeguard their profits and remain competitive by instantly adjusting prices in response to shifting market conditions.
- **Supply Chain Management:** By anticipating possible interruptions and streamlining logistics, AI and ML simplify supply chain operations. AI, for instance, can forecast weather that may have an impact on shipping schedules and recommend alternate routes or delivery options. This feature guarantees that goods arrive at shelves on schedule, preserving a constant supply of goods and avoiding delays that can affect sales.

Example: Recommendation Systems

It has been shown that recommendation systems are especially successful at boosting client satisfaction and sales. These algorithms look analyze a customer's past purchases and browsing habits to identify things that the customer is probably going to like. For example, the recommendation system may promote new organic items, cookbooks, or related kitchen appliances to a consumer who regularly purchases organic food. By highlighting pertinent products, this not only increases sales but also improves the shopping experience by making it more engaging and personalized.

Table 5: Impact of AIbased Recommendation Systems on Sales

Month	Sales without AI (in $)	Sales with AI (in $)	Percentage Increase (%)
January	50,000	60,000	20%
February	45,000	55,000	22%
March	55,000	67,000	21.8%

As a result, the retail industry has become more dynamic, responsive, and customerfocused with the incorporation of AI and ML. These cuttingedge data science solutions help retailers predict and meet customer needs more effectively, manage resources more effectively, and ultimately increase profitability. The retail industry will likely see even more advancements and improvements as a result of these technologies' continued development.

4. Transportation

AI and MLbased data science applications in the transportation sector are transforming logistics, maintenance, and vehicle operations. Predictive maintenance is one of the key uses, where AI systems examine sensor data from infrastructure and automobiles to identify possible problems before they arise. This proactive strategy lowers maintenance costs, saves downtime, and improves the general dependability of transportation networks. For example, maintenance can be planned precisely in time to prevent expensive and inconvenient failures by using ML models to anticipate when a train component is likely to fail.

Another disruptive use is route optimization. Here, massive volumes of data, such as traffic patterns, weather, and delivery schedules, are processed by ML algorithms to identify the most effective transportation routes. By guaranteeing ontime delivery, this lowers fuel usage and travel time while simultaneously increasing customer satisfaction. Delivery services, for instance, can use AI to dynamically modify routes in realtime to account for unforeseen delays or traffic jams.

One innovative use of AI in transportation is autonomous vehicles. These cars use sophisticated AI algorithms to process data from multiple sensors, including radar, LIDAR, and cameras. In order to make driving judgments, artificial intelligence (AI) analyzes this data in realtime. This allows selfdriving cars to drive on roadways, avoid obstacles, and obey traffic laws. In addition to lowering human error and improving road safety, this technology offers mobility alternatives for people who are unable to drive.

Additionally, public transportation planning and management makes use of data science. Here, AI and ML are utilized to manage fleet operations, improve schedules, and evaluate ridership patterns. This results in decreased operating costs, increased service frequency, and more effective use of resources. To make sure that capacity meets demand, transit authorities, for example, can utilize data analytics to identify peak travel times and modify bus or train timetables accordingly.

Overall, by optimizing resource consumption and lowering emissions, the application of data science in transportation not only simplifies operations but also advances sustainable practices. In this industry, the application of AI and ML technologies is opening the door to more intelligent, secure, and effective transportation systems.

5. Marketing

Applications

- **Sentiment Analysis:** Opinion mining, or sentiment analysis, uses artificial intelligence (AI) to assess social media posts, customer reviews, and other textual data in order to ascertain the sentiment underlying the words. Through the classification of these emotions as either good, negative, or neutral, companies can obtain uptodate knowledge about consumer attitudes and brand recognition. Marketing teams may swiftly summarize public opinion about a product launch by using an AIdriven sentiment analysis tool, which can scan millions of tweets. This information allows the teams to modify their strategy.
- **Campaign Optimization:** AI and ML are essential tools for marketing campaigns since they optimize strategies and maximize return on investment. Machine learning algorithms examine past campaign data to find trends and forecast which approaches are most likely to be effective. These models recommend the optimal timing to launch a campaign, the most efficient channels to use, and the best content style by taking into account a number of variables, including audience demographics, engagement metrics, and past campaign success. With the aid of this predictive skill, marketers can

develop audienceresonant campaigns that are highly targeted and successful.

- **Churn Prediction:** One crucial use of data science in marketing is churn prediction, which determines which consumers are most likely to discontinue using a product or service. Predictive models are used to identify atrisk customers by examining transaction history, interaction patterns, and customer behavior. This enables companies to proactively engage with these clients by making tailored offers, incentives, or interventions. Churn prediction, for instance, may be used by a subscription service to provide a discounted cost to users who exhibit signs of disengagement, therefore lowering the total churn rate and preserving a loyal client base.

Example: Sentiment Analysis

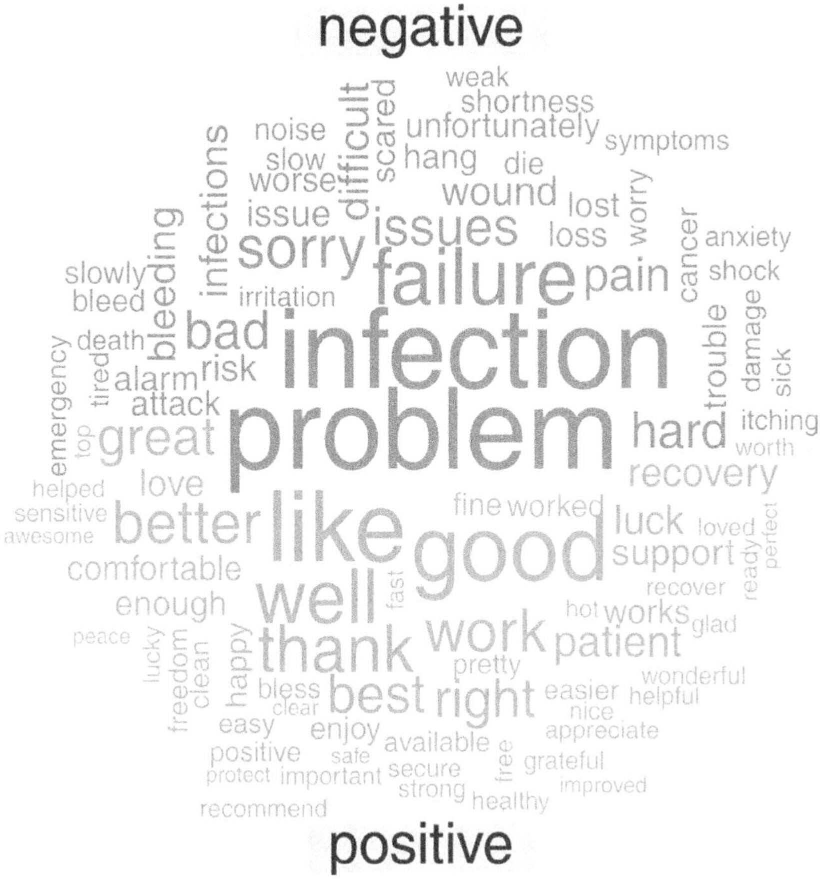

Imagine that a business has just introduced a new product. The marketing team may examine hundreds of client evaluations from many platforms by utilizing AIpowered sentiment analysis. A graphic representation of a word cloud that highlights often used terms in both positive and negative reviews can give a brief summary of consumer opinions. This helps the business make datadriven decisions by enabling it to determine which features of the product are wellreceived and which ones need to be improved.

A table that contrasts the accuracy of machine learning models with that of classic statistical models can be used to demonstrate the efficacy of churn prediction.

Table 6: Churn Prediction Accuracy

Model	Accuracy (%)
Traditional Model	75
ML Model	90

This table highlights the importance of integrating advanced analytics into marketing strategy by showcasing the greater accuracy of machine learning (ML) models in predicting client attrition.

RealWorld Case Studies

1. **Netflix:** To enhance content delivery and personalize suggestions, Netflix leverages AI and ML. By using watching habits analysis, their recommendation engine makes recommendations for movies and TV series that dramatically boost viewer engagement and lower attrition rates.
2. **CocaCola:** CocaCola uses AI to monitor social media sentiment, which enables them to quickly respond to customer comments and adjust marketing initiatives in realtime.
3. **Amazon:** A large percentage of Amazon's sales are generated by its AIpowered recommendation engine, which makes product recommendations based on browsing and historical purchase activity.

Businesses may revolutionize their marketing strategies by utilizing AI and ML to make sure they are proactive rather than reactive and that they provide individualized experiences that increase consumer happiness and loyalty. This innovative marketing strategy demonstrates the significant influence of data science on contemporary corporate operations.

Conclusion

Data science's incorporation of AI and ML has transformed a number of sectors by improving procedures, personalizing experiences, and making predictions that are more accurate. The chapter's applications highlight how modern technologies can have a profound impact on society.

2

Data Collection and Preprocessing

2.1 DATA COLLECTION TECHNIQUES

In data science, the data collecting process is the cornerstone that supports all other analysis and models. The chapter delves into diverse methods of gathering data, stressing their significance, approaches, and optimal procedures in relation to applications of Artificial Intelligence (AI) and Machine Learning (ML).

Importance of Data Collection

In the context of AI and ML, the value of data collecting cannot be emphasized because it provides the foundation for defensible, perceptive analyses and predictions. First, the robustness and dependability of models are directly impacted by the quality of the data. Poorquality data might result in inaccurate or misleading findings, whereas highquality data guarantees that the patterns and trends found by AI and ML algorithms are significant and actionable.

Second, the effectiveness of AI and ML models is highly dependent on the volume of data. While quality is crucial, algorithms can better forecast outcomes and withstand outliers when they have access to a large enough number of data that allows them to generalize patterns across many contexts. When gathering data, this balance between quantity and quality is always taken into account.

Furthermore, ethical issues play a significant role in data collection procedures. To keep people's confidence and accountability, data gathering practices must be open, equitable, and compatible with laws like the GDPR. In addition, biases included in data sources or sampling techniques must be carefully addressed to avoid biased results that reinforce social injustices or inaccurate model predictions.

In the end, efficient data collecting underpins both the wider societal consequences of AI and ML as well as their technological components. Organizations and researchers may fully utilize AI and ML to spur innovation, enhance decisionmaking, and have a positive impact on a range of industries, from healthcare and finance to education and beyond, by gathering and using data responsibly. Therefore, in today's datadriven environment, investing in sound data gathering procedures is essential to achieving the transformative potential of AI and ML.

Techniques and Methodologies

Data Collection

AI and ML data gathering techniques comprise a range of approaches designed to extract useful insights for predictive modeling and decisionmaking from a variety of data kinds.

1. Surveys and Questionnaires

Conventional but efficient means of obtaining structured data directly from people or organizations include surveys and questionnaires. When obtaining both quantitative and qualitative information on consumer behavior, market trends, or user preferences, these techniques are quite helpful. In order to get precise data for statistical analysis and model training, researchers create surveys. Surveys, for instance, can reveal customer satisfaction metrics or demographic trends in market research that are essential for developing business strategies.

2. Web Scraping

Web scraping is the process of automatically extracting data from websites using tools and scripts to gather data from web pages. This method is essential for combining big datasets from industries like finance, research, and ecommerce. Web scraping, for example, makes it possible to obtain realtime data on stock prices, news mood, or economic indicators in the financial markets, giving analysts access to the most recent information for investing strategies and predictive modeling.

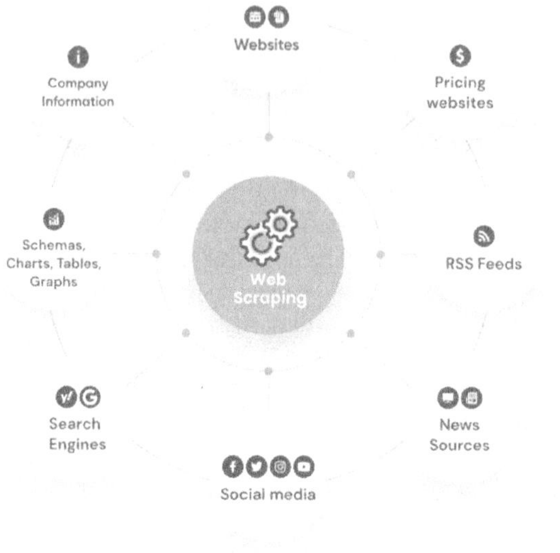

3. Sensor Data Collection

Sensor data collecting has become essential in many areas, such as manufacturing, environmental monitoring, and healthcare, with the rise of the Internet of Things. Sensorequipped Internet of Things (IoT) devices record temperature, humidity, motion, and other data in real time, allowing for predictive maintenance and ongoing monitoring. Wearable technology, for instance, is used in the healthcare industry to gather physiological data such as heart rate and activity levels, which helps with illness management and individualized healthcare interventions.

4. Social Media Mining

Social networking sites produce enormous volumes of unstructured data that are incredibly insightful about trends, sentiment, and public opinion. Text, sentiment, and network analysis are all used in social media mining techniques to extract useful data for governments and corporations. Sentiment analysis on Twitter, for example, can be used to inform policy decisions or marketing efforts by determining how the public feels about a political issue or brand.

Best Practices

- First and foremost, Data Security and Privacy is crucial. To protect personal data, it entails abiding by laws like the General

Data Protection Regulation (GDPR). By putting strong security measures in place, users' and stakeholders' trust is preserved and data is protected from breaches and illegal access.

- Second, to deal with errors, missing values, and inconsistencies in raw data, Data Cleaning is crucial. Outlier identification, imputation techniques, and normalizing are some of the procedures used to make sure the dataset is accurate and fit for analysis. Through this procedure, the quality and dependability of the insights produced by AI and ML models are greatly improved.
- Thirdly, Data Augmentation is essential to increasing dataset size and diversity. Through the use of methods like duplication, transformation, or combination, data scientists can create new datasets or expand preexisting ones, which will help their models perform better and more broadly in novel situations.
- Additionally, Version Control and Documentation are essential for reproducibility and transparency. Maintaining thorough documentation of data collecting techniques, preprocessing modifications, and versions of utilized datasets guarantees that studies may be verified and repeated by other investigators or in various settings.
- Last but not least, Continuous Monitoring and Evaluation of data collection procedures is required to maintain data quality and adjust to changing requirements. Over time, regular audits, feedback loops from model performance, and stakeholder involvement help to sustain the relevance and dependability of AI and ML applications by quickly identifying and resolving issues.

By implementing these best practices, data gathering initiatives can maximize the value and utility of the insights gained while supporting the moral application of AI and ML technologies. Organizations and researchers may reduce risks, improve their capacity for making decisions, and stimulate innovation across a range of industries by promoting a disciplined approach to data collecting.

Case Studies

Healthcare

Data gathering is essential to the healthcare industry's revolution in patient care, medical research, and operational effectiveness. Healthcare providers utilize a range of data gathering methodologies to obtain insights from heterogeneous sources, including wearable technology, medical imaging, and electronic health records (EHRs).

Data Sources

- **Electronic Health Records (EHRs):** The medical history, treatments, and results of each patient are contained in these extensive digital records. Personalized medicine and predictive analytics are made possible by data scientists who examine electronic health records (EHRs) to find trends in patient outcomes, treatment effectiveness, and disease progression.
- **Wearable Devices:** Wearable technology, such as fitness trackers and medical sensors, is revolutionizing the healthcare industry by providing realtime data on vital signs, physical activity, and sleep habits. Proactive interventions and early health issue detection are supported by continuous monitoring via these devices.

Applications

- **Predictive Analytics:** AI models can identify atrisk groups, forecast illness risks, and suggest preventive actions by examining past patient data from EHRs. Predictive models, for instance, can estimate the risk of readmission in light of lifestyle, medical history, and patient demographics.
- **Clinical Decision Support:** Making evidencebased judgments is made easier for physicians when AIpowered decision support tools are integrated with EHR data. To recommend the best course of action and lower diagnostic errors, these systems examine the symptoms of the patient, the results of their tests, and their treatment regimens.

Example Scenario

Consider a situation where a medical professional uses AI to review diabetic patients' electronic health records. Artificial intelligence systems are able to forecast the likelihood of diabetes problems like retinopathy or neuropathy by analyzing data on blood glucose levels, medication compliance, and lifestyle choices. By adopting a proactive strategy, healthcare providers can enhance patient outcomes, modify treatment plans, and execute focused treatments.

Finance

Techniques for gathering data are essential to risk management, fraud detection, and customer analytics in the financial sector. Large amounts of transactional and market data must be collected, processed, and analyzed by financial institutions using reliable data pipelines.

Data Sources

- **Transactional Data:** Purchases, withdrawals, and transfers are just a few of the consumer contacts that banks and financial institutions gather transactional data from. Transactional pattern analysis aids in anomaly detection, fraud identification, and customer experience personalization.
- **Market Data:** Extensive data on stock prices, exchange rates, commodity prices, and economic indicators are produced by financial markets. Financial analysts gather realtime market data through web scraping and API integration to guide their investment strategies and risk evaluations.

Applications

- **Fraud Detection:** Transactional data is analyzed by AI algorithms to find anomalous spending patterns, fraudulent transactions, and identity theft. Financial institutions can avoid financial losses and safeguard customer assets by utilizing machine learning models.
- **Algorithmic Trading:** Highfrequency trading companies analyze market data using algorithms powered by artificial intelligence (AI) to execute deals at the best prices and volumes. To predict market trends and enhance trading methods, these algorithms make use of technical indicators, sentiment analysis of news, and historical data.

Example Scenario

Imagine a situation where a financial organization analyzes transactional data for credit card fraud by using machine learning techniques. The model gains the ability to identify patterns suggestive of fraudulent activitysuch as atypical spending patterns or transactions that deviate from the cardholder's customary behaviorby means of algorithmic training on historical data. These AI models for realtime monitoring allow for timely intervention to improve security and reduce fraud threats.

Conclusion

The effectiveness of AI and ML applications is largely dependent on efficient data collection. Data scientists can guarantee the validity and applicability of the insights gained by using the right methods and following best practices, which will promote creativity and wellinformed decisionmaking across a range of industries.

2.2 DATA CLEANING AND PREPARATION

The foundation of any effective analysis in the field of data science is the cleaning and preparation of data. It entails converting unstructured raw data into a tidy format that may be used for modeling and additional research. This chapter examines several methods and best practices that are necessary to guarantee the accuracy and dependability of data.

Importance of Data Cleaning

When it comes to applying AI and ML to transform raw data into usable insights, data cleaning is a crucial step in the data science process. Its significance is immeasurable since any study or model's dependability and quality depend on how clean the data it is based on is. Impurities such missing numbers, inconsistencies, errors, and outliers are frequently present in raw data. These problems may result from data input errors made by humans, broken sensors, or simply random fluctuations in the data collection procedures. These flaws have the potential to seriously impair the accuracy and efficacy of later assessments and forecasts if they are ignored.

Data scientists make sure the data appropriately depicts the realworld event it is meant to portray by thoroughly cleansing the data. Errors must be found and fixed, missing values must be filled in using the proper imputation techniques, and outliers that could skew statistical studies or machine learning model training must be eliminated or corrected. Additionally, data cleaning improves the dataset's general quality, which facilitates exploration and the extraction of insightful information. It makes it possible to create strong predictive models that perform well when applied to previously undiscovered data and to make more trustworthy comparisons across various datasets.

Essentially, data cleansing is a fundamental component of data science activity rather than just a preliminary measure. It guarantees that later studies and machine learning assignments are constructed upon a strong and reliable foundation, which eventually results in more precise conclusions and betterinformed choices across a range of industries, from marketing to finance and healthcare, among others. Effective data cleansing plays an increasingly important role in optimizing the value and usability of datadriven approaches in AI and

ML applications as data continues to expand in volume and complexity.

Techniques and Methods

Now let's take a closer look at the strategies and tactics applied to data preparation and cleaning:

1. Handling Missing Data

Missing data is a prevalent problem in datasets and can be caused by a number of things, including purposeful nonresponses, sensor problems, and data input errors. Reliability and integrity of analyses depend on handling missing data effectively.

- **Imputation Techniques:** One method is to use statistical measures from the corresponding column, such as the mean, median, or mode, to fill in the missing data. This approach is easy to use and maintains the data's overall distribution.
- **Advanced Techniques:** Predictive models, like as decision trees or regression, can be used for more complex handling in order to forecast missing values based on other connected features. Although it necessitates careful evaluation of model assumptions and data structure, this approach can produce estimations that are more accurate.

Methods for Handling Missing Data

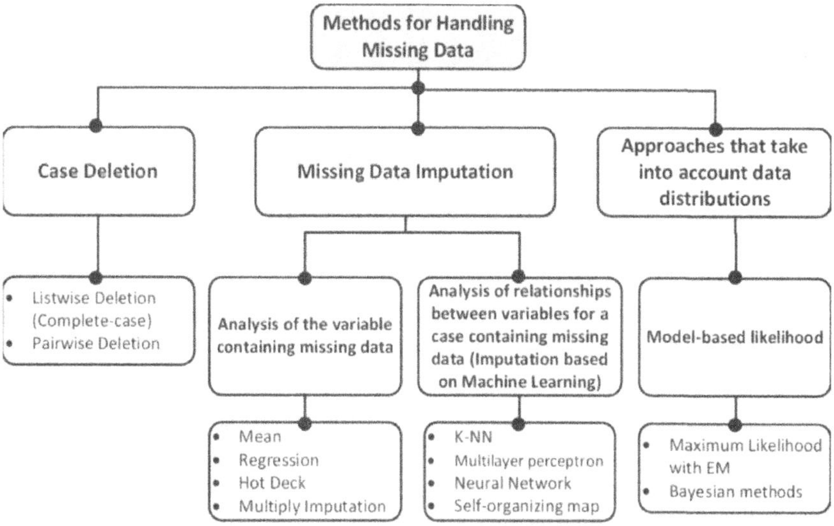

2. Dealing with Outliers

Data points known as outliers can cause statistical studies and machine learning models to be skewed because they drastically differ from the rest of the sample. For data integrity to be maintained, outliers must be identified and dealt with properly.

- **Statistical Methods:** Based on how different an outlier is from the mean or median, methods such as the Zscore or the Interquartile Range (IQR) approach can be used to identify them. Afterward, outliers can be changed or eliminated based on context and subject expertise.
- **Visualization:** Histograms, box plots, and scatter plots are useful visual aids for locating outliers. Data scientists can identify anomalies with these charts and decide how best to treat them.

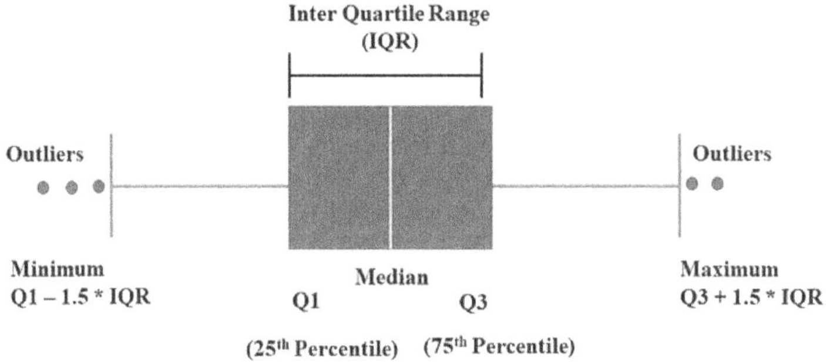

3. Data Transformation

Data transformation is the process of transforming unprocessed data into a form that is better suited for modeling and analysis. To make sure that various data kinds (numeric, category, and text) are in a common format, this step is frequently required.

- **Normalization:** Applying standardization methods like Zscore normalization or scaling numerical data to a standard range, say between 0 and 1. By taking this step, you can make sure that every variable contributes equally to the study and that no single variable uses its size to its advantage.
- **Encoding:** Many machine learning techniques depend on the numerical transformation of categorical data. Algorithms can effectively comprehend categorical data by using techniques like label encoding, which assigns numerical values to categories, or onehot encoding, which creates binary columns for each category.

4. Handling Text Data

Because text data is unstructured, it poses special obstacles that must be overcome in order to extract useful features for analysis and modeling.

- **Tokenization:** By considering text as numerical data, breaking it down into smaller units like words or ngrams (contiguous sequences of n items) makes subsequent analysis easier.
- **Stopword Removal:** Eliminating frequent, superfluous words (stopwords) that don't add anything to the text's meaning. By doing this, the data's noise is reduced and the analysis is narrowed to more pertinent concepts.

These methods are crucial for cleaning and preparing data so that it is comprehensive, accurate, and presented properly for analysis. Gaining proficiency in these techniques enables data scientists to extract insightful information and create reliable machine learning models that adapt well to fresh data. To improve the quality and dependability of the study, each stage necessitates carefully weighing the particular dataset and domain expertise.

Practical Implementation

1. Initial Exploration and Understanding

To fully grasp the structure and properties of the dataset, preliminary exploratory data analysis (EDA) must be carried out before moving on to data cleaning. For example, while working with the Iris dataset, our first step would usually be to look at the mean, median, and standard deviation for the numerical columns (sepal length, petal width, etc.). In order to spot any abnormalities or unusual patterns, we would also use density plots or histograms to illustrate the distributions of these attributes.

2. Handling Missing Data

Missing data is a prevalent problem in realworld datasets that must be fixed before moving on to additional research. The type and quantity of missing data will determine which approach is best. For example, simple methods such as mean or median imputation can work well if only a small percentage of the entries are missing. However, in order to effectively estimate missing values, more complex techniques like multiple imputation or predictive modeling may be required for larger volumes of missing data.

3. Dealing with Outliers

Machine learning models and statistical analysis can be severely distorted by outliers. In order to find outliers in numerical parameters like sepal length or petal width in the Iris dataset, we may employ visualization approaches like box plots or scatter plots. Once located, outliers can be treated in one of two ways: either by modifying them using methods like winsorization or resilient scaling, or by eliminating them if they are errors or extreme numbers that do not accurately reflect the underlying distribution.

4. Data Transformation and Encoding

We frequently need to correctly transform and encode features in order to make sure that our data is suitable for machine learning algorithms. To bring all characteristics to a similar scale and stop some features from dominating others, normalization techniques for numerical features, such as MinMax scaling or standardization (Zscore scaling), can be used. Encoding techniques like onehot encoding or label encoding can be used to transform categorical values into a numerical format that machine learning algorithms can handle efficiently for categorical variables like species in the Iris dataset.

5. Iterative Process and Validation

Data cleaning and preparation is an iterative process that incorporates technique refinement based on early insights and input from later investigations. It is not a onetime operation. Verifying the efficacy of cleaning and preprocessing stages is crucial, and this can be done by evaluating how they affect tasks that come after, like model performance or result interpretability. To make sure that our preparation procedures translate effectively to fresh data and increase the resilience of our models, crossvalidation approaches might be utilized.

Conclusion

Data preparation and cleansing are iterative procedures that need for significant thought and subjectmatter expertise. Through the appropriate application of these methodologies, data scientists may guarantee the robustness and reliability of their studies, laying the groundwork for the development of precise machine learning models.

2.3 HANDLING MISSING DATA

1. Understanding Missing Data

In the fields of data science and machine learning, comprehending missing data is essential since it has a direct impact on the accuracy and dependability of analytical findings. The absence of values in a dataset that are supposed to be there is referred to as missing data. There are several categories into which missing data can fall:

1. **Missing Completely at Random (MCAR):** This kind of missing data happens when there is no connection between the missingness and any variables, either observed or unobserved. The missing data points are essentially a random subset of the data that don't depend on the data or other variables.
2. **Missing at Random (MAR):** MAR happens when the observable variables determine the likelihood of missing data but not the missing data itself. Put differently, there are other factors in the dataset that can account for the missingness.
3. **Missing Not at Random (MNAR):** MNAR happens when the probability of data being missing is correlated with the missing value. In other words, MNAR occurs when the missingness is tied to the missing values themselves. Improper handling of this could result in biased outcomes.

It is crucial to comprehend the kind of missing data as it affects the methods chosen to address it. Simple methods like listwise deletion, which removes rows with missing data, may be appropriate in the case of MCAR, for example, without significantly increasing bias. To maintain the integrity of the data and the reliability of later analyses, more complex methods, such as imputation (changing missing values with estimated values) or the use of specialist models that take missingness patterns into account, might be required for MAR and particularly MNAR.

Missing data has practical consequences for decisionmaking and model performance in addition to statistical ones. Inadequate data can cause biased parameter estimations, lower the power of statistical tests, and worsen the variance or decrease the predicted accuracy of machine learning models. Therefore, in order to guarantee the validity and trustworthiness of datadriven insights in AI and ML applications, strong solutions for addressing missing data are crucial.

Data scientists may improve the quality and utility of their analyses and eventually contribute to more accurate and meaningful insights from complicated datasets by grasping the subtleties of missing data and using the right techniques.

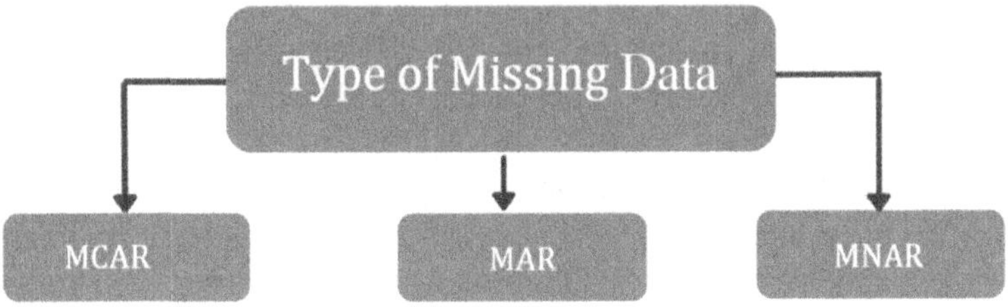

2. Impact of Missing Data on Analysis

Missing data has a significant and complex impact on analysis, affecting machine learning model performance as well as the statistical integrity of results. A number of serious problems can occur when data points are missing, endangering the validity and dependability of inferences made from the dataset.

- First of all, statistical studies become biased when there are missing data. The results are skewed towards the observed subset due to bias, which arises from the possibility that the given data is not representative of the complete population or dataset. In the event that survey responses are absent for specific demographic groups, inferences made from the residual data might not precisely represent the beliefs or actions of those groups.
- Second, the effectiveness and strength of machine learning algorithms and statistical tests are diminished by missing data. The ability of a test to identify an effect when one exists is known as statistical power, and missing data can lower this power by decreasing the size of the effective sample. This decrease in power makes it more difficult to find significant links or patterns in the data, which could result in findings that are not entirely accurate.

Furthermore, summary statistics like means, variances, and correlations might be distorted by the existence of missing data. For example, the mean of a variable derived from the incomplete dataset might not correctly reflect the genuine population average if missing values are not handled appropriately.

Furthermore, missing data might interfere with the training process and reduce the predicted accuracy of models in the context of machine learning. In order to prevent errors during training and prediction, many machine learning algorithms require preprocessing procedures like imputation, which fills in missing information, or specific handling.

Effectively handling missing data necessitates giving significant thought to its patterns and methods (whether missing entirely at random, at random, or not at random). Depending on the type and degree of missingness in the dataset, several procedures are used, such as deleting incomplete cases, imputation using statistical techniques or machine learning models, or even more complex techniques like multiple imputation.

3. Techniques for Handling Missing Data

A crucial component of data preprocessing in data science and machine learning is handling missing data. Missing values are frequently encountered while working with realworld datasets for a variety of reasons, including human error, problems with data collection, or malfunctions in the system. If missing data is not correctly managed, it can have a substantial negative influence on the accuracy and dependability of analytical findings and machine learning models.

1. **Deletion:** Removing incomplete rows or columns from the dataset is a simple method of handling missing data. Although this approach is straightforward and eliminates the need for imputation, it may result in the loss of important data and a smaller sample size. To ensure that the removal does not skew the analysis, deletion is usually employed when missing data is either negligible or randomly dispersed throughout the dataset (MCAR).
2. **Imputation:** Imputation is the process of substituting estimated values based on the remaining data for missing values. Typical methods consist of:
    - **Mean, Median, Mode:** The average, median, or most frequent value of the corresponding feature can be used to fill in any missing values using these straightforward statistical methods. They can maintain the statistical characteristics of the data and are easy to apply, but they could miss the underlying correlations between the variables.
    - **Prediction Models:** More sophisticated imputation techniques use machine learning models like kNearest Neighbors (KNN), Decision Trees, or linear regression to

forecast missing values. When the missing data mechanism (MAR or MNAR) is not entirely random, these models are particularly helpful since they use the links between variables to estimate missing values more precisely.

- **Multiple Imputation:** Through the use of numerous possible values, this technique adds uncertainty into the process of imputation for each missing data point. By taking into account the variability in imputed values, it increases the robustness of the study and works especially well with complicated datasets.

3. **Advanced Methods:** In addition to fundamental imputation strategies, additional methods encompass:
    - **Interpolation:** This technique, which assumes a smooth relationship between observations, estimates missing values based on nearby data points.
    - **ExpectationMaximization (EM) Algorithm:** It maximizes the likelihood of observed data by iteratively estimating a statistical model's parameters when some data are missing.
    - **Data Augmentation:** Adding extra data or external datasets to improve the accuracy of imputation.

The type of missingness, the distribution of the data, and the particular objectives of the analysis or modeling all play a role in selecting the best method for handling missing data. It's critical to assess how handling missing data will affect later analyses and make sure the selected approach complies with the dataset's requirements and underlying assumptions.

Data scientists can improve the resilience and reliability of their analyses and machine learning models by using efficient ways for addressing missing data. This will ultimately improve the decisionmaking and insight production from datadriven approaches.

4. Best Practices and Considerations

In the context of data science employing AI and ML, when talking about "Best Practices and Considerations" for handling missing data, it's important to explore the subtle tactics and tenets that direct efficient data management and model construction:

1. **Data Understanding and Analysis:** Understanding the type and patterns of missingness in the dataset is essential before making decisions about how to handle missing data. To find out which variables have missing values, how much of them are missing, and whether there are any obvious patterns or

relationships with other variables, exploratory data analysis (EDA) must be performed. Through acquiring a more profound comprehension of the reasons behind missing data (MCAR, MAR, and MNAR), data scientists may make more informed choices on the management of these gaps.

2. **Selection of Imputation Methods:** One popular method for dealing with missing data is imputation, or filling in the blanks. However, the accuracy and dependability of later studies and machine learning models can be strongly impacted by the imputation method selection. While easy to use, basic imputation techniques such as mean, median, or mode may not adequately represent underlying data patterns. On the other hand, more advanced methods like predictive modeling (regressionbased imputation, kNearest Neighbors, etc.) can take use of correlations between variables to produce estimates that are more accurate. The distribution of the data, the existence of outliers, and the particular goals of the research should all be taken into account when choosing the imputation method.
3. **Evaluation of Imputation Impact:** It is crucial to assess how these choices will affect the overall quality of the data and the performance of the model after imputing missing values. This entails contrasting the outcomes of the imputation procedure with those obtained without it, evaluating modifications to statistical measures (such as variance and mean), and keeping an eye out for any biases that may have been inadvertently introduced. In machine learning pipelines, crossvalidation approaches can be utilized to verify the resilience of imputed data.
4. **Expertise and Domain Knowledge:** When dealing with missing data, domain and subject matter expertise come in very handy. Comprehending the circumstances surrounding the data's generation might offer valuable perspectives on justifiable causes for absent values and direct the choice of suitable imputation techniques. In addition, domain experts can help evaluate the data and make sure that the imputed values match the realworld events that the data depicts.
5. **Transparency and Documentation:** For repeatability and transparency purposes, it is imperative to record the procedures used when addressing missing data as well as the reasoning behind these choices. Information about the preprocessing of the data, the imputation methods used, any assumptions made, and the results of sensitivity tests carried out to evaluate

the stability of the imputed data should all be included in this documentation.

Data scientists may efficiently handle the issues of missing data in AI and ML systems by following these best practices and considerations, which will result in more dependable insights and improved decisionmaking abilities. In the data science process, handling missing data is not just a technological issue but also an essential one that calls for careful evaluation of statistical approaches and domainspecific knowledge.

Conclusion

In summary, managing missing data involves more than merely closing gaps; it also entails making wise choices that protect the accuracy and dependability of datadriven insights. Data scientists may successfully limit the impact of missing data on analysis and maintain robust model performance by utilizing appropriate methodologies and understanding the nature of missing data.

2.4 DATA TRANSFORMATION AND NORMALIZATION

The Data Transformation and Normalization chapter provides an essential basis for preparing data for modeling and analysis in the field of data science. The main ideas, strategies, and real-world applications covered in this chapter will all be covered in detail in this review.

Key Concepts Covered

The chapter on data transformation and normalization is essential to improving the quality and usability of data for analytical insights and machine learning models in the field of data science. The term "data transformation" refers to a range of methods used to alter raw data in order to improve its suitability for analysis further on. This entails dealing with problems including outliers, skewed distributions, and inconsistent scales between variables. Log transformation is a basic method that works well for handling data with extremely skewed distributions because it expands small values and compresses large ones to help create a more normal distribution.

Standardization, or Zscore normalization, is another important idea. Using this method, data is transformed to have a standard deviation of 1 and a mean of 0. It is especially helpful in situations where the data shows different scales, making sure that every feature adds the same amount to the study. Standardization, for example, facilitates the comparison of variables that initially have multiple units or scales of measurement in statistical modeling or clustering methods.

Another widely used technique is minmax scaling, which involves scaling data to a predetermined range, usually between 0 and 1. This method works well for algorithms like support vector machines and neural networks that need the input data to be on a bounded interval. All features are scaled evenly, and the relative relationships between data points are preserved.

To further reduce the impact of outliers on the scaling procedure, robust scaling is used. Robust scaling is resistant to extreme values that could otherwise bias the scaling of the entire dataset by employing the median and interquartile range in place of the mean and standard deviation.

These methods are invaluable in a variety of data science applications and disciplines. For instance, normalization in image processing makes ensuring that pixel intensities are consistent between images, which makes precise comparison and analysis possible. Predictive analytics and risk assessment are aided in financial modeling by the transformation and normalization of financial variables, which allow for meaningful comparisons between organizations or time periods.

To sum up, data scientists may efficiently preprocess and prepare data for later analysis and modeling tasks by learning data transformation and normalization procedures. These fundamental abilities help extract useful insights and make defensible conclusions from complicated information, in addition to improving the precision and dependability of machine learning models.

"Data Science Using AI and ML" offers thorough examples and exercises that reinforce key concepts for additional study and realworld applications. This ensures competency in utilizing data transformation and normalization for advanced analytics and machine learning projects.

Practical Applications

Data transformation and normalization have several realworld applications in data science and machine learning, all of which highlight how important these methods are for improving data quality and model performance.

Normalization methods, such scaling pixel intensities to a fixed range (like 0 to 1), are crucial in image processing, for example. Because of this standardization, robust performance is made possible in tasks like object detection and picture classification by ensuring that characteristics produced from images are comparable across datasets. Furthermore, skewed pixel distributions can be handled by transformation techniques such logarithmic scaling, which raises the accuracy of computer vision models.

Normalization is essential in financial modeling, as datasets frequently include a variety of metrics, including stock prices, market indexes, and economic indicators. Analysts can efficiently compare trends and fluctuations over time or between various financial instruments by scaling these variables to a common range. This procedure guarantees that the model's predictions stay precise and reliable in addition to helping to find connections and trends.

Natural Language Processing (NLP) transforms textual input into numerical representations appropriate for machine learning algorithms, primarily through the use of data transformation techniques. Fundamental methods include tokenization, which divides text into discrete units like words or ngrams, and vectorization, which turns these units into numerical vectors. Text features are normalized thanks to normalization techniques, which improve the efficiency of tasks like sentiment analysis, text categorization, and language modeling.

Data transformation and normalization have a wide range of practical applications in a variety of fields and data science applications. These methods not only expedite the preprocessing of data but also greatly enhance the precision, dependability, and comprehensibility of machine learning models, thereby enabling data scientists to derive substantial insights and arrive at wellinformed conclusions from intricate datasets.

Visual Aids

The use of visual aids is essential for improving comprehension and memorization of the main ideas covered in the Data Transformation and Normalization chapter. Let's examine these visual components' contributions to a thorough understanding of the subject in more detail.

Tables and Comparison

Technique	Description	Use Case
Log Transformation	Converts skewed distributions into normallike distributions	Financial data analysis
Standardization	Centers data around mean, scales by standard deviation	Statistical modeling
MinMax Scaling	Scales data to a range (e.g., [0, 1])	Neural network training

Technique	Description	Use Case
Robust Scaling	Scales data by removing the median and scaling according to the interquartile range	Handling data with outliers

Application Scenarios

Visual aids are also useful in placing theoretical conversations in the context of real-world applications. Visuals can illustrate the practical applications of data transformation and normalization techniques, for example, in the domains of image processing and financial modeling. An example of image processing may present the before and aftereffects of normalizing pixel intensity, while an example of financial modeling could highlight the effects of standardizing financial measures for different companies or periods of time. These visual aids not only highlight the value of data preparation methods in a variety of contexts but also encourage originality in the way they might be applied in different data science topics.

Conclusion

In conclusion, any data scientist or machine learning practitioner must have a solid understanding of data transformation and normalization techniques. These techniques enhance model performance, promote more lucid insights from data analysis, and increase data quality.

Professionals may efficiently preprocess data to unleash its full potential in AI and ML applications by learning these strategies.

For more investigation, consult the thorough examples and exercises in "Data Science Using AI and ML," which will guarantee that you fully understand these basic ideas.

2.5 FEATURE ENGINEERING AND SELECTION

A key component of machine learning data preparation is feature engineering. It entails converting unprocessed data into features that help the prediction models better understand the underlying issue and perform better as a result. The many methods and factors in feature engineering and selection are covered in this chapter.

Key Topics Covered

1. **Feature Extraction:** This includes techniques for extracting significant characteristics from unprocessed data, making sure they record pertinent details needed for predictive

modeling. Tokenization, TFIDF (Term FrequencyInverse Document Frequency), and word embeddings like Word2Vec are some of the methods used for text data; edge detection, color histograms, or pretrained convolutional neural networks (CNNs) for deep learningbased feature extraction are some of the methods used for image data; statistical aggregations, timeseries decomposition, or Fourier transformations are some of the methods used for temporal or sensor data. Every method seeks to extract key features from the data in order to enable precise model predictions.

2. **Feature Transformation:** The feature transformation procedure guarantees that the data is appropriate for machine learning techniques. By adjusting the range of numerical characteristics to a consistent scale, techniques like scaling (e.g., MinMax Scaling, Standardization) stop prominent features from overshadowing others during model training. In order to transform categorical data into a numerical format that computers can understand, handling categorical variables requires the use of encoding techniques like label encoding and onehot encoding. Additionally, data normalization methods guarantee that the distributions of features are constant, which is essential for algorithms such as logistic regression and Kmeans clustering.
3. **Feature Selection:** Techniques for feature selection seek to separate out and preserve the most relevant features for modeling from superfluous or unnecessary ones. Among the strategies are wrapper methods (e.g., LASSO regularization) that use predictive models to evaluate subsets of features, filter methods (e.g., correlation coefficients) that statistically measure the importance of features, and embedded methods (e.g., recursive feature elimination) that integrate feature selection into the model training process. By concentrating on the most significant predictors, efficient feature selection not only increases model interpretability by lowering computational complexity and overfitting but also improves model performance.
4. **Dimensionality Reduction:** To minimize the number of features while maintaining the maximum amount of information, methods such as Principal Component Analysis (PCA), tDistributed Stochastic Neighbor Embedding (tSNE), and Linear Discriminant Analysis (LDA) are utilized. Techniques for reducing dimensionality are very helpful in managing highdimensional data, easing the burden of dimensionality,

and enhancing computing effectiveness. These techniques help with tasks like clustering, classification, and visualization by converting data into lowerdimensional spaces.

Importance of Feature Engineering

Because feature engineering has a significant impact on model performance, interpretability, and scalability, it is extremely important in the fields of machine learning and artificial intelligence. Fundamentally, feature engineering is the process of converting unprocessed data into useful characteristics that accurately depict the underlying issue. This is an important step since a machine learning model's ability to learn patterns and generate predictions is directly influenced by the quality and relevancy of its features.

The potential of feature engineering to improve model correctness is one of the main reasons it is essential. Data scientists can greatly enhance prediction results by creating features that capture the key elements of the data, such as finding pertinent variables or changing variables to conform to model assumptions (such normality). For instance, word embeddings (e.g., Word2Vec) or TFIDF (Term FrequencyInverse Document Frequency) approaches can be used to turn text into numerical characteristics, which enables models to analyze and extract meaning from textual input efficiently in natural language processing applications.

Additionally, by increasing the transparency of the links between input variables and output predictions, feature engineering improves the interpretability of the model. It is simpler to comprehend which elements affect the model's judgments and how changes in those aspects affect predictions when features are developed appropriately. This interpretability is very important, especially in areas where judgments made using machine learning models need to be justified or compliant with laws.

Furthermore, overfittinga typical problem in machine learningis mitigated in large part by feature engineering, wherein models perform well on training data but badly on unseen data. Data scientists can construct more resilient models that perform better when applied to fresh, untested data by choosing or developing characteristics that are wellgeneralized across various datasets. This procedure involves key techniques including handling missing values, outlier detection, and feature scaling, which make sure the model learns from the inherent patterns in the data rather than noise or unimportant information.

Furthermore, scalability in machine learning systems is supported by feature engineering. Effectively designed features can lower memory consumption and computational complexity, allowing models to handle bigger datasets and realtime processing demands more successfully. In contemporary applications, such Internet of Things (IoT) devices, where computing resources are scarce and data quantities are enormous, scalability is essential.

Illustrative Examples

Our comprehension of the importance of feature engineering and selection strategies in data science and machine learning can be improved by using illustrative examples that offer more indepth insights into how these methods are used in realworld settings.

Feature Extraction Techniques

Feature extraction is the process of converting unprocessed data into a format that machine learning algorithms can understand. For example, in image processing, methods such as edge detection extract contours and edges, which are essential for tasks like segmentation or object recognition. In contrast, color histograms show how colors are distributed within an image and reveal details about its overall composition. These techniques reduce complicated data and draw attention to significant visual patterns that support precise model predictions.

Feature Transformation

To enhance model performance, features frequently need to be altered once they are extracted. Common methods for standardizing numerical features that guarantee each variable contributes equally to model training are scaling and normalization. To prevent biases in the model towards particular characteristics, scaling, for example, makes sure that features with wider numerical ranges do not dominate those with lower ranges. Data visualization both pre and postnormalization can provide a clear picture of how these treatments alter data distributions to better fit the needs of machine learning algorithms.

Feature Selection Strategies

The goal of feature selection is to eliminate superfluous or unnecessary characteristics while identifying the most relevant ones that have a substantial impact on model performance. The methods used vary from basic statistical techniques like correlation analysis to more complex ones like feature significance scores generated from ensemble techniques like Random Forests or Recursive Feature

Elimination (RFE). Data scientists may make wellinformed decisions about which characteristics to include or exclude based on clear insights into which features have the biggest impact on predicting accuracy thanks to visual representations like feature relevance scores on graphs.

Dimensionality Reduction

Principal Component Analysis (PCA) and other dimensionality reduction techniques are used to condense large datasets of features while maintaining the relevant information. By finding orthogonal components that account for the majority of the variance in the data, PCA reduces the number of dimensions without significantly compromising predictive ability. The amount of information that each component retains can be shown through visualizations of explained variance ratios vs the number of principal components, which can help find the ideal balance between model complexity and performance.

These illustrations highlight how feature engineering and selection in data science are iterative and exploratory processes. Data scientists may increase the interpretability of models, extract valuable insights from data, and ultimately boost the effectiveness of machine learning applications in a variety of fields by carefully utilizing these approaches.

Conclusion

Iterative procedures like feature engineering and selection call for creativity, domain expertise, and a thorough comprehension of the dataset. Effective use of these methods can help data scientists improve model performance, lessen overfitting, and obtain datadriven insights that are essential for making decisions in AI and ML applications.

2.6 TOOLS FOR DATA PREPROCESSING

A critical phase in the data science pipeline is data preparation, which entails preparing raw data for analysis by cleaning and formatting it. In order to create reliable AI and ML models, this chapter examines a variety of data preprocessing tools and methods.

1. Data Cleaning

In data science and machine learning, data cleaning is a fundamental component of data preprocessing. To guarantee the quality and dependability of the dataset for analysis, it entails locating and fixing flaws or inconsistencies. Usually, the procedure consists of several crucial steps:

First, it's important to handle missing data. Missing values are frequently present in datasets for a variety of reasons, including measurement errors, equipment malfunctions, or a lack of data collection. There are various methods for dealing with missing data, such as:

- **Mean or median imputation:** This technique substitutes the feature's available data mean or median for any missing values.
- **Forward or backward filling:** The process of filling in missing values by using either the next accessible value (backward) or the last known value (ahead).
- **Advanced techniques:** As an illustration, consider predicting missing values based on other features using machine learning methods like KNearest Neighbors (KNN).

Furthermore, removing duplicates prevents bias in analysis by guaranteeing that each data point is distinct.

Thirdly, managing outliers is essential to avoiding their skewing of machine learning models or statistical studies. Outliers are suitably identified and eliminated using methods including scatter plots, box plots, and Zscore analysis, as well as the Interquartile Range (IQR) method.

In addition, correcting inconsistencies entails assuring data integrity across various sources or formats, standardizing data formats, and resolving differences in naming conventions or units of measurement.

Last but not least, handling noise in data is crucial, especially when dealing with datasets that are taken from realworld settings where data can be tampered with or contain unrelated information. Robust statistical approaches, smoothing, and binning are among techniques that can assist reduce noise and enhance the quality of data.

Data cleaning improves the quality, consistency, and dependability of datasets, which is a critical component of the data preprocessing pipeline. It prepares the groundwork for later processes like feature engineering and model construction, which eventually result in data science and machine learning applications with more precise and trustworthy insights and forecasts.

2. Data Transformation

Within the fields of data science and machine learning, data transformation is an essential part of data preprocessing. Its main goal is to transform unprocessed data into a format better suited for analysis and training models. Several crucial methods that improve the data's quality and usability are used in this process:

1. **Scaling and Normalization:** The process of normalizing numerical data involves either standardizing it to have a mean of 0 and a standard deviation of 1, or scaling it to a standard range, usually between 0 and 1 (minmax scaling). By doing this, it is ensured that every characteristic contributes equally to the analysis and that no feature will dominate because of its size.

Normalization, for instance, brings features with different measurement unitsfor instance, thousands and single digitsto a same scale, enhancing model convergence and performance.

2. **Managing Classification Variables:** Discrete values, such as colors, categories, or labels, are represented by categorical variables. Transformation is required because many machine learning algorithms cannot handle category data directly. One popular technique is onehot encoding, in which a binary feature column is created for every category. An alternative method involves mapping categories to integer values via label encoding. The decision is based on the algorithm being utilized as well as the type of data.

Onehot encoding, for example, would produce distinct binary columns for each product category for assessing customer preferences across various categories, making comparisons and predictions more meaningful.

3. **Engineering Features:** Feature engineering is the process of generating new features from preexisting data to improve the models' capacity for prediction. This can involve aggregations, interaction terms, or mathematical transformations.

Feature engineering, for instance, can entail developing additional features like moving averages, trend markers, or seasonal adjustments to better capture underlying patterns in a time series dataset tracking sales.

4. **PCA, or Principal Component Analysis:** By reducing the dimensionality of the data while preserving as much variance as possible, PCA is a dimensionality reduction approach. It finds patterns in data, cutting down on characteristics without sacrificing important details.

For example, principal component analysis (PCA) can ease subsequent modeling work by reducing the number of correlated variables in a dataset into a smaller set of main components that explain the variance in the data.

3. Feature Engineering

In machine learning and data science, feature engineering is a crucial component of data preparation. The objective is to convert unprocessed data into useful features that can dramatically enhance the accuracy of predictive models. Choosing, extracting, and even producing new features from the current dataset are all part of this process. The idea of feature engineering is to enrich the model with more discriminative and relevant data, which will improve the model's capacity for precise classification or prediction.

A key strategy in feature engineering is dimensionality reduction, which is frequently accomplished using techniques like Singular Value Decomposition (SVD) and Principal Component Analysis (PCA). By converting them into a smaller collection of principle components that yet capture the crucial variation of the data, these strategies reduce the number of input variables. This not only reduces computation time but also aids in handling feature multicollinearity.

Feature scaling and normalization, which standardizes the range of numerical features, is another important component. When features are scaled uniformly, algorithms such as Support Vector Machines (SVM) or Kmeans clustering perform better since fewer characteristics can dominate due to their greater range.

Furthermore, feature selection methods are essential for improving model performance since they help find the features that are most pertinent and useful for the prediction task. Only the most significant features are identified and kept, thanks to techniques like Recursive Feature Elimination (RFE), which iteratively eliminates the least significant features, and feature importance scores from decision tree-based algorithms (like Random Forest).

Moreover, text preprocessing is crucial for tasks involving natural language processing, wherein unprocessed text input is converted into numerical feature vectors by means of TFIDF (Term FrequencyInverse Document Frequency), stemming, and tokenization.

Effective feature engineering in realworld applications necessitates a thorough comprehension of the domain and problem context. In order to make sure that the designed features both enhance model performance and generalize well to new data, it is common practice to conduct iterative experimentation and validation.

The foundation of any successful machine learning project is feature engineering. To convert unprocessed data into a format that optimizes the predictive ability of machine learning algorithms, a blend of domain expertise, ingenuity, and methodical techniques are required. Data scientists may create reliable models that provide precise and useful insights by fully utilizing their data by becoming proficient in feature engineering approaches.

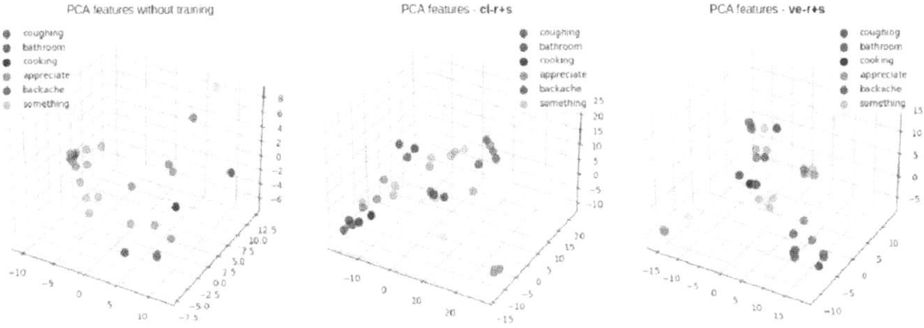

PCA visualization for feature extraction

Conclusion

By guaranteeing data relevance and quality, efficient data preprocessing creates the groundwork for effective AI and ML models. Through the implementation of suitable instruments and methodologies covered in this section, data scientists can augment the precision and efficacy of their models.

3

Exploratory Data Analysis

3.1 DESCRIPTIVE STATISTICS

Data organization and summarization techniques are offered by descriptive statistics. It facilitates the understanding of a dataset's primary properties by data scientists and analysts, including distribution, variability, and central tendency.

Key Concepts Covered

Let's go into more detail about the main ideas discussed in the "Descriptive Statistics" chapter within the framework of "Data Science Using AI and ML".

- **Measures of Central Tendency:** Central tendency measures shed light on a dataset's typical or central value.
- **Mean:** the total of all values divided by the number of observations to determine the arithmetic average of a set of data. Although it offers a balanced measurement of the dataset's center, it is sensitive to outliers.
- **Median:** The middle value, either ascending or descending, in a dataset. It provides a reliable indicator of central tendency and is less susceptible to extreme values than the mean.
- **Mode:** The value or values that appear most frequently in a dataset. It can show the typical category or value and is helpful for categorical data.
- **Measures of Variability:** These metrics characterize how data points are distributed or scattered about the central tendency.

- **Range:** The variation in a dataset's maximum and minimum values. Although it gives a straightforward assessment of the spread, outliers can have a significant impact.
- **Variance:** The mean of the squared deviations from the mean. It is utilized in inferential statistics to quantify the dispersion of data points around the mean.
- **Standard Deviation:** The variance's square root is the standard deviation. It provides a standardized measure of the spread by calculating the degree of variance or dispersion from the mean.
- **Data Distribution:** Comprehending the data distribution is essential for analyzing its properties and arriving at wellinformed conclusions.
- **Histograms:** Histograms divide numerical data into intervals, or bins, and display the number of observations in each bin to represent the frequency distribution of the data. They shed light on the distribution's form, center, and dispersion of data.
- **Box Plots:** Based on five important statisticsthe minimum, first quartile (Q1), median, third quartile (Q3), and maximumbox charts provide an overview of the data distribution. In addition to highlighting anomalies, they display the distribution's skewness and spread.
- **Tables of Frequencies:** Numerical data that is categorized or grouped into categories is shown in frequency tables along with the number of observations (frequency) in each category. They give an understandable synopsis of the distributions of categorical data.

These fundamental ideas serve as a foundation for more complex analysis and modeling strategies in data science and machine learning, in addition to aiding in the efficient summarization of data. Through the mastery of descriptive statistics, data scientists are able to discern patterns, identify anomalies, and extract significant insights from intricate datasets. This ability to make informed decisions and facilitate predictive modeling in AI and ML applications is made possible.

Visual Representations

Descriptive statistics greatly benefit from the intuitive insights that visual representations offer into the distribution, central tendency, and variability of data. These graphical tools help stakeholders and decisionmakers comprehend complex statistical information more easily and communicate it to them more effectively.

Histograms are essential for illustrating the distribution of numerical data because they illustrate the number of observations inside each bin and divide the data into bins or intervals. Exam results, for example, can show whether they are skewed, regularly distributed, or show other patterns by looking at their histogram. The distribution and concentration of data points over various value ranges can be evaluated with the use of this visualization.

Box charts, sometimes referred to as boxandwhisker plots, work very well at summarizing data skewness and spread. They present the summary in a condensed fashion using five numbers: minimum, first quartile, median, third quartile, and maximum. For the purpose of comparing distributions among several groups or categories, box plots are especially helpful. A box plot, for instance, that displays the salary distribution among different departments can be a useful tool for highlighting differences and anomalies.

Frequency tables present the categories or bins together with their corresponding frequencies or counts, organizing classified or grouped numerical data into tabular form. These tables offer a concise summary of the distribution of data among several groups or time intervals. For example, demographic trends and prospective market segments can be identified by using a frequency table that divides customers into age groups (0–10, 11–20, etc.) and displays the number of customers in each category.

These visual aids for data exploration and comprehension are also effective tools for presenting results and bolstering datadriven choices in applications of AI and ML. Data scientists may spot patterns, unearth hidden insights, and effectively explain statistical findings by using histograms, box plots, and frequency tables.

Practical Appliations

Beyond simple data summarization, descriptive statistics have numerous practical uses in the context of AI and ML. Here's a more thorough investigation:

- In many realworld AI and ML applications, descriptive statistics is essential. Feature selection is a notable application. Identifying the most significant variables that contribute to forecast accuracy is often necessary for data scientists prior to training machine learning models. Understanding the distribution and significance of various variables within a dataset is made easier with the use of descriptive statistics, such as measures of central tendency and variability. For instance, examining descriptive statistics of customer demographics, purchase history, and engagement metrics in a predictive model for customer turnover might identify which elements are most indicative of churn behavior.

- Outlier detection is another useful application. Data points that substantially differ from the rest of the dataset are called outliers. If these outliers are not appropriately handled, they may skew statistical analysis and machine learning models. Box plots and zscores are two examples of descriptive statistics methods that are useful for locating outliers. For example, use descriptive statistics to analyze transaction quantities in financial fraud detection might aid in identifying anomalous transactions that can point to fraudulent activity.
- Descriptive statistics also help with data preprocessing chores that are necessary for training machine learning models successfully. To convert data into a uniform format appropriate for machine learning algorithms, methods like normalization and standardization rely on descriptive statistics like mean and standard deviation. By ensuring that various features are similar and contribute equally to the model's learning process, this preprocessing step enhances the accuracy and performance of the model.
- Descriptive statistics help firms segment their consumer base efficiently in realworld settings like customer segmentation in retail or marketing. Through the examination of descriptive facts pertaining to consumer behavior, purchasing trends, and demographics, enterprises can devise focused marketing approaches customized for distinct customer groups. Descriptive data, for instance, may show that elders and young individuals have different shopping behaviors. This information could lead companies to create tailored product offerings or promotional activities to suit the needs of each market segment.
- All things considered, descriptive statistics' useful applications in AI and ML highlight how crucial it is to comprehend, prepare, and use data for predictive modeling and decisionmaking. Data scientists may create effective business outcomes in a variety of domains, refine machine learning models, and extract insightful information from data by becoming proficient in descriptive statistical approaches.

Case Study: Customer Segmentation

One of the most important uses of descriptive statistics in data science, especially in the context of AI and ML, is customer segmentation. It entails segmenting a clientele into groups according to shared traits, customs, or requirements. Businesses may improve consumer satisfaction, refine product offers, and customize marketing techniques thanks to this segmentation.

Descriptive statistics are essential for client segmentation in realworld applications. Analysts divide up their client base into several segments using metrics like as average purchase amount, frequency of purchases, demographics (age, gender, location), and customer lifetime value. For example, descriptive statistics can be used by a retail business to identify highvalue clients who spend more than a given amount or make repeated purchases.

The distribution of these data across various client categories can be shown using graphical representations like box plots or histograms, which offer a clear picture of the behaviors and preferences of these customers. A histogram, for instance, might show how customers' ages are distributed among each category, showing demographic trends that affect consumer behavior.

Through the use of descriptive statistics to group comparable clients, machine learning algorithms can improve customer segmentation even further. Effective customer grouping is achieved by using measures of central tendency and variability via techniques such as kmeans clustering or hierarchical clustering. By providing tailored incentives and suggestions, this datadriven strategy not only strengthens marketing efforts but also improves individualized consumer experiences.

All things considered, client segmentation serves as an example of how descriptive statistics support sophisticated analytical methods in AI and ML. Businesses may boost client retention, streamline operations, and eventually spur growth in cutthroat marketplaces by utilizing these insights.

Conclusion

The foundation of exploratory data analysis (EDA) in data science is descriptive statistics. Data scientists can get important insights into the underlying patterns and properties of the data by using appropriate graphical and tabular representations. This helps to create the foundation for more advanced analyses and modeling approaches in AI and ML.

3.2 DATA VISUALIZATION TECHNIQUES

Data visualization is a key component in the field of data science that uses AI and ML to connect raw data with actionable insights. This chapter examines a number of methods and ideas that are crucial to efficient data visualization, enabling data scientists to explain complicated information in a way that is both understandable and natural.

Importance of Data Visualization

Let's explore data visualization's significance in the context of data science with artificial intelligence and machine learning.

By converting complicated datasets into visually appealing and useful representations, data visualization plays a fundamental role in the field of data science. Its importance stems from a number of crucial elements that improve comprehension and decisionmaking:

Data visualization improves pattern recognition, to start. Visual data presentation makes patterns, trends, and outliers easier to spoteven in big, complex datasets. The capacity to derive significant ideas and hypotheses from raw datawhich may not be immediately apparent from raw numbers or text aloneis vital for data scientists.

Second, communication is aided by effective data display. By providing information in a simple and understandable way, it closes the knowledge gap between technical analyses and non-technical stakeholders, such managers, executives, or clients. Visualizations help stakeholders easily understand difficult concepts, which promotes team alignment and well-informed decisionmaking.

Data visualization additionally facilitates Exploratory Data Analysis (EDA). Visual representations help data scientists discover patterns in the data, identify abnormalities, and generate preliminary hypotheses in the early phases of data exploration. In AI and ML projects, this repeated process of visual exploration frequently yields insights that direct later data preprocessing and model creation.

Visualizations also make comparisons and trend analysis easier. Different types of charts and graphs (such as bar charts, line graphs, and scatter plots) provide intuitive tools for exploring data relationships and making wellinformed predictions, whether it's comparing sales figures across regions, analyzing temporal trends in stock prices, or understanding correlations between variables.

Last but not least, careful application of color, design, and interactivity in visualizations improves comprehension and user engagement. Thoughtful color selection helps draw attention to important ideas or trends, and sound design principles guarantee cohesion and clarity. Users are empowered to examine data from many angles and gain deeper insights that static reports might not be able to provide through interactive features like filtering subsets of data or zooming in on individual data points.

Data visualization is a potent tool that facilitates communication, discovery, and decisionmaking in data science by utilizing AI and ML. It is not merely a way to display data. Data scientists may fully utilize data by utilizing visualizations to turn it into actionable intelligence that spurs creativity and commercial success.

Principles of Effective Data Visualization

Several fundamental ideas that guarantee impact, clarity, and understanding are necessary for effective data visualization. These guidelines affect not only how visualizations are made but also how insights are conveyed and comprehended.

1. **Simplicity and Clarity:** Clarity is the most important rule. Information should be presented in a clear and concise manner in visualizations to reduce viewer confusion and cognitive strain. To do this, provide a clear explanation of the data's meaning through annotations, titles, and labels. Clarity is enhanced by simplicity, which eliminates extraneous details that can mislead or confuse the viewer. Clear design makes it easier for readers to concentrate on the main point that the data is trying to make.

2. **Use of Appropriate Charts:** The successful presentation of various forms of data depends on the choice of chart or graph type. While line graphs are useful for showing patterns over time, bar charts are best for comparing categorical data. Heatmaps are a useful tool for visualizing dense data matrices, while scatter plots can be used to uncover correlations between variables. Selecting the right chart guarantees that the information is displayed in a way that optimizes comprehension and generates new insights.
3. **Color and Design:** Carefully chosen color improves visual appeal and helps a visualization communicate meaning. Colors can be used to show significance, distinguish between groups, and draw attention to key patterns or data points. On the other hand, misinterpretation or confusion may result from the overuse or incorrect use of color. A visualization that is harmonious and simple to navigate is enhanced by design concepts like judicious use of whitespace, a clear visual hierarchy, and consistent formatting. Consistent design decisions are made for every aspect of the visualization, which preserve coherence and direct the viewer's attention to the desired message.
4. **Contextualization and Storytelling:** Good visualizations should do more than just display data; they should also tell a narrative or tell a tale. Putting data in a larger context aids in stakeholders' comprehension of the importance of the insights obtained from the visualization. The viewer's comprehension is enhanced by the additional layers of information provided by annotations, captions, and contextual explanations. Visualizations become effective tools for influencing decisionmaking and motivating action based on datadriven insights when they offer data inside a narrative framework.
5. **Interactivity and Accessibility:** Users can dynamically explore data in interactive visualizations by modifying parameters, focusing in on particular areas, or applying filters. Because of its interactivity, which caters to a variety of user demands and viewpoints, it increases user engagement and permits deeper data analysis. Furthermore, making sure that visualizations are inclusive and understandable to all users, regardless of ability, is ensured by responsive design and compliance with assistive technologies.

Following these guidelines guarantees that data visualizations serve as useful instruments for efficient communication and analysis in addition to being visually beautiful. Data scientists and analysts can fully utilize the power of visualizations to communicate findings, find insights, and inform decisionmaking in the AI and ML domains by implementing accessibility considerations, appropriate chart selection, clarity, and thoughtful design.

Techniques and Examples

Let's examine each of the previously listed visualization techniques in more detail, adding background information and examples as needed:

1. Bar Charts

Bar charts are simple yet effective tools for data comparison in categories. They are made up of bars that change in height or length to indicate the percentage, count, or frequency of each group. Bar charts are a great tool for presenting discrete data points, such sales figures across multiple areas, because of their simplicity, as demonstrated in the example. Viewers can rapidly determine whether region had the biggest or lowest sales by comparing the bar heights, providing quick insights into performance indicators and trends.

2. Line Graphs

The best visual aids for displaying relationships and trends across time are line graphs. They make it simple to observe how variables vary in relation to one another by connecting data points with lines. For example, a line graph can indicate the patterns in the stock market over a year, illustrating changes in indexes or stock prices. In addition to highlighting patterns like seasonal trends or abrupt changes, this visualization style helps predict future behavior based on past data.

3. Scatter Plots

Relationships between two variables can be seen using scatter plots. With one variable on the xaxis and the other on the yaxis, each point on the plot represents an observation from the dataset. This method is very useful for finding outliers, clusters, or relationships in data. A scatter plot, for instance, can show how a set of students' exam scores and study hours correlate. Determining if there is a positive, negative, or no correlation between the two variables can be done by looking at the point distribution. This information can help in choosing study techniques or academic interventions.

4. Heatmaps

Heatmaps provide data a visual representation by displaying the magnitude of values within a matrix as colored bars. Large datasets or intricate matrices, where it may be difficult to quickly understand each individual data point, are especially wellsuited for their utilization. A heatmap showing website traffic during various hours and days is one example. Lighter hues denote slower times, whereas darker ones can indicate periods of increased traffic. Heatmaps help analysts quickly identify trends, peak hours, or anomalies, which helps them make decisions about infrastructure development, marketing campaigns, and resource allocation.

Conclusion

Gaining proficiency with data visualization approaches improves interpretation and decisionmaking, which in turn increases the efficacy of AI and ML models. Data scientists may turn complex data into actionable insights that spur innovation and commercial success by using the concepts covered in this chapter.

In conclusion, data visualization is more than just making eyecatching images; it's about translating data into a language that makes sense to people who must use it to make decisions. You will leave this chapter with the knowledge and resources necessary to fully utilize visualization in your data science endeavors.

3.3 IDENTIFYING PATTERNS AND TRENDS

Finding patterns and trends is essential in the field of data science. Patterns give data insights that make predictions and decisionmaking possible. The main topic of this chapter is the ways in which machine learning (ML) and artificial intelligence (AI) aid in the identification of patterns and trends in data.

1. Understanding Patterns and Trends

The foundation of data analysis is made up of patterns and trends, which provide profound insights into the characteristics of the data and direct strategic choices. In essence, a pattern is an identifiable regularity in the data, like recurrent fluctuations or repeating sequences. There are many other types of patterns that can be seen, such as complex structures like clusters of related data points or cyclic patterns, which are made up of data points that repeat at regular intervals. For instance, seasonal patterns in retail could indicate yearly spikes in sales around the holiday season. Recognizing these trends facilitates inventory control and resource planning.

Conversely, trends show the overall direction that data is going over time. In contrast to patterns, trends tend to be linear or follow a predetermined trajectory rather than being cyclical. The steady rise in global temperatures throughout the previous century, which points to a continuing alteration in climatic circumstances, is an illustration of a trend. Trends can be either longterm, showing more significant changes over longer periods of time, or shortterm, catching current alterations in data.

Predictive analytics relies on patterns and trends to help businesses predict future events by analyzing past data. AI and ML, which can analyze massive amounts of data and reveal intricate, nuanced links that human analysis could overlook, improve this capability. These underlying patterns and trends can be easily identified by machine learning models, especially those that are employed in time series forecasting, anomaly detection, and clustering. This allows for more precise forecasts and wellinformed decisionmaking. Over time, AI and ML systems become more adept at recognizing patterns through ongoing learning and adaptation, yielding evermoreaccurate insights.

2. Role of AI and ML in Identifying Patterns and Trends

The ability to collect and analyze large datasets is one of the many ways that artificial intelligence (AI) and machine learning (ML) play a transformational role in discovering patterns and trends. Fundamentally, artificial intelligence (AI) and machine learning (ML) offer the computational capacity and advanced algorithms required to identify intricate patterns and trends that may be invisible to human analysts.

First of all, data preprocessinga crucial stage that entails cleansing, standardizing, and converting unprocessed data into a format appropriate for analysisis an area in which AI and ML algorithms shine. Ensuring the integrity and quality of the data is an essential step in accurately detecting patterns. Automated methods drastically cut down on time and effort, such as handling missing numbers and outlier detection.

Subsequently, feature selection is improved by AI and ML, wherein algorithms determine which variables are most pertinent to the patterns and trends. Reducing dimensionality and concentrating on important features through the use of techniques like Principal Component Analysis (PCA) and feature importance scores obtained from Random Forest models enhances the interpretability and performance of the model.

Within the field of supervised learning, algorithms like decision trees, neural networks, and linear regression rely on previously labeled data to forecast future results. These models are forecasting and trendidentifying tools that are trained on historical data. Applications where supervised learning excels include stock market prediction, revenue forecasting, and anticipating client attrition.

Algorithms for unsupervised learning such as association rule learning and clustering are essential for discovering hidden patterns in the absence of previous labels. By grouping data points based on similarity, clustering algorithms such as KMeans and DBSCAN reveal logical groupings within the data. This is very helpful for identifying anomalies and segmenting markets. In contrast, association rule learning uncovers intriguing relationships between variables in sizable datasets and is frequently employed in market basket research to identify connections between product purchases.

Furthermore, deep learning methods, which are a subset of ML and AI, advance pattern recognition even further. Convolutional Neural Networks (CNNs) are highly effective at image identification tasks, recognizing patterns in visual data for applications like medical imaging and facial recognition. Because they are made to handle sequential data, recurrent neural networks (RNNs) and long shortterm memory networks (LSTMs) are perfect for time series analysis, where they can accurately forecast patterns over time.

Lastly, anomaly detection is improved by AI and ML. This is important because it helps find odd patterns that can point to fraud, errors, or new insights. In sectors like cybersecurity and quality control, techniques like Isolation Forests and Autoencoders are skilled at identifying departures from the norm and can provide timely alerts.

By automating data preprocessing, improving feature selection, applying both supervised and unsupervised learning approaches, and utilizing deep learning for complicated pattern identification, AI and ML play a critical role in discovering patterns and trends. Businesses and researchers can gain deeper insights and make better decisions with the help of these technologies, which propels progress in a variety of disciplines.

3. Techniques for Identifying Patterns and Trends

Finding patterns and trends in data is essential for getting insightful information and coming to wise judgments. To do this, data scientists use a variety of approaches, each with special benefits and uses.

Time Series Analysis

The focus of time series analysis is on data points that are gathered or recorded throughout time at predetermined intervals. This method works especially well for spotting seasonal patterns and trends. Time series analysis commonly employs Exponential Smoothing and Moving Average. By mitigating shortterm swings, the Moving Average enhances the visibility of longterm patterns. By giving previous observations exponentially decreasing weights, exponential smoothing aids in the predicting of future data points by placing a greater emphasis on more recent data.

Clustering

By assembling comparable data points into clusters, underlying patterns in datasets can be found. Methods such as Hierarchical Clustering and KMeans are commonly employed. KMeans is a valuable technique for market analysis and customer segmentation since it divides data into a predetermined number of clusters based on feature similarity. A tree of clusters is created by hierarchical clustering, and it can be sliced at different levels to produce a variety of cluster forms. Understanding the hierarchical structure of the datasuch as the classification of species or the grouping of documentscan be accomplished with this method.

Association Rule Learning

In big datasets, association rule learning finds intriguing correlations or links between variables. It is widely used to identify products that are frequently purchased together in market basket analysis. For example, the adage "If a customer buys bread, they are likely to buy butter" can be used to guide crossselling tactics and identify product affinity. Association rule generation and analysis are frequently performed using algorithms such as Apriori and Eclat.

Anomaly Detection

The goal of anomaly detection is to locate outliers or odd patterns that drastically depart from the norm. Applications such as fraud detection, network security, and quality control require this technology. Anomaly detection techniques like Isolation Forest, OneClass SVM, and Autoencoders are widely used. In order to isolate anomalies, Isolation Forest first randomly selects a feature, and then it randomly selects a split value between the feature's maximum and minimum values.

Finding uncommon and rare events in a dataset is a specific strength of this strategy.

Dimensionality Reduction

By lowering the number of variables under consideration, dimensionality reduction techniques like Principal Component Analysis (PCA) and tDistributed Stochastic Neighbor Embedding (tSNE) aid in pattern recognition. Keeping as much variability as feasible, principal component analysis (PCA) converts the data into a set of linearly uncorrelated variables known as principal components. In contrast, tSNE is a nonlinear dimensionality reduction method that works well for two or threedimensional data visualization on highdimensional data. These techniques are useful for complex dataset visualization, noise reduction, and feature extraction.

Machine Learning Algorithms

Based on past data, supervised learning algorithms provide predictions about the future, such as Linear Regression, Decision Trees, and Neural Networks. When predicting continuous outcomes, such as property prices, based on the connection between factors, linear regression is employed. Decision trees are straightforward to understand and helpful for classification problems since they divide the data into subgroups according to the input feature values. In huge datasets, neural networksespecially deep learning modelsperform exceptionally well at identifying intricate patterns, like in speech and image recognition.

These methodologies provide distinct perspectives and advantages, rendering them vital instruments inside the data scientist's arsenal. Businesses and researchers can find hidden patterns, predict future trends, and make more confident datadriven decisions by utilizing these techniques.

4. Case Study: Retail Sales Analysis

Objective

This case study's main objective is to identify patterns and trends in retail sales data in order to improve marketing tactics and inventory management. The analysis attempts to deliver actionable insights that help promote corporate growth and efficiency by utilizing AI and ML methodologies.

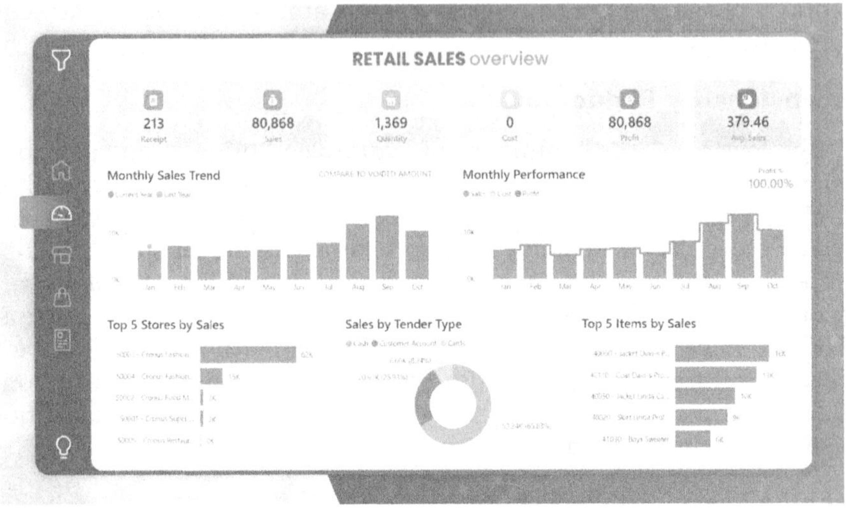

Methodology

1. **Data Collection:** Obtaining comprehensive historical sales data from multiple retail locations is the first stage in the process. Daily sales numbers, product categories, client demographics, and transaction specifics are all included in this data.
2. **Data Preprocessing:** Raw data is frequently disorganized and lacking. Therefore, data preparation techniques are used to clean and organize it. In order to maintain consistency, missing values are handled, outliers are found and dealt with, and data is normalized.
3. **Time Series Examination:** This is looking at sales data over an extended period of time to find longterm trends and seasonal patterns. To reduce oscillations and draw attention to important patterns, methods like exponential smoothing and moving averages are used. For example, a retailer may notice slower times in offpeak months and more sales during the holiday seasons.
4. **Clustering:** Based on their purchase habits, clients are divided into groups using clustering methods such as KMeans. This aids in the identification of discrete customer segments, including discount hunters, highvalue clients, and infrequent purchasers. To increase sales, customized marketing campaigns can then be directed towards each sector.
5. **Association Rule Learning:** This method is employed to find connections between items. An examination of market baskets,

for instance, may show that consumers who purchase bread also frequently purchase butter. By using these insights, marketers may better arrange products and encourage buyers to buy similar products together.

Results

The analysis yields several valuable insights:

- **Seasonal Trends:** A distinct trend appears that indicates higher sales over the holidays and during exclusive promotions. This gives the business the opportunity to get ready by creating focused marketing efforts and storing up on popular items.
- **Customer Segments:** Different client segments are identified using the clustering analysis. Highvalue clients might be targeted with loyalty programs and special offers if they frequently make highvalue purchases. Discounts, on the other hand, can encourage infrequent customers to make more purchases.
- **Product Associations:** Pairs or groups of products that are frequently purchased together are identified using association rule learning. For example, it may be discovered that consumers who purchase pasta also frequently purchase pasta sauce. Through group placement or package discounts, the shop can increase sales of both products.

5. Tools and Technologies

There are many tools and technologies available in the field of data science that make it easier to spot patterns and trends. Programming languages and specific libraries and frameworks are among the most important tools.

Programming Languages

Because of its ease of use and vast selection of libraries designed specifically for data manipulation, analysis, and machine learning, Python is the most popular language in the data science field. NumPy is a crucial library for numerical calculations, Pandas is used for data management, and Scikitlearn is used to develop machine learning methods. Python is a versatile language that can be used by both novices and experts.

R is an additional potent language created especially for statistical visualization and analysis. It is well known for its reliable statistical packages and how simple it is to use tools like ggplot2 to create sophisticated representations. When working on complicated data analysis jobs, statisticians and data scientists frequently choose R.

Libraries and Frameworks

A Google open-source library called TensorFlow is essential for deep learning applications. It enables data scientists to create and train neural networks for a variety of applications, including natural language processing, picture and speech recognition, and more. TensorFlow is the preferred option for deep learning projects due to its scalability and broad community support.

The AI Research lab at Facebook created PyTorch, a more adaptable method for creating machine learning models. Because of its dynamic computation structure, which facilitates more efficient and intuitive model development, it is especially wellliked by researchers and projects that call for quick prototyping and experimentation.

A complete Python machine learning library is Scikitlearn. With a welldesigned API that supports a variety of machine learning methods, including as classification, regression, clustering, and dimensionality reduction, it offers straightforward and effective tools for data mining and analysis. Because Scikitlearn integrates with other Python libraries such as NumPy and Pandas, it is a vital tool for evaluating models and prepping data.

Apart from these fundamental technologies, data scientists frequently utilize additional tools like Apache Spark for managing largescale data processing and machine learning, Tableau and Power BI for generating dynamic visual analytics, and Jupyter Notebooks for interactive data exploration and visualization.

When combined, these tools and technologies enable data scientists to analyze data effectively, find hidden patterns and trends, and make defensible conclusions based on insights from the data.

Conclusion

Using AI and ML to spot patterns and trends is a potent way to comprehend and make use of data. Utilizing methods like as clustering, association rule learning, and time series analysis, firms are able to make competitive and performanceboosting datadriven decisions.

3.4 CORRELATION AND CAUSATION

Understanding the link between variables is essential for data scientists to make wellinformed decisions and forecasts. Two basic ideas are covered in this chapter: correlation and causality. Although these terms are frequently used synonymously in daily speech, in the fields of statistics and data analysis, they have different meanings. Understanding these distinctions is crucial for precise data interpretation and analysis, particularly when applying machine learning (ML) and artificial intelligence (AI) methods.

Correlation

A key idea in statistics and data science, correlation quantifies the direction and strength of a linear relationship between two variables. The correlation coefficient, generally represented as \(r \), is a number that ranges from 1 to 1. It is used to quantify this relationship. A complete positive linear relationship, where one variable grows proportionately to another, is indicated by a correlation coefficient of 1. A complete negative linear relationship, on the other hand, is denoted by a correlation coefficient of 1, meaning that a rise in one variable results in a corresponding reduction in the other. A correlation value of zero indicates that there is no linear relationship between the variables, meaning that variations in one do not necessarily correspond to variations in the other.

Different sorts of relationships can be described by various forms of correlation:

- **Positive Correlation:** This happens when there is a consistent movement of both variables. For instance, test scores typically rise in tandem with an increase in study hours.
- **Negative Correlation:** This is the situation in which one variable rises and the other falls. Test scores, for instance, may decline with an increase in TV viewing hours.
- **Zero Correlation:** This denotes that there is no connection or pattern between the variables.

Scatter plots are a useful tool for visualizing correlations, in which each point represents a pair of values. A visual representation of the relationship's intensity and direction can be obtained from the point pattern. Points grouped around a line that slopes upward, for example, indicate a positive correlation, whereas points grouped around a line that slopes downward, indicate a negative correlation.

It's crucial to remember that a connection does not indicate a cause. It is possible for two variables to be connected by chance or for a third variable to influence both of them. For instance, there may be a correlation between ice cream sales and drowning cases because both increase in the summer, but eating ice cream does not lead to drowning.

For nonlinear relationships or ordinal data, additional correlation measurement techniques such as Kendall's tau and Spearman rank correlation are employed in addition to the Pearson correlation coefficient. These metrics offer various perspectives on the connections between variables and are selected in accordance with the particular needs of the study as well as the features of the data.

Comprehending correlation is essential in multiple domains, such as finance, healthcare, and social sciences, since it facilitates the identification of connections and trends within data. Understanding correlation in the context of AI and ML helps with feature selection, preprocessing data, and model interpretation, all of which lead to the creation of predictive models that are more accurate in the end.

Causation

Causation is the establishment of a causeandeffect relationship over and above the simple association between variables. Put differently, when we suggest that one variable causes another, we are implying that modifications to the first variable will necessarily affect modifications to the second. Because it helps us understand the mechanics underlying different phenomena and make predictions, this relationship is crucial to many scientific domains.

Researchers frequently use experimental designs like randomized controlled trials (RCTs) to prove causation. Confounding variables are reduced in an RCT by randomly assigning participants to either the treatment or control groups. By isolating the treatment's effect, this randomization offers compelling proof of causality in the event that notable variations are noted between the groups.

Even though they are less controlled, observational studies can nevertheless demonstrate causation by using techniques like longitudinal studies, which gather data over a protracted period of time. This method demonstrates that the cause comes before the effect in time, which aids in establishing temporal precedencea crucial requirement for causality.

In more complicated cases, endogeneity problems in regression models are addressed by academics through the inclusion of instrumental variables (IV). A third variable known as an instrumental variable is one that is connected to the cause but not the effect directly; it serves to weed out irrelevant factors and bolster the case for causality.

Take the connection between smoking and lung cancer, for instance. Smoking promotes lung cancer, according to a large body of research that used RCTs, longitudinal studies, and instrumental variable methodologies. Consistent data, even after adjusting for other risk variables, indicates that smokers have a markedly increased risk of lung cancer compared to nonsmokers.

Understanding causation is essential for creating models in the fields of data science and machine learning that can produce accurate predictions and suggestions. To identify causal linkages from massive datasets, methods such as counterfactual reasoning and causal inference models are used. By revealing the underlying causal mechanisms, these techniques assist data scientists in going beyond the identification of patterns and correlations to produce more insightful and useful results.

To sum up, causality is the study of understanding and demonstrating how one action or occurrence directly causes another. Although establishing causation necessitates meticulous experimental planning, thorough analysis, and frequently complex statistical approaches, it is crucial for decisionmaking and comprehending the real dynamics of the systems we investigate.

Correlation vs. Causation

In the realm of data science, knowing the difference between correlation and causation is essential, especially when using AI and ML approaches. A statistical relationship between two variables that shows how they move together is called a correlation. This shift does not, however, suggest that one variable influences the other. For example, there may be a direct link between summertime drowning incidents and ice cream sales. It would be incorrect to assume that purchasing ice cream results in drowning, even though both rise during the summer months. This is an illustration of a spurious correlation, in which a third variable, like temperature, has an impact on the relationship between the variables.

But causation suggests a causeandeffect connection in which an occurrence (the cause) immediately leads to another (the consequence). It is significantly more difficult to establish causation and needs extensive testing and confirmation. For instance, a number of studies have established a link between smoking and lung cancer. In these situations, scientists prove that smoking causes lung cancer by means of controlled trials, longterm investigations, and statistical techniques, as opposed to only a correlation.

Understanding and using the right techniques is essential to separating correlation from causation. When determining causality, Randomized Controlled Trials (RCTs) are regarded as the gold standard. Researchers can minimize the impact of confounding variables and isolate the effect of the intervention by randomly assigning subjects to treatment and control groups. Longitudinal studies, in which participants are followed for extended periods of time, are useful in determining if changes in one variable eventually influence changes in another. In addition, econometrics and time series analysis employ sophisticated methods such as instrumental variables and Granger causality tests to deduce causation from observational data.

While algorithms in the fields of AI and ML may find patterns and connections in vast datasets, deciphering these links needs critical thought. Although domain knowledge and strong statistical methods are necessary to validate these results, machine learning models have the ability to identify plausible causal relationships. An ML algorithm may, for example, find a strong association between a set of characteristics and a target variable in predictive modeling. Nevertheless, additional research and testing are necessary to ascertain whether these characteristics causally affect the goal.

Although correlation can offer significant understanding of the connections between variables, it is insufficient to establish causality. Data scientists may distinguish between simple correlations and real causal linkages using rigorous experimental designs and sophisticated statistical techniques, producing more precise and useful insights. To guarantee the accuracy and dependability of forecasts and decisions based on data, it is essential to comprehend this distinction.

AI and ML in Determining Relationships

In data science, artificial intelligence (AI) and machine learning (ML) are essential for figuring out how variables relate to one another. These technologies are particularly good at finding connections and patterns in large datasets that human analysts might not see right away. AI and ML can reveal intricate links that conventional statistical methods might miss by utilizing advanced algorithms.

In real life, AI and ML models are capable of carrying out operations like predictive modeling, in which they use past data to learn and forecast future results. For example, machine learning algorithms can forecast future moves in the financial markets by analyzing historical stock prices and economic factors. Likewise, artificial intelligence (AI) in healthcare can examine patient data to find relationships between symptoms, interventions, and results, supporting tailored medicine and therapy suggestions.

In AI and ML applications, separating correlation from causation is still a major difficulty. While these tools are excellent at identifying correlations between variables, proper experimental design and extra domain knowledge are frequently needed to prove causal links. To go beyond correlation and identify causal relationships, methods like randomized controlled trials (RCTs), counterfactual reasoning, and causal inference models are used.

Additionally, largescale datasets with highdimensional features can be explored with the use of AI and ML, leading to the discovery of subtle correlations that improve predictions and insights. The capacity of AI models to derive significant associations from data is further improved by methods like ensemble learning and feature engineering.

All things considered, AI and ML are indispensable instruments in contemporary data science, enabling analysts and researchers to unearth complex linkages, reach wise conclusions, and spur breakthroughs in a range of sectors. These technologies will become more and more crucial in comprehending and forecasting intricate interactions between factors as they develop.

Conclusion

In data science, knowing the difference between correlation and causation is essential. While AI and ML are capable of spotting patterns in data, it is imperative to use the right methods to ascertain whether these patterns actually represent causal relationships. In a variety of industries, including banking and healthcare, accurately determining causation can result in more accurate forecasting and more effective decisionmaking.

3.5 HYPOTHESIS TESTING

A key idea in data science, artificial intelligence, and machine learning is hypothesis testing. It allows data scientists to draw conclusions about a population from sample data, supporting or contradicting presumptions and theories that come from data analysis. This chapter covers a variety of topics related to hypothesis testing, including approaches, uses in AI and ML, and realworld examples.

Key Concepts

1. Null and Alternative Hypotheses

Creating two hypotheses is the first step in the hypothesis testing process:

- **Null Hypothesis \(H_0 \):** This hypothesis postulates the absence of any meaningful variation or impact. It stands for the current situation or the presumption that variables have no relationship.

- **Alternative Hypothesis \(H_1 \):** This hypothesis suggests that there is a relationship, effect, or difference between the variables, which is in contrast to the null hypothesis.

To ascertain whether there is sufficient evidence to reject the null hypothesis in favor of the alternative, these hypotheses are tested using sample data.

2. Significance Level (α)

The chance of rejecting the null hypothesis when it is true is known as the significance level, and it is commonly represented by the symbol \(\alpha \). Levels like 0.05 (5%) and 0.01 (1%), for example, are often utilized. The danger of incorrectly rejecting a genuine null hypothesis or neglecting to reject a false null hypothesis, respectively, is balanced by selecting a significance threshold.

3. Test Statistics and Pvalue

- **Test Statistics:** A quantitative analysis of the data that gauges how much the sample data deviates from the null hypothesis. The type of data and the hypothesis being tested determine which test statistic is used (e.g., zscore for proportions, tstatistic for means).
- **Pvalue:** In the event that the null hypothesis is correct, the likelihood of seeing the test statistic or more severe outcomes. A smaller pvalue denotes more evidence that the null hypothesis is false, implying that the observed data is unlikely to support the null hypothesis.

4. Types of Hypothesis Tests

- **Parametric Tests:** These tests make certain assumptions about the data's distributions, including normality. ANOVA for comparing several groups and ttests for comparing means are two examples.
- **Non-parametric Tests:** No assumptions regarding the data's underlying distribution are made by these tests. When the distribution of the data is uncertain or non-normal, they are employed, as in the case of the Wilcoxon ranksum test for comparing medians.

Comprehending these fundamental ideas enables data scientists to employ hypothesis testing suitably in diverse situations, guaranteeing that inferences derived from data scrutiny are both statistically sound and dependable. Through meticulous selection of appropriate hypothesis tests and interpretation of outcomes using significance levels and pvalues, researchers can arrive at wellinformed conclusions and suggestions for AI and ML applications.

Applications in AI and ML

Hypothesis testing has several uses in AI and ML beyond simple statistical validation; it is essential to many stages of model creation, assessment, and optimization. A principal use case is model comparison. Data scientists can use hypothesis testing to assess the statistical significance of performance metrics differences between two or more models. For example, hypothesis testing can verify if an algorithm really performs better than another or if the difference is just the result of chance when comparing the accuracy of various algorithms on a classification task.

The selection of features is an additional crucial aspect. The performance of the model is greatly impacted by choosing the appropriate features, or variables, in machine learning. Finding the features that have a statistically significant impact on the model's predictions is made easier with the use of hypothesis testing. Data scientists can prioritize features that actually matter by evaluating the alternative hypothesisthat a certain feature contributes to the model's accuracyagainst the null hypothesis, which states that the feature does not.

Moreover, hypothesis testing is a crucial component of A/B testing, a popular technique for service and product optimization. A/B testing, as used in AI and ML contexts, is experimenting with various iterations of a model or algorithm to see which one produces better results. Businesses can utilize hypothesis testing to assist them make datadriven decisions about which variant to adopt by quantifying the observed differences in KPIs like user engagement or conversion rates.

Data scientists can make wellinformed decisions based on statistical evidence rather than gut feeling or anecdotal observations thanks to hypothesis testing in AI and ML. It makes sure that inferences made from data analysis are solid, repeatable, and indicative of actual results, which improves the dependability and efficiency of AI and ML applications across a range of industries.

Practical Example: A/B Testing in Ecommerce

A/B testing is a critical approach in ecommerce that is used to assess how changes in website structure, product placement, or even button color affect user behavior. Let's say a fictitious internet merchant want to know if their "Buy Now" button's red instead of blue color changes impact conversion rates. The steps for applying hypothesis testing are as follows:

1. Formulate Hypotheses:

Null Hypothesis (HO): There is no discernible impact of button color changes on conversion rates.

Alternative Hypothesis (H1): Changing the color of the button influences conversion rates in a positive or negative way.

2. Design Experiment:

Split website users into two groups at random; the control group sees the blue button, while the experimental group sees the red button.

3. Collect Data:

Track important indicators like impressions, button clicks, and real conversions (purchases) for both groups during a predetermined time frame.

Variant	Impressions	Clicks	Conversions	Conversion Rate
Blue Button	1000	150	30	0.03
Red Button	1100	165	45	0.04

4. Calculate Test Statistics

Using the observed data, calculate a test statistic (such as the zscore or tstatistic). The disparity in conversion rates between the two groups is measured by this statistic.

5. Determine Pvalue

Assuming the null hypothesis is true, find the pvalue, which represents the likelihood of witnessing the data. Stronger evidence against the null hypothesis is indicated by a lower pvalue.

6. Make Inference:

Examine the pvalue in relation to the selected significance level (e.g., $\alpha = 0.05$). Reject the null hypothesis and conclude that altering the button color has a statistically significant impact on conversion rates if the pvalue is smaller than α.

Draw Conclusion

Make an informed decision about whether to permanently deploy the modification throughout the website based on the statistical significance and the practical significance (magnitude of the effect).

In our example, the conversion rate for the red button was higher than the blue button's, at 4% as opposed to 3%. Assume that the pvalue, which represents statistical significance, is less than 0.05. If so, we may declare with confidence that there is a rise in conversion rates when the button color is changed from blue to red.

Conclusion

In AI and ML, hypothesis testing offers a strict framework for datadriven decisionmaking. Data scientists may evaluate models, validate assumptions, and optimize processes based on empirical facts by comprehending its ideas and methodology.

Practitioners of AI and ML can make sure that their results are replicable and statistically valid, rather than merely relying on anecdotal evidence, by including hypothesis testing into their workflow.

3.6 ADVANCED DATA EXPLORATION TOOLS

The foundation of any datadriven decisionmaking process is data exploration. It entails comprehending the properties and organization of data prior to using statistical analysis or machine learning methods. More sophisticated tools improve this process by offering more sophisticated insights and visual aids.

Key Tools and Techniques

A. Principal Component Analysis (PCA):

The dimensionality reduction method known as Principal Component Analysis (PCA) is frequently applied in data exploration. As much variance as possible is preserved as highdimensional data is transformed into a lowerdimensional space. PCA facilitates the visualisation of complicated datasets and the comprehension of their underlying structure by finding principle components, which are linear combinations of the original variables.

PCA is particularly useful for:

- **Visualization:** Charting data points to identify patterns or clusters in a smaller area.
- **Feature Selection:** Determining which variables account for the majority of the dataset's volatility.

- **Noise Reduction:** removing extraneous information and concentrating on the most important details in the data.

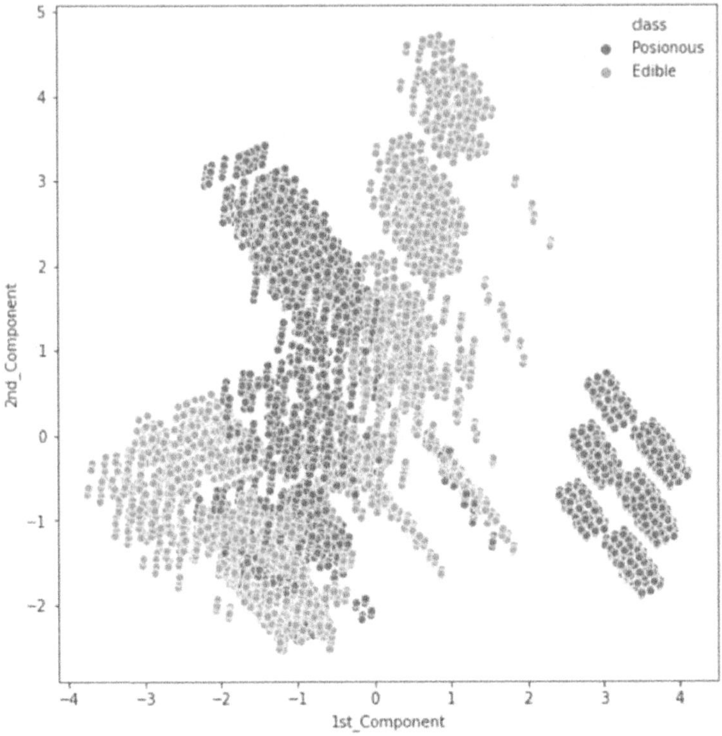

B. tDistributed Stochastic Neighbor Embedding (tSNE):

Another effective method for visualizing highdimensional data is to embed it in a lowdimensional space, such as 2D or 3D, using tSNE. Since tSNE prioritizes maintaining the local structure of data points over PCA, it is a useful technique for locating clusters or groupings that may not be visible in the original dimensions.

Key applications of tSNE include:

- **Cluster Identification:** Emphasizing groups of related data points together.
- **Pattern Recognition:** Highlighting connections between adjacent locations.
- **Anomaly Detection:** Locating anomalies or anomalies in datasets.

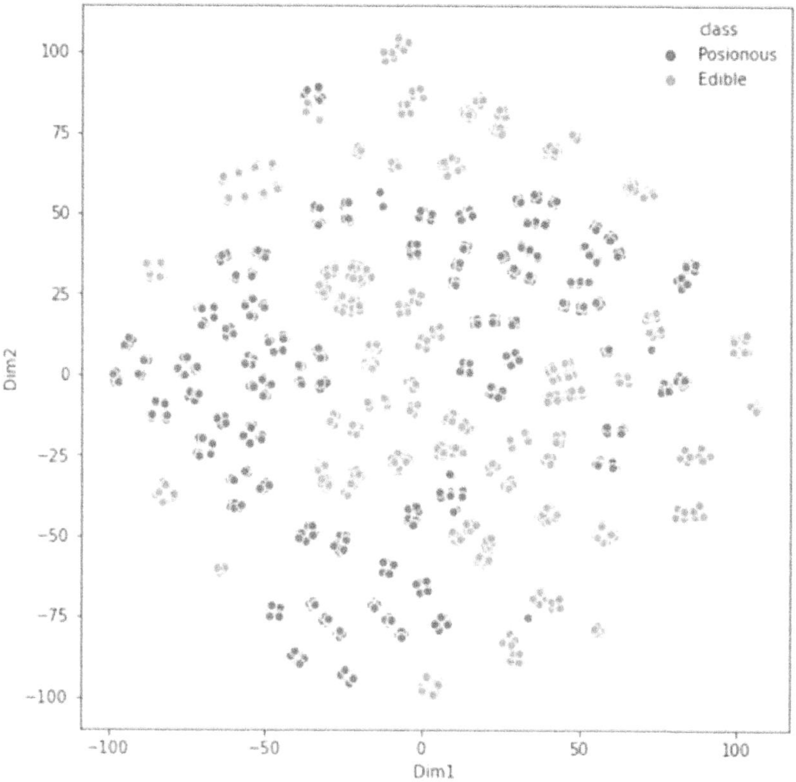

C. Hierarchical Clustering

Using hierarchical clustering, data is arranged according to similarity between data points to create a dendrogram, or treelike structure. Until every data point is a part of a single cluster, the most similar clusters are combined iteratively.

Hierarchical clustering is beneficial for:

- **Cluster Analysis:** Identifying natural groupings within data.
- **Interpretability:** Visualizing relationships between clusters at different levels of granularity.
- **Decision Making:** Providing insights into data structure and groupings.

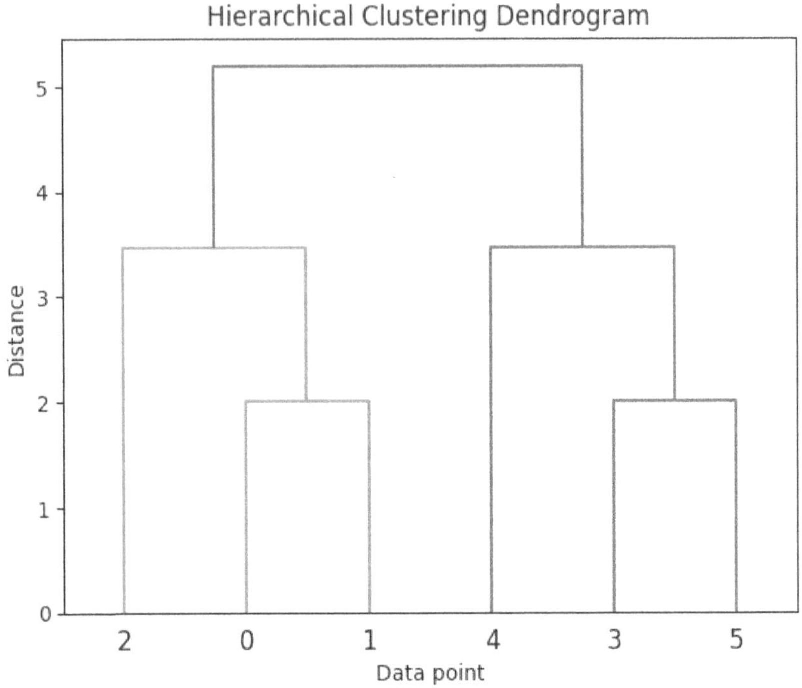

Visualization Techniques

Through the transformation of unstructured data into meaningful insights that are simple to understand and share, visualization plays a critical role in data exploration. In addition to improving our comprehension of complicated facts, advanced visualization techniques can make links, patterns, and trends visible that might not be seen in simple numerical summaries.

a. Heatmaps

Heatmaps are useful tools for simultaneously visualizing correlations and patterns across several variables. Heatmaps enable us to easily detect relationships, clusters, or anomalies within datasets by utilizing color gradients to represent values. A correlation heatmap, for instance, can help with feature selection or the identification of redundant variables in machine learning models by graphically highlighting which variables have a strong or inverse association with one another.

b. Box Plots

Box plots, sometimes referred to as boxandwhisker plots, offer a succinct overview of how a numerical variable or metric is distributed among various groups or categories. They facilitate distribution comparison and the identification of group differences by displaying important statistical metrics including the median, quartiles, and outliers. When conducting exploratory data analysis, box plots are especially helpful for evaluating the distribution and central tendency of data points, spotting any skewness or outliers, and making wellinformed choices regarding model selection or data preprocessing.

c. Scatter Plots with Regression Lines

When attempting to visualize the relationship between two continuous variables, scatter plots are essential. They represent each pair of values from the dataset by a single dot on a graph, which is used to plot data points. Whether a relationship between variables is linear, quadratic, or nonlinear, adding a regression line to a scatter plot aids in determining its direction and strength. Because it enables data scientists to evaluate the fit of a regression model and generate predictions based on observed patterns, this visualization technique is highly beneficial in the fields of predictive modeling and hypothesis testing.

d. Interactive Visualizations

As technology has progressed, interactive visualizations have gained popularity as a means of examining vast and intricate datasets. Users can create dynamic, customisable charts, graphs, and dashboards with tools like Plotly, D3.js, or Tableau, which allow for realtime exploration and analysis. Zooming, filtering, and hovering over data points are examples of interactive features that improve user engagement and offer deeper insights into patterns and trends in the data. Datadriven decisionmaking processes in a variety of industries, including marketing, finance, healthcare, and higher education, greatly benefit from these representations.

e. Geographic Visualizations (Maps)

By turning locationbased data into maps, geographic visualizations enable data scientists to examine spatial distributions, patterns, and trends among various geographic regions. Simple point maps to intricate choropleth maps that colorcode regions according to data values are examples of these kinds of displays. In domains like environmental science, urban planning, and epidemiology, where knowledge of spatial correlations and patterns is crucial for formulating wellinformed policies and decisions, geographic visualizations are especially helpful.

Data scientists and analysts who want to learn more about complicated datasets indepth must have access to sophisticated visualization approaches. Through the use of these strategies, professionals can locate patterns that are hidden, spot anomalies, and successfully inform stakeholders of their results, thus promoting datadriven decisionmaking and innovation in AI and ML applications.

Conclusion

Utilizing sophisticated data exploration instruments like PCA, tSNE, hierarchical clustering, box plots, and heatmaps greatly improves our comprehension of intricate datasets. These technologies help with visualization, but they also offer insights that help with decisionmaking in applications of AI and ML.

4

Machine Learning Fundamentals

4.1 INTRODUCTION TO MACHINE LEARNING

1. What is Machine Learning?

Within the larger field of artificial intelligence (AI), machine learning is a key field that enables computers to learn from data and make predictions or choices without needing to be explicitly programmed for every situation. Fundamentally, machine learning algorithms find patterns and structures in data, which helps computers learn from examples and gradually get better at what they do. Because it enables machines to perform complex tasks that are challenging to explain using conventional programming techniques, this feature is especially transformational.

There are various sorts of machine learning algorithms, each with a specific function:

- Supervised Learning entails using labeled data to train algorithms, matching each input to the appropriate output. Predictive analytics, speech recognition, and image recognition are some of the applications for this kind.
- Unsupervised Learning works with unlabeled data and looks for underlying structures or hidden patterns in datasets. Applications include finding relevant groupings in customer segmentation or grouping related products together in recommendation systems.
- The concept of Reinforcement Learning centers on agents interacting with their surroundings and learning to adjust their behavior in response to feedback from favorable or unfavorable

results. This kind is utilized in robotics, autonomous driving, and gaming (like Go or Chess).

Furthermore, the quality, amount, and relevance of the data are critical to machine learning's efficacy. Cleaning, converting, and selecting characteristics are all part of the data preparation process, which is essential to getting datasets ready for analysis. Machine learning models are rigorously tested using test data after training to determine their correctness, dependability, and generalizability.

Machine learning, in its simplest form, is a paradigm change in computing, where systems learn from experience and adapt in addition to following preset rules. Machine learning applications are spreading quickly across industries, from manufacturing and entertainment to healthcare and finance, as AI and data science breakthroughs quicken. This is radically changing how organizations function and how people engage with technology.

2. Applications of Machine Learning

By enabling systems to learn from data and make predictions or judgments without human interaction, machine learning has transformed a number of sectors. For instance, machine learning algorithms are used in the healthcare industry to evaluate patient data and help with disease diagnosis, outcome prediction, and treatment plan customization. By sorting through enormous volumes of genetic information, imaging data, and medical records, these algorithms can find patterns that human specialists would miss, enhancing patient care and diagnostic precision.

Machine learning is essential to the banking industry because it enables algorithms to identify anomalous patterns in transaction data and immediately identify potentially fraudulent activity. Furthermore, machine learning models are used in risk assessment to evaluate credit scores, loan histories, and market data in order to forecast the probability of default. This helps financial organizations make well-informed lending decisions.

To tailor marketing campaigns and divide consumers into groups, machine learning algorithms examine consumer behavior and interests. Machine learning-powered recommendation systems make content or product suggestions based on a user's previous interactions, improving user experience and raising sales conversion rates.

Autonomous cars, which use sophisticated algorithms to analyze real-time data from sensors like cameras, radar, and lidar to sense their surroundings and make driving judgments, are another significant application of machine learning. By enabling cars to recognize and identify pedestrians, other cars, and traffic signs, navigate through traffic, and adjust to changing road conditions, these algorithms open the door to more effective and safe transportation systems.

Machine learning continues to spur efficiency and innovation in these and many other sectors, revolutionizing business through task automation, enhanced decision-making, and the extraction of previously unobtainable insights from enormous datasets. It will become increasingly important to research and develop in the field of data science and artificial intelligence as machine learning and AI continue to grow because of the potential for new applications and societal effect.

3. Machine Learning Workflow

The machine learning workflow is a methodical procedure that includes multiple essential phases, all of which are necessary for creating efficient models and extracting valuable information from data.

1. Data Collection and Preparation

The first step in the process is data collecting, which entails gathering pertinent datasets from a variety of sources like databases, APIs, and Internet of Things devices. This stage is crucial since the model's performance is directly impacted by the quantity and quality of data. After being gathered, the data is preprocessed. This include fixing any errors in the data, filling in any missing numbers, and formatting it appropriately for analysis. Algorithms can more easily discover patterns when data is standardized, thanks to techniques like feature scaling and normalization.

2. Exploratory Data Analysis (EDA)

To acquire understanding of the dataset, exploratory data analysis, or EDA, is carried out prior to model selection. The purpose of visualization tools like scatter plots, heatmaps, and histograms is to find patterns, correlations, and outliers in the data. EDA facilitates the comprehension of variable distribution and the discovery of correlations that might guide feature selection and engineering choices.

3. Feature Engineering

To enhance the performance of the model, feature engineering entails choosing, extracting, and modifying features (variables) from the dataset. This could entail scaling numerical features, encoding categorical variables, or generating new features from already-existing ones. The objective is to provide the model useful and pertinent input data so that it can learn and become more predictive.

4. Model Selection and Training

The next stage is to choose a suitable machine learning algorithm after the data has been prepared and features have been engineered. The type of task (classification, regression, etc.) and the properties of the data will determine this choice. Neural networks, decision trees, support vector machines (SVM), and ensemble techniques like random forests are examples of popular algorithms. Using the training dataset, models are trained to discover patterns and connections between input variables and desired outputs.

5. Model Evaluation and Validation

Using validation techniques like cross-validation or dividing the data into training and validation sets, the model's performance is assessed after training. Evaluation criteria that quantify the model's performance on unknown data include accuracy, precision, recall, and F1-score. This stage prevents overfitting, which occurs when a model performs well on training data but badly on test dataand guarantees that the model generalizes well to new data.

6. Hyperparameter Tuning

Hyperparameter tuning is carried out to further maximize the performance of the model. Hyperparameters (e.g., learning rate, number of layers in a neural network) are parameters that control the learning process and model complexity. Methods like grid search or randomized search are employed to identify the optimal set of hyperparameters that optimize model efficiency.

7. Model Deployment and Monitoring

When a model is good enough, it is put into use and starts predicting things based on fresh, unobserved data. Integrating the model into already-existing applications or systems is known as deployment. The model's accuracy is maintained throughout time by post-deployment, monitoring, and maintenance. This could entail periodically retraining the model with fresh data or updating it in response to evolving circumstances.

4. Types of Machine Learning Algorithms

There are various types of machine learning algorithms, each intended to handle particular jobs and learning scenarios. These include:

1. **Supervised Learning:** Algorithms learn from labeled data in supervised learning, where each input has a goal output that corresponds to it. In order to enable the algorithm to generate predictions on new data, the objective is to train a mapping function from the input variables (features) to the output variables (labels). Two common supervised learning problems are regression and classification.
    - **Classification:** In this task, new data points are predicted to have a categorical label or class based on previous observations. For instance, determining if an email is spam or not by looking at previously categorized examples.
    - **Regression:** Predicting a continuous numerical value from input features is the goal of regression tasks. For example, estimating the cost of a house depending on its location, size, and number of rooms.
2. **Unsupervised Learning:** When there is no labeling of the data and the objective is to find structures or patterns within the data, unsupervised learning algorithms are employed. These algorithms search through the data and uncover hidden connections or clusters without being told what to look for.
    - **Clustering:** Algorithms for clustering put related instances in groups according to shared traits. This is helpful for jobs like customer segmentation, where clients are put together based on shared behaviors or preferences without the customers' prior knowledge of each other's identities.
    - **Dimensionality Reduction:** These methods seek to minimize the amount of input variables in a dataset while maintaining its significant organizational framework. One common example for data compression and visualization is Principal Component Analysis (PCA).
3. **Reinforcement Learning:** In reinforcement learning, an agent learns how to make choices in a given environment in order to accomplish a particular objective. By obtaining feedback from the environment in the form of incentives or penalties, the agent learns by making mistakes and learning from them.

- **Dynamic Environments:** Reinforcement learning works well in situations where judgments must be made gradually and actions have an impact on future states. Autonomous driving, playing video games (like chess), and robot control are a few examples.

Every kind of machine learning algorithm has advantages and uses, therefore it's critical for data scientists and machine learning professionals to know when and how to use them. While unsupervised learning is useful for examining data and finding hidden patterns, supervised learning is frequently employed for jobs with clear, labeled data. For situations requiring adaptive learning and ongoing engagement with the environment, reinforcement learning is perfect because of its emphasis on decision-making in dynamic environments.

The skills of artificial intelligence and data science can be advanced by practitioners by using their strengths to address a variety of real-world issues in industries like marketing, finance, healthcare, and more by becoming proficient with these kinds of machine learning algorithms.

These ideas form a strong basis for more research and application in "Data Science Using AI and ML" and are essential to comprehending the field of machine learning and its applications.

Conclusion

In data science, machine learning is a potent technology that lets systems automatically pick up new skills and get better with time. The use of AI and ML in real-world situations is growing in frequency and significance as these technologies develop.

4.2 SUPERVISED LEARNING ALGORITHMS

Supervised learning algorithms are essential to the data science and machine learning (ML) fields because they enable the generation of predictions and judgments from labeled data. This chapter explores the basic ideas, methods, and uses of supervised learning, emphasizing the importance of this approach in actual AI systems.

Key Concepts

1. Supervised Learning Overview

In the field of supervised learning, machine learning algorithms are trained on labeled data, or input-output pairs. The primary objective is to extrapolate generalizations from the provided instances to forecast or decide on unknown data. The dataset consists of examples where input variables, or features, are paired with predicted output variables, or targets, so that the algorithm can learn a mapping function that connects inputs to outputs. Through iterative learning, the model is able to improve its predictions over time with the help of a specified set of labeled instances.

2. Types of Supervised Learning Algorithms

- **Classification:** When the target variable is discrete or categorical, this kind of method is applied. Based on previous observations, the model learns to predict the class labels of new instances. Email spam detection, for instance, uses information taken from the email content to classify emails as spam or not.
- **Regression:** Regression methods are applied when the objective variable is continuous, as opposed to classification. These algorithms use input feature information to predict numerical values. Regression problems include, for example, estimating home values depending on location, square footage, and number of bedrooms.

Comprehending these differences is essential, as it determines the selection of algorithms and the methodology for preparing data and assessing models. Algorithms for supervised learning are flexible and can work with both structured and unstructured data. They serve as the basis for a wide range of practical applications in industries like marketing, banking, and healthcare, where it's critical to make precise forecasts based on previous data.

Data scientists may create and implement predictive models that facilitate decision-making and task automation in a variety of sectors by grasping these fundamental ideas. Every algorithm has advantages and disadvantages, therefore it's critical to choose the best one depending on the particular issue at hand and the properties of the data. In order to ensure the model's resilience and dependability in real-world applications, this selection procedure entails comprehending the underlying assumptions, complexity, and processing requirements of each algorithm.

Algorithms Covered

1. Linear Regression

A key technique in supervised learning is linear regression, which forecasts a continuous numerical value from input information. The dependent variable (output) and the independent variables (inputs) are assumed to have a linear relationship. Using techniques like Ordinary Least Squares (OLS), the model computes coefficients (slope and intercept) that minimize the difference between anticipated and actual values. Because of its ease of use and interpretability, linear regression is frequently employed in situations where it can be used to forecast sales trends based on advertising expenditures or estimate patient recovery times based on medical data.

2. Decision Trees

Models that are flexible enough to tackle challenges involving both regression and classification are decision trees. They use a hierarchical structure of nodes to organize the data, with each node standing for a feature and each branch for a decision rule. The dataset is divided at each node of the tree recursively according to the feature that best separates the data based on a selected criterion (e.g., mean squared error for regression or Gini impurity for classification). Decision trees are useful in fields like marketing consumer segmentation and disease diagnosis based on clinical signs since they are simple to understand and depict.

3. Support Vector Machines (SVM)

Strong supervised learning models for classification and regression applications include Support Vector Machines (SVM). SVMs maximize the margin between classes by locating a hyperplane in a high-dimensional space that best divides classes. By using kernel functions to translate input data into a higher-dimensional space, they can handle both linearly and non-linearly separable data with effectiveness. When complicated decision limits are needed, SVMs are very helpful in tasks like biological classification, text categorization, and image classification.

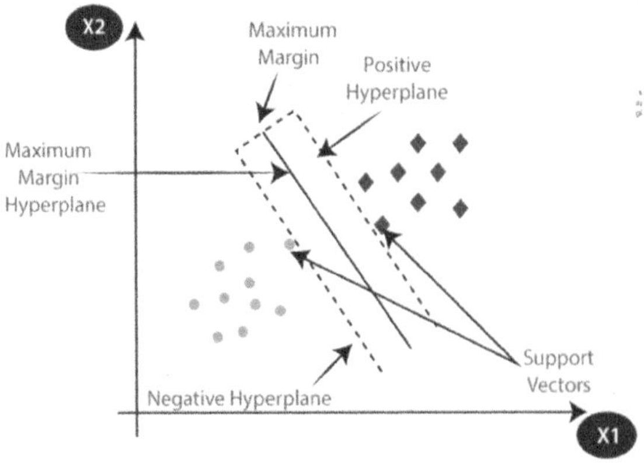

Since each of these algorithms has advantages and disadvantages, they can be applied to various problem domains and data types. To apply them to real-world datasets in data science and machine learning projects, it is essential to comprehend their fundamental principles, parameters, and tuning approaches. Through the mastery of these algorithms, practitioners may create resilient predictive models that drive informed decision-making processes in a variety of sectors and applications by extracting significant insights.

Practical Applications

Because supervised learning algorithms can generate predictions and classifications from labeled data, they are widely used in a variety of industries. These algorithms are essential in finance for activities like credit scoring, where models forecast default risk by analyzing past financial behavior data from debtors. In a similar vein, supervised learning algorithms in fraud detection examine transaction patterns to spot unusual activity suggestive of fraudulent activity, assisting financial institutions in safeguarding their clients' money.

Supervised learning is essential to the healthcare industry since it helps with medical diagnosis and forecasts the course of diseases. Predictive models, for example, can use patient data analysis to predict how diseases like cancer or diabetes would progress, which helps medical professionals create individualized treatment strategies. Furthermore, supervised learning algorithms in image analysis allow for automated interpretation of medical images, including MRIs and X-rays, helping radiologists identify problems more accurately and efficiently.

Supervised learning algorithms power customer segmentation and targeted marketing techniques in retail and e-commerce. These algorithms classify customers into different groups according to their purchasing habits and demographics by examining their behavior and preferences. Businesses can customize product recommendations and promotional offers thanks to this segmentation, which raises client happiness and increases sales.

Moreover, natural language processing (NLP) applications like sentiment analysis and language translation depend on supervised learning approaches. The attitudes expressed in reviews and social media posts can be effectively classified by models trained on labeled textual data, offering useful insights for market sentiment analysis and brand reputation management.

All things considered, supervised learning algorithms have several real-world uses in a variety of industries, enabling businesses to automate procedures, make data-driven decisions, and provide customers with improved services. These algorithms are anticipated to have a major impact on industry efficiency, innovation, and consumer experience in the years to come as they develop in tandem with advances in AI and machine learning.

Conclusion

Aspiring data scientists and AI developers must become proficient with supervised learning methods. Professionals that are knowledgeable about these methods are better equipped to create precise prediction models and glean insightful information from data.

4.3 UNSUPERVISED LEARNING ALGORITHMS

Unsupervised learning methods are essential for deriving valuable insights from data in the fields of data science and machine learning without the need for explicit direction from labeled outputs. This chapter explores the many approaches and strategies used in unsupervised learning, highlighting their benefits and uses.

Key Concepts

1. The aim of clustering, a basic unsupervised learning method, is to organize data points into clusters according to commonalities in their feature space. Finding naturally occurring groupings in data without first knowing the class names is the core of clustering. By repeatedly assigning each data point to the cluster with the closest centroid, for example, K-Means clustering divides data into K clusters and eventually converges to clusters that minimize intra-cluster distance.
    - In contrast, hierarchical clustering creates a hierarchy of clusters that resembles a tree by iteratively joining or dividing clusters according to how close they are to one another. Density-Based Spatial Clustering of Applications with Noise, or DBSCAN, finds clusters using density-connected regions, making it appropriate for datasets with noise and asymmetric forms.
    - Applications for clustering can be found in many different fields, including computer vision, cybersecurity, and

marketing, where it is used for picture segmentation and customer segmentation. It facilitates the discovery of hidden patterns in data, allowing for insights and defensible choices.

2. Dimensional understanding Reduction strategies try to keep important information in a dataset while reducing the number of variables or features. The curse of dimensionality frequently affects high-dimensional data, increasing processing complexity and noise. By identifying the greatest variance across attributes, dimensionality reduction techniques like Principal Component Analysis (PCA) convert data into a lower-dimensional space. This helps with two- or three-dimensional data visualization in addition to streamlining data representation.
   - Another potent method for visualizing high-dimensional datasets in a lower-dimensional space is t-Distributed Stochastic Neighbor Embedding (t-SNE), which is especially useful for tasks like visualizing complex datasets or clustering analysis. It focuses on maintaining local relationships between data points.
   - These techniques are essential for better decision-making in a variety of applications, including image processing, bioinformatics, and natural language processing, by preparing data, enhancing model performance, and deciphering data structures.
3. The Association Regulation Through learning, one might find intriguing correlations or interactions across variables in sizable datasets. It is especially helpful in market basket analysis, where the objective is to identify common item sets or combinations of items that consumers buy together. Using an iterative process to generate candidate itemsets and prune those that do not match minimal support requirements, the Apriori method, for instance, finds frequently occurring itemsets.
   - Another effective method is FP-Growth (Frequent Pattern Growth), which expedites the mining process by building the FP-tree, a compact data structure, to mine frequent itemsets without explicitly producing candidate itemsets.
   - Applications for association rule learning include cross-selling tactics, recommendation systems, and e-commerce and retail industry awareness of consumer behavior patterns. Businesses can use it to improve marketing strategy and operational efficiencies by extracting meaningful insights from transactional data.

Applications in Business and Research

Because unsupervised learning algorithms may find underlying patterns and structures in data without the requirement for labeled samples, they are widely used in both research and business.

In Business Applications

1. **Customer Segmentation:** Companies might divide their clientele into various groups according to their interests, demographics, or purchase patterns. Improved consumer happiness, tailored recommendations, and focused marketing techniques are all made possible by this segmentation.
2. **Churn Prediction:** Businesses trying to hold onto their customer base must be able to predict customer attrition. Algorithms for unsupervised learning can recognize trends that point to the likelihood of client attrition, allowing for focused intervention and proactive retention tactics.

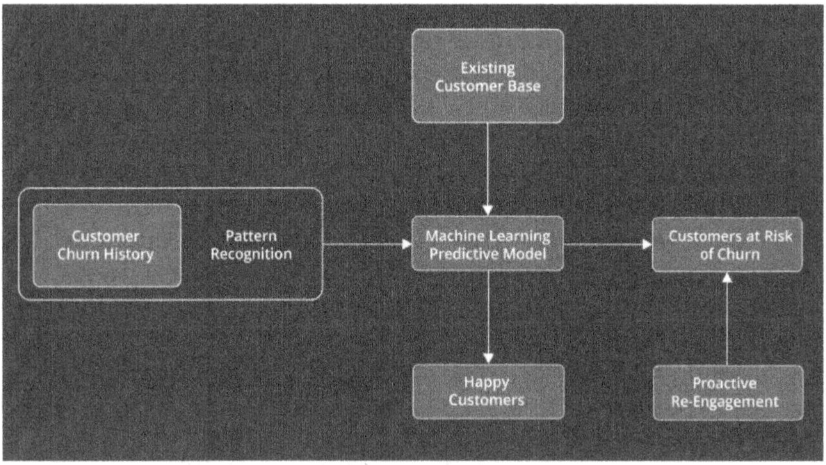

3. **Recommendation Systems:** Based on user behavior and preferences, unsupervised learning is used by platforms such as Netflix and Amazon to recommend content and goods. Through user preference clustering, these systems improve user pleasure and engagement.
4. **Anomaly Detection:** Finding abnormalities or outliers in datawhich may indicate fraudulent transactions, cybersecurity risks, or operational inefficienciesis made easier with the use of unsupervised learning techniques. By doing this, businesses may reduce risks and raise security levels all around.

In Research Applications

1. **Analysis of Biological Data:** Unsupervised learning is utilized in the analysis of gene expression data, discovery of gene clusters with related functions or regulatory patterns, and molecular understanding of biological processes.
2. **Analysis of Astronomical Data:** Astronomers can better comprehend the structure and history of the universe by using clustering algorithms to discover celestial objects with similar properties, categorize galaxies, or find patterns in cosmic microwave background radiation.
3. **Analysis of Social Networks:** Through the clustering of nodes, which can be individuals or entities, inside a social network according to shared qualities or connectivity patterns, researchers can obtain valuable insights into the dynamics of information diffusion, community structures, and influential nodes.
4. **Market Basket Analysis:** To identify recurring item groupings and uncover purchasing patterns, retailers and e-commerce platforms use association rule learning to analyze transaction data. Pricing plans, cross-selling opportunities, and inventory management are all informed by this information.

Unsupervised learning plays a vital role in fostering innovation, allowing informed decision-making in both commercial and research contexts, and extracting actionable insights due to its versatility and application across multiple domains. Future data science and AI-driven applications should continue to be relevant and influential as long as algorithms and computer power remain high. This is because complicated datasets can be mined for fresh insights.

Challenges and Future Directions

It's important to take into account a number of important factors that influence the efficacy and practicality of unsupervised learning algorithms when debating their difficulties and potential future directions.

Challenges in Unsupervised Learning

1. Interpretability of Results

Interpreting the clusters or patterns found by algorithms is a major problem in unsupervised learning. Unsupervised approaches rely on intrinsic data structures, as contrast to supervised learning, where the goal variable offers explicit instruction. Thus, guaranteeing the appropriate interpretation of links and clusters continues to be a major challenge. To overcome this difficulty, strategies like domain knowledge integration and visualizations are essential.

2. Scalability with Large Datasets

The scalability of many unsupervised learning techniques is a challenge when dealing with huge data sets. To handle large data effectively, algorithms like K-Means or Hierarchical Clustering can become computationally expensive and may need specialized implementations or distributed computing frameworks. Optimizing algorithmic efficiency and utilizing parallel processing techniques are key components in addressing scalability challenges.

3. Quality and Preprocessing of Data:

An important factor influencing the effectiveness of unsupervised learning systems is the caliber of the input data. Incomplete or noisy data sets can provide untrustworthy association or clustering patterns. Normalization, outlier detection, and feature engineering are examples of data preprocessing techniques that are essential for boosting algorithm robustness and elevating the caliber of insights obtained.

Future Directions

1. Enhancing Algorithm Robustness:

The goal of future unsupervised learning research is to create algorithms that can withstand fluctuations in noise and data distribution. Techniques like robust statistical methods that reduce the influence of outliers and ensemble clustering, which integrates many clustering algorithms, are potential approaches.

2. Incorporating Deep Learning Approaches:

Although deep learning has transformed supervised learning tasks, its applicability in unsupervised situations has been limited because of the difficulties in training without explicit labeling. In the future, deep learning architectures specifically designed for unsupervised taskslike generative adversarial networks (GANs) for artificial data generation or autoencoders for dimensionality reductionwill be developed.

3. Advancing Interpretability and Explainability:

Enhancing the interpretability of outcomes from unsupervised learning continues to be a crucial topic of attention. Research endeavors are examining methods to furnish comprehensible explanations for patterns of clustering or association, like incorporating rule-based systems or creating visualization instruments that enable interactive investigation of clustering results.

4. Handling High-Dimensional and Heterogeneous Data:

To effectively manage high-dimensional and diverse data, unsupervised learning algorithms need to evolve as datasets continue to grow in size and complexity. The creation of algorithms that can comprehend intricate links between many data kinds, including text, photos, and time-series data, is one of the future directions.

Although unsupervised learning algorithms are incredibly effective at revealing hidden patterns and structures in data, their wider adoption and efficacy depend on resolving issues with interpretability, scalability, and data quality. Subsequent investigations will focus on improving interpretability, deep learning approaches, algorithmic resilience, and adaptability to changing data difficulties. These efforts should open up new application domains.

Conclusion

Algorithms for unsupervised learning are always developing, providing strong resources for drawing conclusions and trends from data in a world growing more interconnected by the day. Gaining an understanding of these methods gives data scientists the tools they need to effectively address challenging real-world issues.

4.4 REINFORCEMENT LEARNING

In the machine learning branch of reinforcement learning (RL), an agent picks up decision-making skills through interaction with its surroundings. RL learns from the results of its actions rather than labeled datasets like supervised learning does. The use of RL in data science, AI, and machine learning is examined in this chapter.

Key Concepts in Reinforcement Learning

Let's examine the fundamental ideas of Reinforcement Learning (RL) in the context of machine learning and data science in more detail.

Strengthening The core of learning is an agent interacting with its surroundings to accomplish predetermined objectives. Fundamentally, RL differs from supervised learning in that it doesn't rely on labeled datasets. Rather, the agent gains experience via trial and error and gets feedback in the form of incentives or sanctions depending on what it does.

The agent, the environment, actions, rewards, and objectives are the essential elements of reinforcement learning. In the environment, the agent is the decision-maker whose goal is to maximize cumulative rewards over time by choosing the right actions based on its present state. These activities have an impact on the environment, which has an impact on the agent's incentives. Learning a policy, or strategy or collection of rules, that determines what to do in each given state to maximize long-term rewards, is the agent's ultimate goal.

The idea of rewards is central to reinforcement learning (RL), as it gives the agent instant feedback following each action. In terms of the agent's objectives, rewards can be zero, negative, or positive, indicating how desirable the action was. In reinforcement learning (RL), the goal is usually to maximize the cumulative reward throughout multiple interactions with the environment, as opposed to attaining a single accurate output as in supervised learning.

The difference between exploration and exploitation is crucial in RL. While exploitation consists of selecting courses of action that are known to result in positive results based on prior experience, exploration entails trying out various courses of action to determine which give the largest rewards. Effective learning in dynamic and uncertain situations requires striking a balance between exploration and exploitation.

Moreover, value functions and policy optimization are two methods that RL algorithms frequently use to aid in decision-making. Value functions aid in the agent's decision-making by estimating the expected cumulative reward from a given state while adhering to a specified policy. Policy optimization techniques seek to enhance the agent's policy with time by modifying its behavior in response to observed rewards and action results.

Reinforcement learning offers a strong framework for discovering the best course of action in dynamic settings when explicit supervision is either unfeasible or unavailable. This paradigm is particularly useful in the context of data science and machine learning. RL agents are suited for a wide range of applications, from robotics and gaming to finance and healthcare, because they can adapt and enhance their performance over time through continual learning from interactions with the environment.

Algorithms in Reinforcement Learning

Reinforcement Learning Algorithms Through contact with their surroundings, agents can learn optimal behavior through a variety of techniques to learning. A few of well-known algorithms that are worth discussing are Q-Learning and Deep Q-Networks (DQN).

One of the fundamental algorithms of reinforcement learning is Q-Learning. It works by updating action-value functions iteratively.

These functions calculate the expected return, or future rewards, that an agent can anticipate from performing a specific action in a specific state. Since this approach doesn't need a model of the dynamics of the environment, it can be used in situations where accurate models of the environment are hard to come by or unavailable. By balancing exploration and exploitationtypically using an epsilon-greedy policywhich takes random actions with a small probability epsilon and otherwise selects the action that maximizes the estimated returnQ-Learning makes sure that the agent explores the state-space effectively.

By utilizing deep neural networks, Deep Q-Networks (DQN) expand Q-Learning to handle complicated and high-dimensional situations. Deep Q-Networks use a neural network to approximate the action-value function, combining deep learning capabilities with classical Q-Learning. In applications where classic tabular methods like Q-Learning are unfeasible, like video games or robotics, this methodology has shown great performance in solving jobs with large state spaces.

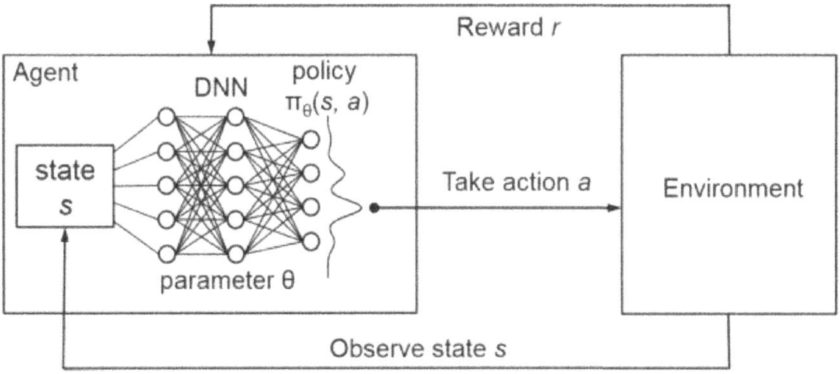

In DQN, the neural network receives the environment as it is at any given time as input and produces Q-values for every action that may be taken. Experience replay and a target network are added to the Q-Learning variation used to train the network in order to stabilize training. Experience replay is a technique for training a network by randomly selecting batches of experiences from a replay buffer containing the agent's experiences (state, action, reward, and future state). By supplying more consistent targets during training, a target network that is frequently updated with the main network's characteristics contributes to the improvement of learning stability.

These algorithms show how reinforcement learning has developed from straightforward tabular approaches to intricate deep learning strategies, empowering agents to take on progressively challenging tasks and domains. Their use in a variety of industries, such as gaming, robotics, and autonomous systems, highlights their adaptability and potential to completely transform AI-driven data science decision-making processes.

Gaining an understanding of these algorithms lays a strong basis for investigating more complex subjects in reinforcement learning, like policy gradients and actor-critic techniques, and how they are applied in real-world situations where learning from interactions is crucial.

Applications in Data Science

In the field of data science, reinforcement learning (RL) has found several useful applications by utilizing its capacity to learn from interaction and enhance decision-making procedures. Game playing is one well-known application area where RL algorithms have shown impressive results. For example, DeepMind's AlphaGo used reinforcement learning (RL) techniques to beat human champions in the difficult game of Go, demonstrating the system's capacity to handle large decision spaces and execute real-time strategy.

Robotics uses reinforcement learning (RL) to help robots learn and improve their actions on their own through trial and error. This makes RL a vital tool for tasks like item handling, robotic navigation, and even humanoid mobility. Robots can function more effectively and dependably in dynamic and unexpected environments because to reinforcement learning (RL) algorithms, which can adjust and get better over time based on input from their surroundings.

Furthermore, reinforcement learning (RL) is essential for maximizing user interactions in recommendation systems. RL algorithms can improve engagement metrics and personalization by learning from user feedback and making adjustments to recommendations iteratively. This can result in more efficient content distribution across a range of channels, including streaming services and e-commerce.

Furthermore, resource management situations like inventory control and dynamic pricing have shown benefits using RL. These uses make use of RL's capacity to strike a balance between exploration and exploitation tactics, optimizing choices to optimize long-term gains while adjusting to shifting consumer behavior and market conditions.

Moreover, RL approaches are being investigated more and more in healthcare, where they help with customized treatment planning, delivering adaptive therapy, and streamlining patient management procedures. These applications show how reinforcement learning (RL) can transform decision-making in important domains by learning from real-world data and gradually improving results.

Essentially, the adaptability of Reinforcement Learning in data science applications highlights its revolutionary potential in a variety of industries, propelling improvements in efficiency, automation, personalization, and decision-making skills. The importance of reinforcement learning (RL) research and development on the creation of AI-driven solutions in complex and dynamic situations is growing.

Challenges and Future Directions

Notwithstanding its encouraging uses and achievements, Reinforcement Learning (RL) still faces a number of obstacles, and there are still many important areas for further study and advancement.

The careful balance between exploration and exploitation is one of the main problems in reinforcement learning. RL agents need to take advantage of existing actions that have produced positive results in the past as well as investigate novel actions to find possibly superior tactics. The effectiveness and efficiency of RL algorithms can be greatly impacted by determining the best trade-off between these two, particularly in complex and high-dimensional environments where exploration can be expensive or time-consuming.

The problem of sample efficiency is still another crucial difficulty. For RL algorithms to develop good policies, they usually need to interact with the environment quite a bit. In real-world applications, where interactions may be costly, risky, or time-sensitive, this requirement for vast amounts of data may be prohibitive. Research is still ongoing to determine how to increase sample efficiency using methods like transfer learning, meta-learning, or more complex exploration methodologies.

The application of RL systems also heavily weighs ethical issues. Ensuring these systems behave ethically and safely becomes critical as they are increasingly integrated into real-world applications such as financial trading, healthcare decision-making, and autonomous vehicles. Gaining the public's trust and regulatory clearance requires addressing issues with justice, accountability, transparency, and the unintended effects of RL acts.

Another topic that needs consideration is how scalable RL algorithms are for handling complex, large-scale problems with enormous state and action spaces. Deep reinforcement learning (DRL) has made strides toward addressing these problems by using deep neural networks to approximate policy representations or value functions. Ensuring these models' stability, robustness, and interpretability, however, continues to be a research priority.

Looking ahead, RL has a lot of great things in store. Further improvements in algorithmic robustness, interpretability, and efficiency will probably increase RL's application in a wider range of fields. Advances in merging reinforcement learning (RL) with other machine learning methods, including imitation learning or multi-agent systems, are anticipated to augment its potential and tackle current constraints.

Conclusion

Without explicit supervision, Reinforcement Learning offers a potent framework for learning how to make decisions in dynamic contexts. Its uses in AI and data science are still growing, offering creative answers to challenging issues in a range of fields.

4.5 MODEL EVALUATION AND SELECTION

In data science, getting the best outcomes depends on your ability to assess and choose the most suitable models. Using the combined powers of artificial intelligence (AI) and machine learning (ML), this chapter focuses on the methods and approaches used in the assessment and selection of machine learning models.

Key Concepts

Evaluation Metrics:

When evaluating a machine learning model's performance, evaluation measures are essential. They offer numerical metrics to assess a model's prediction accuracy on a given dataset. Typical measurements consist of:

- **Accuracy:** The percentage of true findings (true positives and true negatives) in relation to all cases that were looked at.
- **Precision:** The proportion of accurately anticipated positive observations to all positive predictions. It provides an answer to the following query: What proportion of all occurrences classified as positive are truly so?
- **Recall (Sensitivity):** The proportion of all observations in the actual class that were accurately predicted to be positive. It provides a response to the following query: Of all genuinely positive situations, what proportion are accurately identified?

- **F1-Score:** A single metric that strikes a balance between recall and precision, calculated as the harmonic mean of the two.
- **ROC Curve (Receiver Operating Characteristic Curve):** A graphical depiction showing how a binary classifier system can be diagnostically altered by varying its discrimination threshold.
- **AUC (Area Under the ROC Curve):** A larger value denotes better model performance. It provides a single value summary of the information shown in the ROC curve.

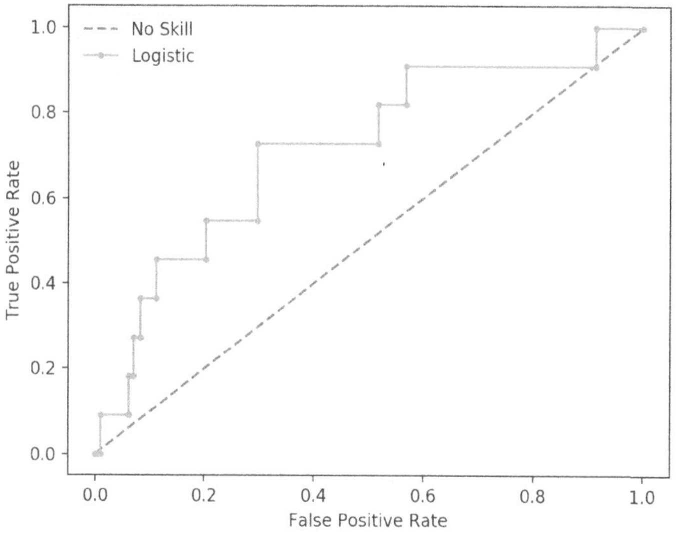

ROC Curve

Cross-Validation:

One statistical technique for estimating a machine learning model's skill is cross-validation. It is mostly employed in machine learning to estimate a model's performance on unknown data. The most popular type, known as k-fold cross-validation, involves dividing the dataset into k equal-sized folds at random. The model is tested on the last fold after being trained on k-1 folds for each fold. Every fold is utilized as a test set exactly once during the k iterations of this operation. Next, an average of the outcomes is obtained to generate a single performance estimate.

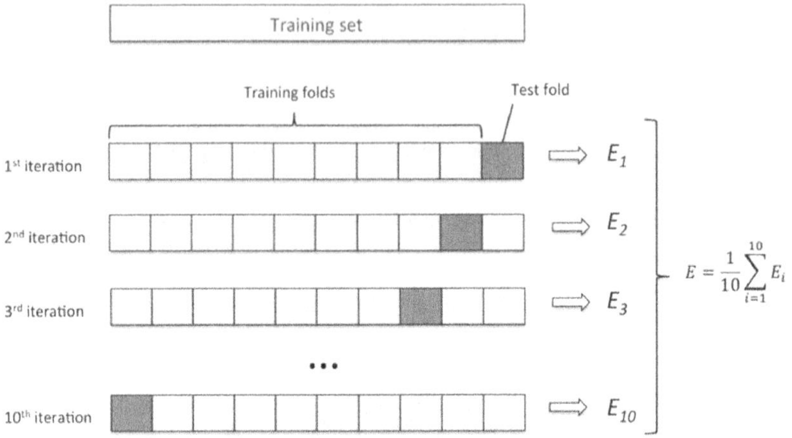

K-fold Cross-Validation

Confusion Matrix

A tabular representation of a classification algorithm's performance is called a confusion matrix. The algorithm's performance can be shown by summarizing the number of accurate and inaccurate predictions. The matrix consists of:

- **True Positives (TP):** The number of correctly predicted positive observations.
- **True Negatives (TN):** The number of correctly predicted negative observations.
- **False Positives (FP):** The number of incorrectly predicted positive observations.
- **False Negatives (FN):** The number of incorrectly predicted negative observations.

Table 1: Confusion Matrix

Predicted/Actual	**Positive**	**Negative**
Positive	TP	FP
Negative	FN	TN

Bias-Variance Tradeoff

A fundamental idea in machine learning, the bias-variance tradeoff characterizes the trade-off between two kinds of error that impact model performance:

- **Bias:** Inaccuracy brought on by excessively basic models. When a model is underfitted, it is unable to fully represent the underlying trends in the data due to high bias.
- **Variance:** Inaccuracy brought on by overly intricate models that are susceptible to noise in the training set. Overfitting, in which the model performs well on training data but badly on unseen data, can be brought about by high variation.

The objective is to maximize the model's generalizability and reduce overall error by striking a balance between bias and variance.

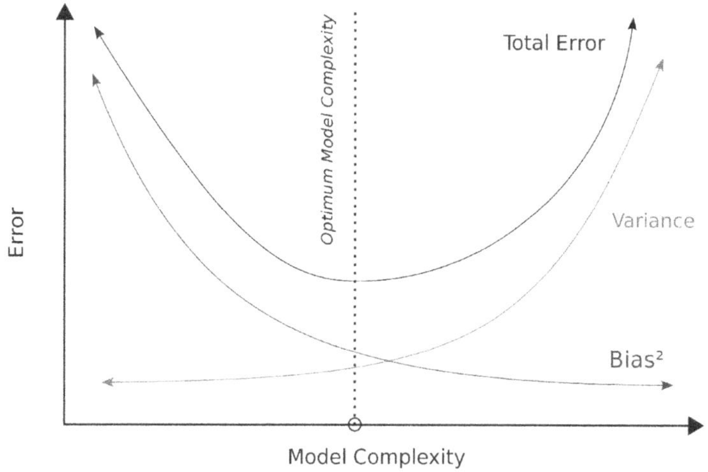

Bias-Variance Tradeoff

Techniques for Model Selection

A key component of machine learning is model selection, which guarantees that the model of choice fits the training data well and generalizes to new data in an efficient manner. The following are a few comprehensive model selection techniques:

1. **Grid Search:** Grid Search is an all-inclusive hyperparameter tuning technique. To identify the best-performing model, it entails defining a collection of hyperparameters and methodically going through every potential combination. Through repeated division of the dataset into training and validation sets, the model is trained and validated on these sets as part of the cross-validation process. Finding the ideal hyperparameters may be done with confidence thanks to this thorough search. It can, however, be computationally costly, particularly when there are a lot of alternative values and hyperparameters.

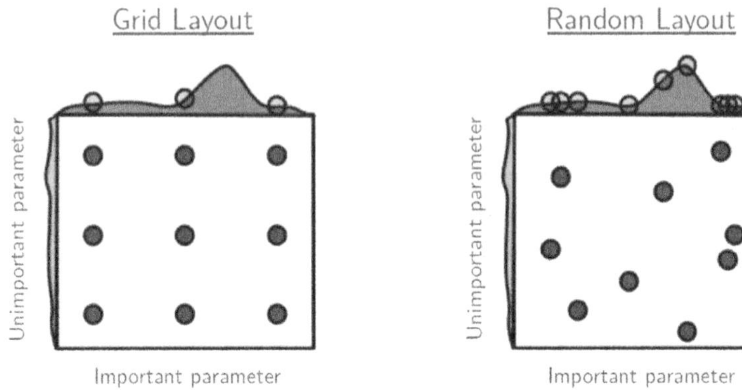

2. **Random Search:** Random Search randomly samples the hyperparameter space as opposed to Grid Search, which assesses every conceivable combination. This method may be more effective, especially if the search space is broad or if some hyperparameters have little effect on performance. Research has demonstrated that Random Search is a useful substitute for Grid Search in that it can frequently identify the optimal hyperparameters more quickly.
3. **Bayesian Optimization:** This is a more sophisticated method that selects the most promising hyperparameters to assess by creating a probabilistic model of the objective function. By taking into account past evaluations, it seeks to identify the minimum of a function in fewer steps than Grid and Random Search. This approach is especially helpful for costly functions where a substantial amount of computing power is needed for each evaluation.

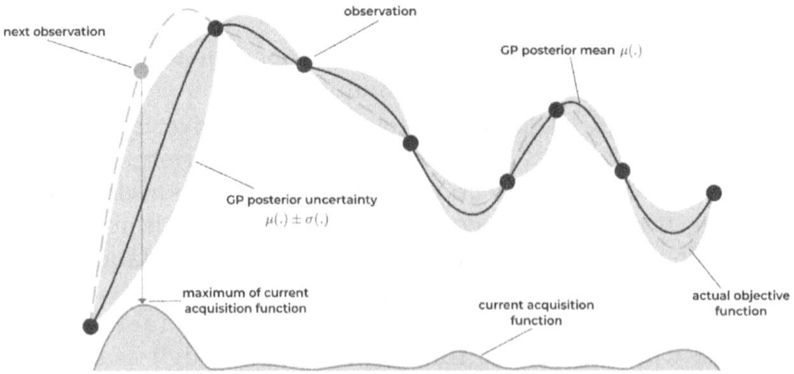

Bayesian Optimization

4. **Automated Machine Learning (AutoML):** Model selection and hyperparameter tuning are automated with the use of autoML tools. They combine methods such as Bayesian optimization, Random Search, and Grid search, and frequently use meta-learning (i.e., learning from prior model assessments) to make the process more efficient. The time and knowledge needed to create high-performing models can be greatly decreased with autoML, opening up machine learning to a wider audience.

AutoML Workflow

5. **Cross-Validation:** Although not a model selection method in and of itself, cross-validation is essential for assessing how well various models perform and guaranteeing a reliable selection process. Methods such as leave-one-out cross-validation and k-fold cross-validation are useful in determining how well a model will generalize to a different dataset. This aids in avoiding both underfitting and overfitting, directing the choice of a model that strikes a balance between bias and variance.

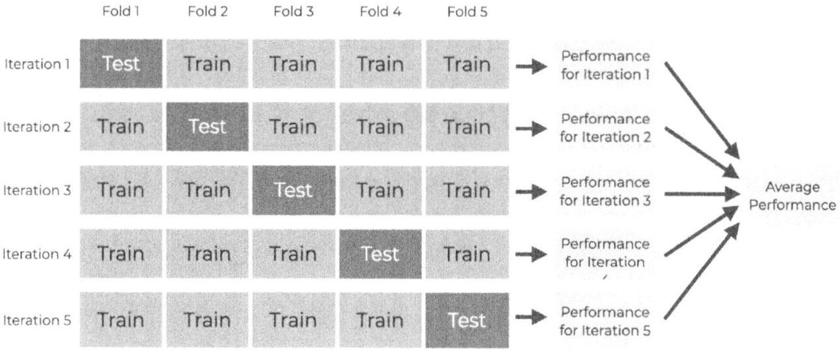

Cross-Validation Method

Data scientists can effectively and methodically determine which models and hyperparameters perform optimally for their particular objectives by utilizing these strategies. The deployment of durable, scalable, and accurate models is ensured by this methodical approach to model selection.

Conclusion

The process of turning raw data into actionable insights depends critically on the evaluation and selection of effective models. Data scientists can improve their models' performance and resilience and make them more suitable for real-world applications by utilizing cutting-edge AI and ML techniques.

4.6 OVERFITTING AND UNDERFITTING

Building strong prediction models in the field of data science, especially in machine learning (ML) and artificial intelligence (AI), requires a grasp of the concepts of overfitting and underfitting. The effectiveness and applicability of a model to fresh, untested data are greatly influenced by these events.

Overfitting

Overfitting is the result of a machine learning model that is too intricately tuned to the training set, collecting noise and outliers in addition to the underlying patterns. Because the model has effectively "memorized" the training dataset rather than learning the generalizable features, this phenomena leads to a model that performs incredibly well on the training data but poorly on fresh, unseen data. A significant difference between training and validation performance indicators is frequently a sign of overfitting.

Overfitting can be caused by a number of things. The complexity of the model is one of the main causes; deep neural networks and other models with a large number of parameters or that are highly flexible can overfit if they are not adequately regularized. Furthermore, when the training data is too tiny, overfitting can happen and the model learns the particulars of the small sample size rather than broad trends.

Since the ultimate goal of machine learning is for the model to be able to generalize to new data, overfitting poses a serious difficulty. Reducing the model's complexity by choosing fewer features or easier algorithms, using regularization strategies like L1 or L2 regularization, and employing cross-validation to make sure the model performs consistently across various data subsets are some ways to mitigate overfitting. Cross-validation aids in evaluating the model's performance on several data segments, assuring its robustness, while regularization penalizes the model's complexity to prevent it from fitting noise.

Moreover, overfitting can be avoided by employing strategies like dropout in neural networks, which ignores randomly chosen neurons during training. Another useful technique in decision trees is pruning, which involves removing branches that don't add much strength to the model's predictions. Ultimately, creating machine learning models that work requires striking a compromise between generality and model complexity.

Underfitting

When a machine learning model is too basic to identify the underlying trends and patterns in the data, it is said to be underfitted, which results in less than ideal performance. This occurs when there is inadequate capacity for the model to understand the data structure, leading to considerable mistakes and high bias on both the training and validation datasets. When extremely basic algorithms are used for complicated tasks, such linear regression on a substantially non-linear dataset, underfitting is usually seen.

Several factors contribute to underfitting:

1. **Model Complexity:** Underfitting occurs when models are used that are too simplistic for the complexity of the data. For example, a poor fit will occur when a linear regression model is used to data that shows a quadratic or higher-order relationship.
2. **Feature Selection:** The model will find it difficult to identify the underlying relationships in the data if significant features are left out or if the features that are included have poor prediction ability.
3. **Insufficient Training:** Underfitting can occur when a model is trained with insufficient epochs or iterations, especially in complicated models like neural networks when the model does not have enough time to learn from the data.
4. **Regularization:** An excessively aggressive regularization strategy (such as an excessively high regularization parameter value) may impede the model's ability to learn adequately, resulting in underfitting.

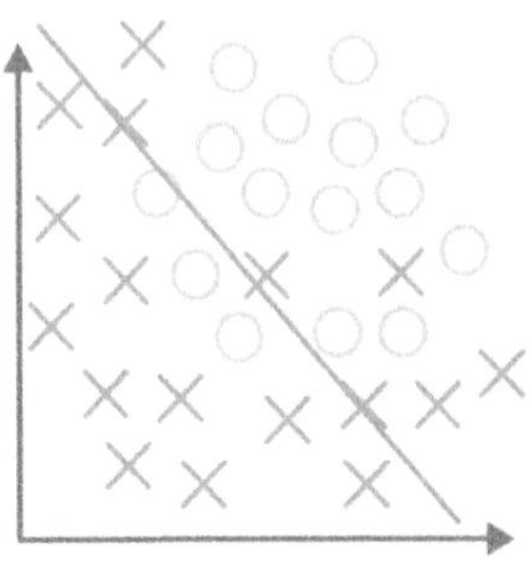

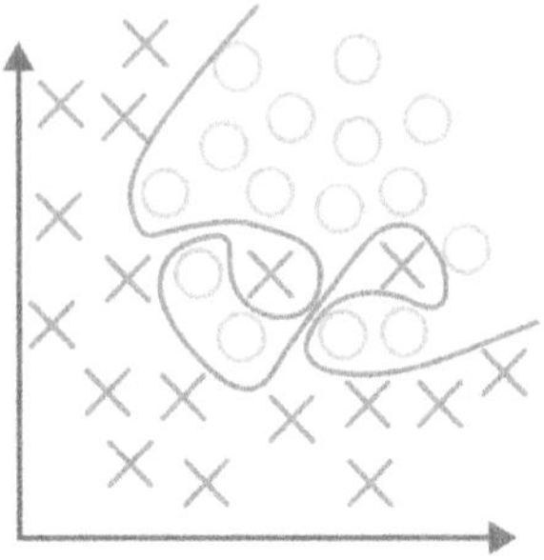

Detailed Example

Imagine having to forecast the price of a home based on a variety of factors, such as the house's age, size, location, and number of bedrooms. For this assignment, a basic linear regression model may not be able to adequately represent the intricate correlations that exist between these characteristics and the price. For example, location may have a non-linear effect on price and interact with other variables in ways that are not captured by a linear model. This oversimplified method would result in continuously inaccurate predictions, with high error rates on both the training and test datasets.

Preventing Underfitting

1. **Increase Model Complexity:** To capture non-linear relationships, use more sophisticated models such as neural networks, decision trees, or polynomial regression.
2. **Feature Engineering:** Improve the dataset by adding new features that more accurately capture the data's underlying trends. This could entail generating polynomial characteristics, interaction terms, or data aggregation that emphasizes significant trends.
3. **Extended Training:** Make sure the model has received sufficient training. This could imply deeper trees or more trees in an ensemble for tree-based models, and more epochs for neural networks.
4. **Appropriate Regularization:** Use regularization strategies sparingly to prevent unduly restricting the model's ability to learn. Finding the ideal balance can be aided by carefully adjusting the regularization value.

To sum up, the process of correcting underfitting include building a more complicated model, improving feature representation, making sure that training is sufficient, and fine-tuning regularization. Data scientists may fully utilize AI and ML in predictive analytics by creating models that are more accurate and broadly applicable by comprehending and addressing underfitting.

Balancing Overfitting and Underfitting

When creating machine learning models, it is important to strike a balance between overfitting and underfitting. A model that is overly complicated and captures noise and fluctuations in the training data but does not generalize to new data is said to be overfitting. As a result, there is poor performance on validation or test sets but great training accuracy. On the other hand, underfitting occurs when a model performs poorly on both training and test sets because it is too basic to identify the underlying patterns in the data. In order to achieve equilibrium, multiple tactics may be utilized:

1. **Cross-Validation:** In this method, the dataset is divided into several subsets. The model is trained on some of the subsets while being validated on others. A popular method is called "K-fold cross-validation," in which the data is split into k parts and the model is trained and validated k times, using a different subset as the validation set each time. This helps identify instances of overfitting or underfitting and guarantees that the model's performance is independent of any specific collection of data.
2. **Model Selection:** It is essential to select the right model. Overly complex models may overfit, while simple models may underfit. For example, a non-linear dataset may be underfit by linear regression whereas it may be overfit by high-degree polynomial regression. As a result, it is essential to choose a model that corresponds with the data's complexity.
3. **Hyperparameter Tuning:** Performance can frequently be enhanced by adjusting the parameters of models. Finding the ideal set of parameters is the goal of hyperparameter tuning, which is typically accomplished using methods like grid search or random search. By balancing model complexity and performance, this method can lessen the likelihood of both overfitting and underfitting.
4. **Regularization:** A penalty is added for higher coefficients in the model using regularization approaches like L1 (Lasso)

and L2 (Ridge) regularization. This improves generalization by discouraging the model from fitting the training data too closely.

5. **Ensemble Methods:** Performance can be enhanced by combining several models. Combinations of techniques like stacking, boosting, and bagging provide a composite model that frequently outperforms individual models. While boosting lowers bias by successively training models that concentrate on the mistakes of earlier ones, bagging minimizes variance by averaging predictions from many models trained on diverse subsets of data.
6. **Feature Engineering and Selection:** Model performance can be greatly enhanced by developing additional features that more accurately represent the underlying patterns and by choosing the most pertinent features. By giving the model additional useful data, this procedure can aid in reducing both underfitting and overfitting.

Data scientists can create models that work well on training data and efficiently generalize to new, untested data by utilizing these techniques. Achieving this equilibrium is crucial for developing dependable, useful, and precise machine learning models.

Conclusion

To sum up, the data science process requires that overfitting and underfitting be understood and addressed. Building reliable models that adapt effectively to new data requires careful model selection, parameter tuning, and performance validation. This allows one to fully utilize AI and ML in the solution of challenging problems.

5

Advanced Machine Learning Techniques

5.1 ENSEMBLE METHODS

Because of the bias-variance trade-off, no single machine learning model is ideal for every situation. In order to address this, ensemble approaches combine several models to produce an improved composite model. This methodology capitalizes on the advantages and minimizes the drawbacks of distinct models.

Types of Ensemble Methods

Machine learning ensemble approaches can be broadly divided into three types: stacking, boosting, and bagging. Every kind uses a different process to combine the predictions of several models in order to improve performance as a whole.

Bagging (Bootstrap Aggregating)

Bagging, often known as bootstrap aggregating, is an ensemble method used to lower a model's variance. It accomplishes this by creating several iterations of a model and making decisions based on the combined predictions of those iterations. Using a technique called bootstrapping, multiple subsets of the training data are first created by randomly choosing and replacing them. After that, each subset is used to train a different modeloften a decision treeof the same kind. For regression, the final prediction is usually obtained by averaging the forecasts, and for classification, the majority vote from all models. The Random Forest approach, which creates a large number of decision trees during training and outputs the mean prediction (for regression) or mode (for classification) of the individual trees, is one of the most often used bagging techniques.

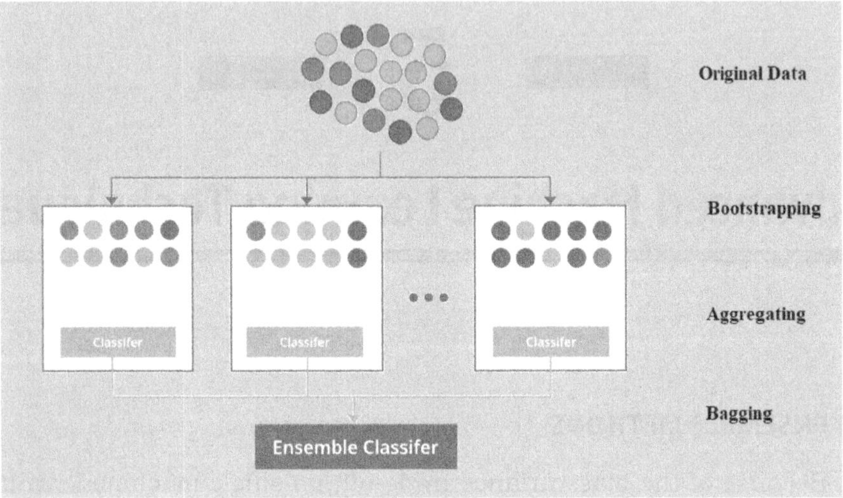

Boosting

Boosting is an additional potent ensemble strategy that creates models in a sequential fashion, trying to fix the mistakes of its forerunners. Boosting aims to improve performance by assigning greater weight to cases that were previously misclassified, in contrast to bagging, which develops models independently. First, a model is fitted to the data; thereafter, more models are added, each of which fixes the mistakes of the preceding models. A weighted majority vote or aggregate is used to combine the predictions. Boosting approaches include Gradient Boosting Machines (GBM), which uses gradient descent techniques to optimize a loss function across iterations, and AdaBoost, which modifies the weights of examples that are erroneously categorized to concentrate more on challenging cases. Two sophisticated gradient boosting implementations that are well-known for their effectiveness and performance are XGBoost and LightGBM.

Stacking

A more advanced ensemble technique called stacking, or stacked generalization, entails training many base models and then using the predictions of those models as input characteristics for a meta-learner, a higher-level model. The original dataset is utilized to train the base models, which can come in several varieties, and the meta-learner is then trained using the base models' outputs. By using a two-layered method, the meta-learner might possibly rectify any biases in the basic models by learning how to integrate their predictions in the best possible way. By combining the advantages of multiple models and reducing the drawbacks of each one alone, stacking can greatly improve prediction performance. In contrast to bagging and boosting, stacking offers greater flexibility in model selection and combination because it does not require the base models to be of the same type.

These ensemble techniques help data scientists create models that are more reliable, accurate, and scalable. By averaging predictions across numerous models, bagging lowers variance; progressively correcting errors, boosting lowers bias; and integrating various varied models, stacking enhances predictions. Ensemble methods are a flexible and vital tool in the field of data science and machine learning since each method has its advantages and can be applied to different kinds of challenges.

Applications of Ensemble Methods

Because ensemble approaches can improve prediction accuracy and robustness, they are widely used in a variety of disciplines. These techniques are used in the banking industry for risk assessment, where combining predictions from many models aids in recognizing fraudulent activity and projecting financial hazards more precisely. For example, ensembles can combine lessons from multiple models in credit scoring to assess a borrower's creditworthiness more accurately than a single model method.

Ensemble methods are essential in healthcare for medical image analysis and disease prediction. Healthcare professionals can accomplish early illness detection and more reliable diagnosis by combining the results from various models. For instance, by combining various variables taken from patient data and medical imaging, ensemble approaches are utilized in cancer detection to provide faster and more precise diagnosis.

Ensemble methods are used in marketing and consumer analytics for recommendation systems and customer segmentation. Through the amalgamation of forecasts from several models that were trained on distinct subsets or depictions of consumer data, marketers can proficiently divide their clientele according to behavioral patterns and inclinations. This segmentation increases client satisfaction and engagement and makes individualized marketing techniques possible. In a similar vein, recommendation systems are powered by ensemble approaches, which combine predictions from different algorithms to offer content or items based on the interests of specific users, improving user experience and raising conversion rates.

Generally, by utilizing the benefits of numerous models to minimize shortcomings and deliver more accurate insights and forecasts, ensemble approaches play a critical role in improving model performance and reliability across a variety of sectors. The increasing complexity and volume of data has made ensemble techniques vital for data scientists and machine learning practitioners trying to efficiently address real-world problems due to their adaptability and efficacy.

Evaluating Ensemble Methods

It is not sufficient to compare the prediction performance of ensemble approaches to that of individual models when evaluating them. While measures like recall, accuracy, precision, F1-score, and ROC-AUC are important for evaluating their efficacy, deeper evaluation considerations explore a number of important areas.

- First and foremost, ensemble diversity is essential. The variety of base models is what gives ensemble approaches their strength. To ensure that the ensemble can generalize effectively beyond the training data, each base model must make mistakes in distinct regions of the feature space. This can be quantified using metrics like base model correlation or diversity measures like Cohen's kappa.
- Second, it's imperative to ensemble calibrate. Predicted probabilities are made guaranteed to closely match actual occurrence probabilities by calibration. Reliable uncertainty estimates are provided by well-calibrated ensembles in classification tasks, which can be important in situations where judgments are based on probability estimates rather than discrete forecasts. Ensemble outputs can be calibrated with the aid of methods like isotonic regression and Platt scaling.
- Thirdly, while assessing ensemble approaches, stability and robustness are crucial. For real-world applications, it is crucial to make sure that minor adjustments to the model's parameters or training data do not significantly affect the ensemble's performance. Measures of stability, like perturbation analysis or stability selection techniques, can evaluate how resilient an ensemble is to changes in the training set.

Furthermore, scalability and computational efficiency are pragmatic factors to take into account, particularly when implementing ensembles in large-scale production systems. In resource-constrained situations, ensembles can become more practical through methods like model trimming, ensemble distillation, or parallelization procedures that reduce computing overhead.

Finally, interpretability is still a problem with ensemble approaches, particularly when combining predictions from many models. Understanding the relative contributions of various features to ensemble forecasts can be aided by approaches such as feature significance analysis across base models or model-agnostic techniques like SHAP (SHapley Additive exPlanations) values.

Advantages and Challenges

Ensemble approaches are widely used in data science and machine learning because of their many benefits, but there are certain difficulties that practitioners must overcome.

Advantages

The capacity of ensemble approaches to outperform individual models in terms of prediction is one of their main benefits. Ensembles successfully minimize variation and improve accuracy by merging many base learners, each trained on separate subsets of data or with different techniques. This is especially helpful when there is noise in the data or when there is a complex and nonlinear relationship between the input features and the target variable.

Another significant benefit is the enhanced resilience of ensemble models. When a model learns to memorize the training data instead of drawing generalizations from it, it is called overfitting, and they are typically more resilient to it. This is accomplished by ensemble approaches, which smooth out individual mistakes and biases that may exist in any single model by combining predictions from numerous models.

Moreover, ensemble approaches are flexible and can be used for a wide range of machine learning tasks, such as regression, classification, and even unsupervised learning issues like clustering. This adaptability results from ensemble approaches' ability to combine many basic model typeslike decision trees, neural networks, or support vector machinestailored to the particulars of the data and issue at hand.

Challenges

Ensemble approaches are useful, but they also have some drawbacks that should be taken into account. The growing complexity of model construction and interpretation is one major obstacle. Managing several models, each with a unique set of parameters and hyperparameters, is a common task for ensembles, which can make the overall architecture and debugging procedure more difficult.

Furthermore, there can be a significant computing expense involved in using ensemble methods. It takes more time and computer resources to train many models sequentially (like in boosting) or concurrently (like in bagging and stacking) than it does to train a single model. This might be a constraining aspect, particularly when deploying models in real-time applications where performance is critical or when working with big datasets.

If not adequately controlled, overfitting could become a problem as well. Even though overfitting is somewhat reduced by ensemble approaches, poorly chosen or tuned base models can still produce models that perform well on training data but badly on unobserved data. This emphasizes how crucial it is to use careful parameter adjustment and strong validation procedures when putting ensemble methods into practice.

Ensemble approaches provide significant advantages over individual methods in terms of resilience, precision, and adaptability; yet, there are drawbacks as well. These include the need to manage complexity, processing resources, and the possibility of overfitting. Comprehending these benefits and obstacles is crucial for efficiently utilizing ensemble techniques to address intricate real-life issues in data science and machine learning.

Conclusion

A data scientist's arsenal would not be complete without ensemble approaches, which allow for the development of reliable, accurate, and broadly applicable models. Through comprehension and utilization of methods like bagging, boosting, and stacking, professionals can greatly improve their predictive modeling skills.

5.2 NEURAL NETWORKS AND DEEP LEARNING

Neural networks and deep learning are among the most potent and adaptable technologies available to us in the field of Data Science Using AI and ML. These innovations have brought about revolutionary changes in a variety of sectors, including natural language processing, autonomous cars, and image and speech recognition. The basic ideas, uses, and developments in neural networks and deep learning are covered in this chapter.

Neural Networks: Basics and Architecture

Neural networks are complex computational models that are intended to replicate the way the human brain processes and learns from data. Neural networks are fundamentally made up of interconnected layers of neurons that process incoming input using basic mathematical processes. These neurons are arranged in layers: an output layer generates the final classifications or predictions, hidden layers use weighted connections to process the raw data or features, and an input layer receives them. Neural networks are unique in that they can learn from data on their own.

Using techniques like backpropagation, the network modifies its internal parameters (weights and biases) during training in order to maximize its capacity for precise prediction by reducing errors between expected and actual results. Neuron activation functions introduce non-linearities that are essential for encapsulating intricate relationships in data, improving the network's ability to represent complex patterns.

Neural networks are effective tools in disciplines like picture and audio recognition, natural language processing, and medical diagnosis because they can learn complex features from large and diverse datasets as they become deeper (more layers) and wider (more neurons per layer). Gaining an understanding of the foundations of neural network architecture is essential to maximizing their potential in the data science and artificial intelligence areas to solve intricate challenges.

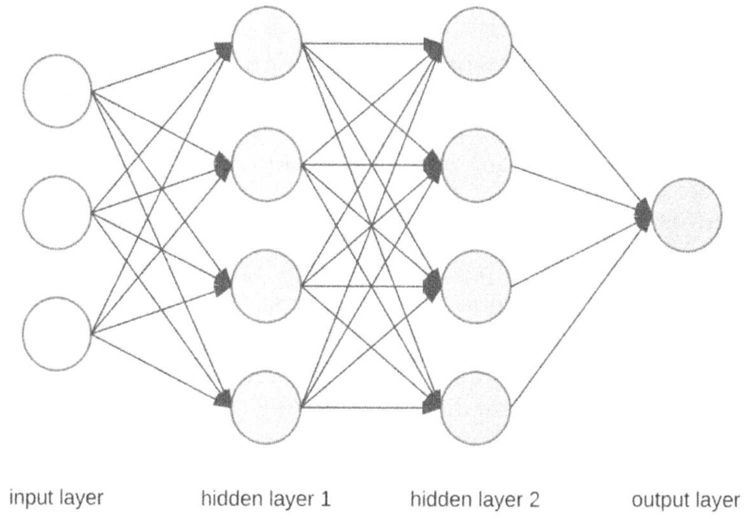

Typical architecture of a neural network

Deep Learning: Advancements and Applications

By allowing computers to recognize intricate patterns in data straight away, deep learning is a subset of machine learning techniques that have completely transformed artificial intelligence. Deep learning models use several levels of abstraction to automatically learn hierarchical representations of data, in contrast to typical machine learning techniques that necessitate feature engineering.

Advancements in Deep Learning

Deep learning has made significant strides in processing and learning from large volumes of unstructured data, including text, audio, and images. Deep neural networks' architecture, which usually consists of numerous layers (hence the word "deep"), is largely responsible for this capacity. It enables the networks to recognize complex patterns and relationships that simpler models could overlook.

Architectural Innovations:

- **Deep Convolutional Neural Networks (CNNs):** These designs are highly effective in learning spatial hierarchies of features, which makes them ideal for tasks like computer vision and image recognition.
- **Long Short-Term Memory (LSTM) and Recurrent Neural Networks (RNNs):** These designs are appropriate for applications like time series prediction, language translation, and speech recognition since they are made for sequential data and maintain recollection of previous inputs.
- **Transformer Networks:** Revolutionized natural language processing tasks like machine translation and text production by introducing attention techniques that allow models to focus on pertinent portions of input sequences.

Applications in Various Domains

Deep learning has impacted several fields and sectors, spurring innovation and resolving challenging issues:

- **Healthcare:** Applications include predictive modeling for drug discovery, individualized therapy recommendations based on patient data, and medical image analysis for diagnosis.
- **Finance:** By evaluating enormous volumes of transactional data, deep learning models are utilized for credit scoring, algorithmic trading, and fraud detection.

- **Automotive:** Deep learning is used by autonomous cars to plan their routes, recognize objects in real time, and make decisions in dynamic surroundings.
- **Retail:** By examining purchase patterns and preferences, recommender systems that are driven by deep learning algorithms tailor the experiences of their customers.

Challenges and Future Directions

Deep learning is not without its problems, though. It requires a lot of labeled datasets, processing power to train complicated models, and outcomes that are easy to understand. Scholars are presently investigating methods to augment the interpretability of models, optimize their efficacy, and expand their capacity to manage multimodal and spatiotemporal data.

Applications in Data Science

Deep learning methods and neural networks have completely changed the field of data science by providing strong answers to challenging issues in a variety of fields. Here, we go into more detail on a few important applications:

Predictive Analytics

Using neural networks, predictive analytics makes predictions about future trends and behaviors by analyzing patterns in previous data. Neural networks, for instance, are used in finance to forecast stock market movements based on historical trading data, economic indicators, and sentiment analysis of the market. In the medical field, they can also predict a patient's outcome using genetic information, medical history, and treatment plans. Neural networks are an excellent tool for predictive modeling tasks because of their capacity to process vast volumes of data and identify subtle trends.

Anomaly Detection

When it comes to spotting odd patterns or outliers in data that diverge from the norm, neural networks are excellent at detecting anomalies. This skill is essential for a number of applications, including financial fraud detection, network security for identifying cyberthreats, and failure prediction and prevention for industrial equipment monitoring. By using past data to identify regular patterns, neural networks can reduce risks and increase operational efficiency by highlighting deviations that could be signs of potential anomalies.

Recommendation Systems

Neural networks are used by recommendation systems to personalize product or content recommendations based on user actions and interests. Neural networks are used in e-commerce platforms such as Amazon and Netflix to evaluate user behavior, past purchases, and browsing habits in order to recommend content or goods that users are likely to find interesting. With time, these systems get more accurate and pertinent as they continue to learn and adjust in response to real-time data.

Natural Language Processing (NLP)

Neural networks have transformed NLP tasks like sentiment analysis, text production, and language translation. Textual data is processed by models such as transformers and recurrent neural networks (RNNs) to understand context, semantics, and syntax. This allows applications to be used, like customer service chatbots, real-time automatic language translation, and sentiment analysis of social media posts for brand reputation management.

Image and Video Analysis

In computer vision applications, neural networks are widely utilized for tasks including object identification, facial recognition, and image classification. Convolutional neural networks (CNNs) automatically learn hierarchical characteristics from pixel-level input, which makes them particularly useful for interpreting visual data. Applications span from real-time obstacle and pedestrian detection in autonomous vehicles to medical imaging for illness diagnosis.

Reinforcement Learning

Reinforcement learning techniques in conjunction with neural networks allow robots to learn by doing and learning how to accomplish certain tasks. This method is used in game playing agents to master complicated games like Go or Chess, in robotics for navigation and manipulation tasks, and in many sectors to optimize resource allocation and decision-making processes.

Conclusion

The fundamental cornerstones of contemporary AI and machine learning are neural networks and deep learning. Their capacity to learn from intricate data structures and make judgments on their own has revolutionized several industries and is still a major source of innovation in data science.

5.3 NATURAL LANGUAGE PROCESSING

A key area of data science is called "natural language processing," or NLP. It uses methods from machine learning (ML) and artificial intelligence (AI) to process, analyze, and extract insights from data related to human language. In the context of AI and ML, this chapter examines the basic ideas, practices, and uses of natural language processing (NLP).

Key Concepts and Techniques

Let's explore some of the fundamental ideas and methods of Natural Language Processing (NLP) in the context of Data Science with Artificial Intelligence and Machine Learning.

The fundamental processes in NLP are tokenization and text preprocessing. In tokenization, unprocessed text is divided into smaller chunks, such words, phrases, or even characters. This procedure converts unstructured text input into a format that machine learning algorithms can handle, making it crucial for additional analysis. Together with tokenization, text preprocessing involves tasks like handling stopwords (common words like "and," "the," etc., which do not significantly contribute to the meaning of a text), converting text to lowercase, removing punctuation, and stemming (reducing words to their root form). These methods tidy and standardize the text, preparing it for further analysis tasks like text categorization, named entity identification, or sentiment analysis.

Human language is understood and produced using statistical language models . By creating probabilistic representations of languagc, these models allow machines to estimate the probability of a word or sentence sequence. Sequences of N contiguous elements, typically words, or N-grams, offer a straightforward but powerful method for modeling language statistics. This is further extended by Hidden Markov Models (HMMs), which are helpful for tasks such as part-of-speech labeling, by including states and transitions between them. Neural language models, such BERT (Bidirectional Encoder Representations from Transformers), have revolutionized natural language processing (NLP) in more recent times. These models use unsupervised learning techniques to capture context dependencies and deeper semantic linkages in text input.

Text including names of persons, places, dates, and other named entities can be recognized and categorized using Named Entity Recognition (NER). This task is widely used in deep learning models like transformers or recurrent neural networks (RNNs) or supervised learning algorithms like Conditional Random Fields (CRFs) to extract structured information from unstructured text. Applications for NER can be found in many different fields, such as entity linking, question-answering systems, and information retrieval.

Sentiment analysis seeks to identify the text's emotional undertone and classify it as either good, negative, or neutral. Completing this work will help you gain insight into consumer feedback, public opinion, and sentiment patterns on social media. Sentiment analysis can be done in a variety of ways. Lexicon-based techniques use predefined dictionaries of words and phrases to assign sentiment scores. More sophisticated techniques use machine learning models such as Support Vector Machines (SVMs), Naive Bayes classifiers, or deep neural networks. With the use of annotated datasets, these models are able to effectively predict sentiment in a variety of textual data types.

Each of these methods is essential to deriving valuable insights from textual data, which helps with applications such as personalized recommendation systems, automated document processing, and customer feedback analysis. The ability to analyze and comprehend human language at scale presents new opportunities for innovation and better decision-making across a variety of industries as NLP continues to develop with breakthroughs in AI and ML.

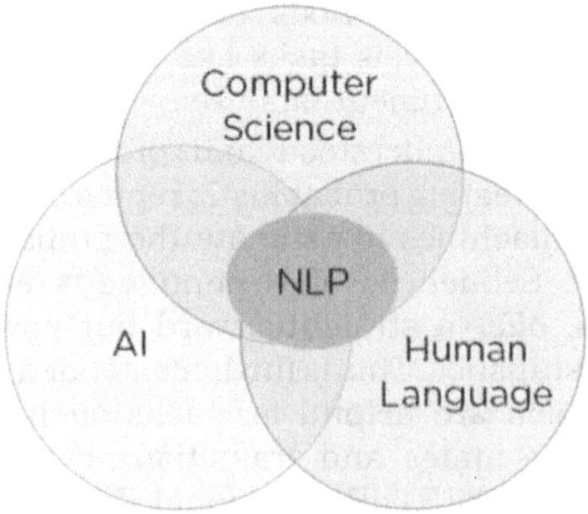

Applications of NLP in AI and ML

Natural language processing (NLP) applications in AI and ML cover a broad range of jobs that use linguistic data to improve and automate different operations. Text classification is a well-known application in which natural language processing (NLP) algorithms classify textual data into specified classifications. Tasks like subject classification in news articles, sentiment analysis on social media posts, and spam detection in emails all depend on this skill. NLP models, for example, can identify if a review reflects a good, negative, or neutral sentiment in sentiment analysis, allowing organizations to assess consumer feedback at scale.

Machine translation is another important application; it allows text to be translated automatically between languages. Sophisticated neural network-based models like Transformers, which can handle intricate linguistic nuances and enhance translation quality, are the result of the evolution of traditional statistical methodologies. These developments are essential for removing linguistic barriers and facilitating cross-cultural communication on a global scale.

Virtual assistants and chatbots are another crucial area where NLP shines. This artificial intelligence (AI) powered systems converse with users in normal language, comprehending their inquiries and providing pertinent answers. Chatbots can offer individualized help in customer service, virtual tutoring, or even medical advice thanks to natural language processing (NLP). In order to provide seamless user experiences, modern chatbot designs incorporate a variety of natural language processing (NLP) techniques, such as entity recognition, intent categorization, and dialogue management.

Additionally, information retrieval and extraction activities benefit greatly from NLP. Text contains names of people, places, and organizations that can be identified and categorized using techniques like Named Entity Recognition (NER). The ability to precisely identify things is crucial for applications such as information extraction from news articles or legal documents, as it greatly improves the accuracy and usefulness of the extracted data.

All things considered, NLP has a wide range of ongoing applications in AI and ML. NLP continues to spur innovation across industries by releasing the potential of unstructured textual data, from improving consumer interactions with chatbots to facilitating cross-lingual communication through machine translation. The breadth and significance of these applications are anticipated to increase with NLP research and development, hence altering the way individuals and organizations use language data in the age of AI-driven technology.

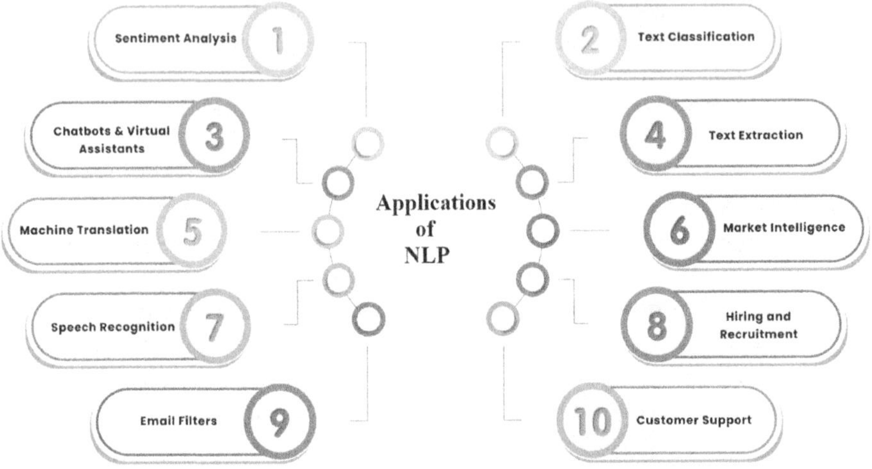

Challenges and Future Directions

The dynamic discipline of Natural Language Processing (NLP) within Artificial Intelligence and Machine Learning (AI and ML) is shaped by a number of emerging difficulties and future prospects. The inherent ambiguity and contextuality of human language is one of the main obstacles. Even while NLP models have advanced significantly in their comprehension of syntax and semantics, clearing up ambiguities in intricate situations is still a difficult undertaking. In order to increase the precision and applicability of NLP applications, future research attempts to improve context-aware NLP models that can more accurately interpret nuances and complexities in language.

NLP that is cross-lingual and multilingual is another crucial area of development. Existing NLP systems mostly work with major languages, which poses difficulties for languages with alternative structures or fewer linguistic resources. Research in this field focuses on building strong multilingual models that can process and comprehend a wide range of languages, enabling wider global applicability and accessibility of NLP technology.

The development of NLP is also heavily influenced by ethical considerations. In order to guarantee equitable and inclusive NLP applications, biases present in linguistic data and algorithms must be addressed. To preserve moral principles and public confidence in

AI-driven language technologies, researchers and practitioners are actively attempting to create techniques that lessen biases and increase transparency in NLP systems.

Furthermore, there are still issues with NLP models' efficiency and scalability. Even though cutting-edge models like Transformers have demonstrated exceptional performance, their training frequently necessitates large amounts of data and processing power. Moving forward, these models will be optimized for efficiency without sacrificing performance, allowing for a wider range of real-world applications.

Last but not least, protecting privacy in NLP applications is still a major worry. Sensitive information is frequently present in textual data, making strong data anonymization and secure processing procedures necessary. Future work will concentrate on creating NLP strategies that protect user privacy and retain the usefulness and efficacy of NLP applications.

NLP has come a long way, but the next wave of AI-driven language technologies will be greatly influenced by how these issues are resolved and what avenues are explored. Through addressing ambiguity, broadening linguistic diversity, promoting ethical standards, enhancing efficiency, and protecting privacy, natural language processing (NLP) is well-positioned to maintain its revolutionary influence on global companies and society.

Conclusion

Neural Language Processing, driven by AI and ML methods, is essential to Data Science. The uses of natural language processing (NLP) in various industries are growing as we learn more about it. This presents both new obstacles and opportunities for utilizing the power of human language data.

5.4 COMPUTER VISION

The branch of artificial intelligence known as computer vision gives machines the ability to perceive, interpret, and comprehend visual data. It includes methods for gathering, handling, deciphering, and comprehending pictures and videos in order to extract valuable data. Computer vision is essential to data science because it can be used for everything from autonomous cars and medical imaging to object detection and facial recognition.

Key Concepts in Computer Vision

Important ideas in computer vision cover a wide range of methods and strategies necessary to get significant information from visual data. Image processing is a basic component that entails modifying photographs to improve their quality or extract particular attributes. For tasks like noise reduction, picture sharpening, or blurring, techniques like image filtering are essential for enhancing the clarity of the images for further analysis. Edge detection is another essential method that locates boundaries in images so that objects may be localized or distinct regions can be distinguished by sudden changes in intensity.

In computer vision tasks, feature extraction is an essential component that goes beyond basic picture processing. This entails locating and measuring distinguishing characteristics or patterns in pictures that are pertinent to the current activity. For example, corner detection finds important locations in an image where the image's intensity abruptly changes; these landmarks are helpful for tasks like object recognition or image registration. Similar to this, the Histogram of Oriented Gradients (HOG) provides a reliable descriptor for object detection tasks in images by displaying the distribution of gradient orientations within local image patches.

Object detection and recognition are essential in computer vision applications as we move toward increasingly complicated tasks. Convolutional neural networks (CNNs) have become indispensable for tasks like object detection and picture categorization with the introduction of deep learning. Models such as YOLO (You Only Look Once) or SSD (Single Shot MultiBox Detector) are excellent at quickly and accurately identifying objects in images, and image classification tasks are well-suited for architectures like ResNet or VGG, which use deep convolutional layers to learn hierarchical representations of visual data.

Additionally, semantic segmentation has become a vital method that allows for picture classification at the pixel level. Semantic segmentation, in contrast to typical object detection, gives semantic labels to each pixel in an image, giving a comprehensive grasp of the composition and spatial layout of scenes. Applications needing accurate picture interpretation, such augmented reality, autonomous driving, and medical imaging analysis, greatly benefit from this capacity.

These fundamental ideas essentially represent the methods and approaches that form the basis of contemporary computer vision systems. The combination of these methods with complex algorithms and models holds the potential to open up new opportunities in a variety of industries, including retail, healthcare, and transportation, among others, as technology develops.

Applications of Computer Vision

Healthcare

Computer vision is essential to enhancing patient care, treatment planning, and diagnosis in the medical field. Computer vision algorithms are used extensively in medical imaging procedures including MRIs, CT scans, and X-rays to help radiologists identify abnormalities and provide correct diagnoses. Deep learning algorithms, for example, are highly precise at identifying cancers, fractures, and other anomalies from medical images. Additionally, computer vision makes telemedicine easier by allowing video analysis to be used for remote patient monitoring. This guarantees prompt intervention and individualized treatment regardless of geographical limitations.

Autonomous Vehicles

The development of computer vision technology is critical to the safe and effective navigation of autonomous vehicles. These cars sense and comprehend their surroundings in real time using computer vision algorithms. Traffic signs, lane markings, cars, and pedestrians can all be identified by AI-driven systems through the analysis of visual data from cameras mounted on the vehicle. Making educated decisions about changing one's speed, dodging hazards, and obeying traffic laws all depend on this capacity. Computer vision is continuously improving object identification, semantic segmentation, and depth estimation to make autonomous driving systems more dependable and safe.

Retail and Commerce

Computer vision transforms customer experiences and operational efficiencies in retail and business. By enabling customers to locate products using photos rather than written descriptions, visual search solutions increase user pleasure and engagement. Users can, for instance, upload a snapshot of a product they like, and artificial intelligence algorithms will suggest related items from the retailer's stock. Additionally, by recognizing objects put in shopping carts, computer vision enables automated checkout procedures, cutting down on wait times and improving the entire shopping experience.

Computer vision is also used by retailers for inventory management, which helps to minimize losses from stolen or lost goods and guarantee precise stock levels.

Surveillance and Security

Computer vision is essential to security and surveillance applications because it can watch and analyze video streams instantly. In public areas, airports, and key infrastructure, video surveillance systems outfitted with computer vision algorithms are capable of identifying suspicious activity, unauthorized entry, or anomalous behaviors. By enabling prompt identification and tracking of persons of interest, facilitating proactive reactions to possible threats, and enhancing security personnel's overall situational awareness, these technologies improve public safety.

Environmental Monitoring and Agriculture

Computer vision helps in the assessment and management of natural resources, crop health, and environmental conditions in agriculture and environmental monitoring. In order to track deforestation, changes in land use, and biodiversity, remote sensing technology can be used in conjunction with computer vision algorithms to evaluate data from drones or satellite imagery. Through the analysis of crop health indicators, the detection of insect infestations, and the optimization of irrigation and fertilizer application, computer vision in agriculture makes precision farming methods possible. These apps assist farmers in making data-driven decisions that increase output, preserve resources, and lessen their influence on the environment.

Entertainment and Media

Through the creation of interactive experiences and content, computer vision improves the media and entertainment sectors. Applications for virtual reality (VR) and augmented reality (AR) use computer vision to superimpose digital data or virtual objects on the physical world, creating immersive experiences for marketing, education, and gaming. Additionally, computer vision algorithms evaluate video content for sentiment analysis, targeted advertising, and content recommendation systems, which aids marketers and content producers in comprehending the preferences and actions of their target audiences.

Computer vision has a wide range of useful applications that have a significant impact on many different industries. These applications include autonomous navigation, healthcare diagnostics, retail customisation, security monitoring, environmental stewardship, and innovative entertainment. Computer vision has the potential to further alter these sectors as AI-driven innovations and technologies expand, offering sustained benefits in efficiency, safety, and user experience.

Challenges and Future Directions

Data Quality and Annotation

Ensuring the quality and diversity of annotated datasets is one of the main problems in computer vision. Accurate model training requires high-quality labeled data, but acquiring and preserving such datasets can be expensive and time-consuming. Additionally, biased training data might provide skewed model predictions, which can undermine fairness in AI applications by reiterating social biases. To overcome these obstacles, rigorous quality assurance procedures to improve dataset diversity and reliability as well as advancements in automated data annotation techniques are needed.

Computational Efficiency

Deep learning models employed in computer vision have high processing requirements, which can be problematic in situations when resources are limited or real-time applications are involved. Methods like quantization, model compression, and effective network topologies (like MobileNet and EfficientNet) are essential for cutting down on computing overhead without compromising model performance. Furthermore, the efficiency and scalability of computer vision algorithms are greatly improved by developments in distributed computing frameworks (e.g., TensorFlow, PyTorch) and hardware accelerators (e.g., GPUs, TPUs).

Ethical Considerations

The rising prevalence of computer vision technologies in society raises ethical questions about privacy, bias, and openness. Prejudices included in training data have the potential to spread via AI systems and provide biased results, especially in applications such as facial recognition and predictive policing. To tackle these ethical quandaries, engineers, policymakers, and ethicists must collaborate collaboratively to create strong frameworks for algorithmic fairness, user permission, and data governance when implementing AI-driven vision systems. Establishing transparency in artificial intelligence decision-making procedures and auditing systems are essential measures in fostering responsibility and confidence in the application of computer vision technology.

Robustness and Generalization

One of the primary research challenges is making sure computer vision models are durable and generalizable in a variety of dynamic contexts. Strong feature representations and domain adaption strategies are necessary since models trained on particular datasets may find it difficult to generalize to new situations or adversarial inputs. Using continual learning techniques, which allow models to learn from new data and change over time, is a promising way to improve the resilience and flexibility of computer vision systems in practical settings.

Interdisciplinary Research and Collaboration

Because computer vision is an interdisciplinary field, cooperation between researchers in computer science, mathematics, cognitive psychology, and domain-specific fields like transportation and healthcare is required. The successful development of context-aware vision systems that can successfully solve societal requirements and real-world difficulties requires the integration of modern AI approaches with domain knowledge. To push the boundaries of computer vision and spur innovation in AI-driven solutions, interdisciplinary research projects and collaborations between government, business, and academia are crucial.

Even while computer vision has advanced significantly in recent years, its full potential in data science employing AI and ML will only be realized by resolving the aforementioned issues and investigating new avenues for research. By encouraging creativity, upholding moral responsibility, and encouraging teamwork, we can open the door for revolutionary computer vision applications in a variety of industries and help create a more advantageous and inclusive AI-driven future.

Conclusion

By giving machines the ability to see and comprehend the visual world, computer vision continues to change various sectors and aspects of daily life. The potential applications of computer vision are endless, offering major contributions to industries like healthcare, transportation, and more as advances in AI and machine learning further improve algorithms and models.

Consult foundational works in the field of computer vision literature as well as current studies in the AI and ML fields for more in-depth analysis of these subjects.

5.5 TIME SERIES ANALYSIS

Understanding and predicting data points gathered over time is the main goal of time series analysis, a critical field in data science and machine learning. It has uses in a number of fields, including economics, finance, and weather forecasting. This chapter examines the basic ideas, methods, and resources utilized in time series data analysis.

Key Concepts Covered

Let's take a closer look at the main ideas discussed in "Data Science Using AI and ML"'s chapter on time series analysis:

1. **Time Series Data:** Sequentially recorded observations throughout time make up time series data. Unlike cross-sectional data, which is based on independent observations, each data point is time-indexed. For the purpose of forecasting, seasonality analysis, and trend analysis, it is imperative to comprehend the temporal sequence.
2. **Time Series Components:** Generally, a time series consists of three primary components:
   - **Trend:** The data's long-term movement or directionality, showing whether values are rising, falling, or staying constant over time.
   - **Seasonality:** Regular patterns, including weekly, yearly, or daily cycles, that recur at predetermined intervals. Data trends can be impacted by seasonality, particularly in domains like retail sales and climatic data.
   - **Noise (Irregularity):** Abrupt variations or anomalies that defy explanations based on seasonality or trend. Noise is the remaining fluctuation in the data after seasonality and trend have been taken into consideration.
3. **Time Series Visualization:** By displaying time series data, one can better comprehend its structures and patterns. Typical visuals consist of:
   - **Line Plots:** Showing trends and seasonal patterns by linking data points over time with a line.
   - **Scatter Plots:** Helpful in determining correlations, these visual aids depict the relationship between two variables over time.

- **Decomposition Plots:** These help with model selection and interpretation by showing how a time series may be dissected into its constituent parts (trend, seasonality, and noise).

4. **Time Series Decomposition:** Techniques for decomposing a time series into its constituent parts include:
   - **Additive Decomposition:** This method summarizes the trend, seasonal, and residual components of the time series. When variations are consistent throughout time, this approach is appropriate.
   - **Multiplicative Decomposition:** Shows the time series as the sum of its residual, seasonal, and trend components. When variations match the series' level, it is employed.
5. **Statistical Models:** Time series analysis makes use of a number of statistical models, such as:
   - **AR (AutoRegressive):** Models that forecast future values by utilizing the series' historical values.
   - **MA (Moving Average):** Models that project values into the future by utilizing historical forecast errors.
   - **ARMA (AutoRegressive Moving Average):** This model combines the moving average and autoregressive models to capture the impacts of both.
   - **ARIMA (AutoRegressive Integrated Moving Average):** Before modeling, a non-stationary time series is made stationary by using differencing.
6. **Forecasting:** Using past data, time series forecasting projects future values. Methods consist of:
   - **ARIMA Models:** Fit for seasonality and autocorrelation in stationary data.
   - **Exponential Smoothing:** Applicable to data lacking a discernible pattern or seasonality.
   - **Machine Learning Algorithms:** These include ensemble techniques and neural networks, which are able to identify intricate patterns in data to make precise predictions.
7. **Evaluation Metrics:** These metrics evaluate time series models' performance:
   - **RMSE (Root Mean Squared Error):** Indicates the predicted error's average magnitude.
   - **MAE (Mean Absolute Error):** Indicates the average absolute differences between the values that were observed and those that were predicted.

- **MAPE (Mean Absolute Percentage Error):** This is a helpful tool for evaluating models on various scales because it calculates the average percentage difference between anticipated and observed values.

Gaining an understanding of these ideas gives data scientists the ability to evaluate and comprehend time series data efficiently, improving forecasting and decision-making across a range of industries.

Illustrative Examples and Visualizations

When analyzing and interpreting time series data, visualizations are essential. Let us expound upon the relevant samples and representations that were previously mentioned:

Example 1: Time Series Decomposition

A technique called time series decomposition divides a time series into its three main parts: trend, seasonality, and residual (or noise). Analysts can better comprehend the underlying patterns in the data by using the decomposition.

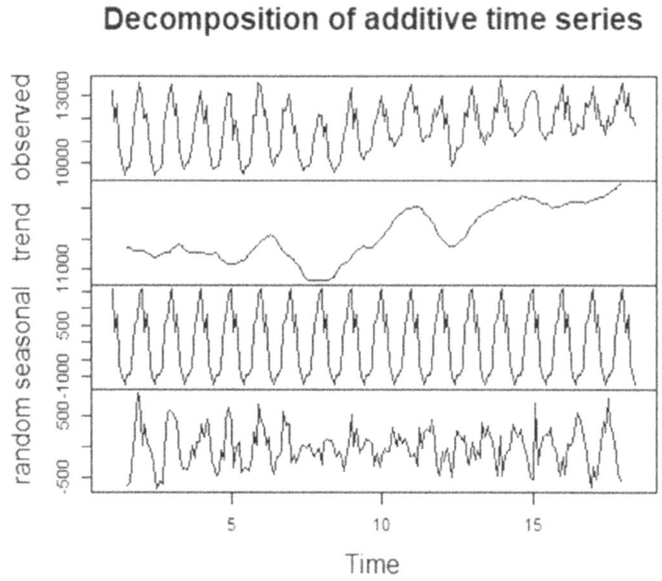

We use the STL (Seasonal and Trend decomposition using Loess) method to the time series decomposition image that is provided. To divide the time series into seasonal, trend, and residual components, this method uses local regression. While the trend records long-term changes in the data, the seasonal component depicts recurrent patterns over a fixed period (e.g., daily, weekly, yearly). The noise or random fluctuations that cannot be related to seasonality or trends are taken into account by the residual component.

Analysts can spot patterns, comprehend seasonal variations, and evaluate the noise or unpredictability in the data by visually examining these elements. This knowledge is essential for creating predicting models that are accurate and for making defensible decisions based on past trends.

Example 2: Forecasting with ARIMA Model

Another crucial use of time series analysis is forecasting future values of a time series. For this, the Autoregressive Integrated Moving Average (ARIMA) model is a widely used technique.

We can see the anticipated values produced by the ARIMA model next to the historical data of a time series in the ARIMA forecasting example image. This model forecasts future values by integrating data from previous observations. To capture the temporal dependencies and patterns in the data, it considers factors like moving average (MA), differencing (I), and autoregression (AR).

Practical Application in Finance

Example 3 – Stock Price Analysis

Time series analysis is a crucial tool used by the financial markets to forecast stock prices, spot patterns, and make wise investment choices.

We can see an example of using time series techniques to examine past stock prices in the stock price analysis graphic. Finding patterns in the data, such as rising or falling trends, seasonal variations (if any), and abrupt shifts (volatility), is made easier by visualizing the data. Based on these historical trends, analysts predict future stock prices using statistical models and machine learning algorithms.

Beyond stock prices, time series analysis is used in finance for risk management, automated trading tactics, portfolio optimization, and trend prediction. For investors and financial professionals, visual representations help in the interpretation of complex financial data and the extraction of useful information.

Conclusion

A fundamental component of data science applications, time series analysis allows precise forecasting and offers insights into temporal patterns. Data scientists can use AI and ML algorithms to derive significant insights from time-dependent data by grasping the principles described in this chapter.

5.6 ANOMALY DETECTION

An essential component of data science is anomaly detection, which looks for odd trends or outliers in data. These anomalies frequently point to important details like mistakes, fraud, or noteworthy occurrences that need more research. This chapter explores a variety of anomaly detection approaches and procedures that make use of machine learning (ML) and artificial intelligence (AI) technologies.

Types of Anomalies

Data anomalies can take many different forms, and each one requires a different method for finding and analyzing them. It is essential to comprehend these kinds in order to create efficient anomaly detection systems:

1. **Point Anomalies:** Individual data points that considerably differ from the remainder of the dataset are referred to as anomalies. A point anomaly, for instance, could appear in a dataset that shows daily temperature measurements if a particular day's temperature is unusually high or low relative to the range that is typically recorded. Statistical techniques like establishing thresholds based on mean and standard deviation or employing clustering algorithms to find outliers are commonly used to discover point anomalies.
2. **Contextual Anomalies:** These are data points that are aberrant only in particular circumstances or contexts, as opposed to point anomalies. This kind of anomaly takes the environment or context of the data point into account. A contextual anomaly could arise, for example, in a manufacturing setting where machines work under various conditions (e.g., temperature, humidity), if a machine responds unpredictably under one set of conditions while performing normally under another. Modeling the connections between variables and taking contextual information into account to determine normal behavior are frequently necessary steps in the detection of contextual abnormalities.
3. **Collective Anomalies:** Although individual data points might not be anomalies in and of themselves, collective anomalies are collections of data points that collectively display unusual behavior. Because it looks for anomalies in the combined behavior of several data points rather than in isolated cases, this kind of anomaly detection is difficult to perform. Collective anomalies, for instance, can appear in a retail sales dataset if sales of several products or regions suddenly decline or increase at the same time. This would point to a systemic problem like a successful marketing campaign or a disturbance in the supply chain.

Every kind of abnormality has different difficulties and needs specific methods for identification and analysis. Improvements in artificial intelligence (AI) and machine learning methodologies, including ensemble approaches for complicated data patterns or deep learning for sequential data, are improving the precision and effectiveness of anomaly detection systems in a variety of fields and applications. Deploying successful anomaly detection technologies that can provide important insights and reduce potential risks in data-driven decision-making processes requires an understanding of these subtleties.

Techniques for Anomaly Detection

Anomaly detection techniques include a range of methods designed for various data kinds and situations. To effectively identify abnormalities, these techniques combine sophisticated machine learning algorithms with statistical concepts.

Anomaly detection relies on Statistical Methods, which set thresholds based on aspects of the data distribution, like mean, standard deviation, or percentiles. Temperature anomalies could be defined as temperatures falling below 19°C (mean - 3 standard deviations) or rising over 31°C (mean + 3 standard deviations) in a temperature monitoring system, for example, if the mean temperature is 25°C with a standard deviation of 2°C. In many situations, statistical approaches are appropriate for initial anomaly detection because they are simple to apply and analyze.

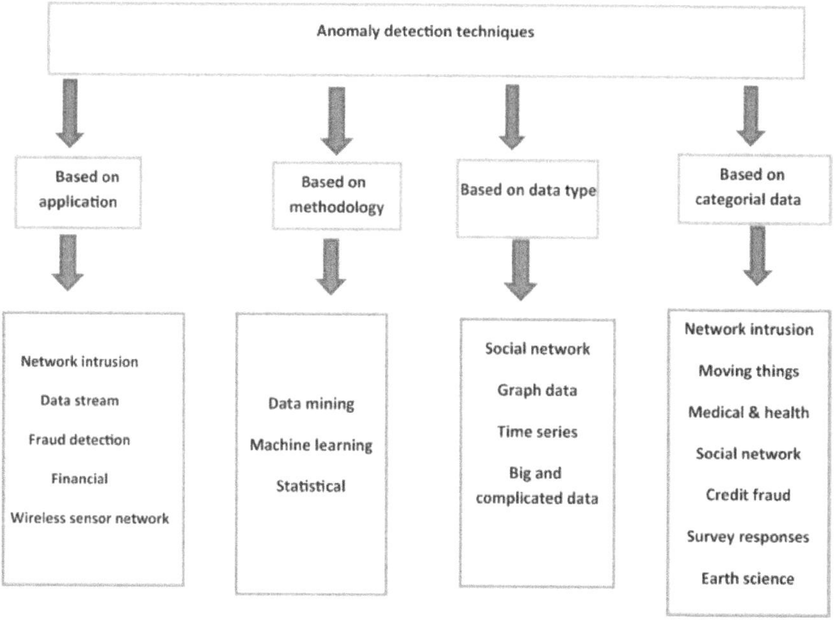

Labeled data is used in Machine Learning Approaches (especially Supervised Learning) to categorize anomalies according to established patterns. This technique makes reliable distinctions between normal and anomalous instances possible by requiring a significant volume of labeled anomaly data for training. Conversely, Unsupervised Learning is useful in situations where labeled data is hard to get by or not available. Assuming that anomalies are uncommon and distinct from regular occurrences, algorithms like Isolation Forests and One-Class SVM (Support Vector Machines) isolate observations that are remote from the bulk of data points in order to identify anomalies. By combining labeled and unlabeled data, Semi-Supervised Learning maximizes the advantages of both methods to enhance anomaly detection performance.

Time Series Anomaly Detection is a crucial tool for identifying irregularities in sequential data, which appear as long-term departures from predicted patterns. It is common practice to employ Moving Average, ARIMA (AutoRegressive Integrated Moving Average), and Deep Learning models, such as Long Short-Term Memory (LSTM) and Recurrent Neural Networks (RNNs). These techniques are appropriate for applications like anomaly identification in stock prices, network traffic, or health monitoring since they capture temporal dependencies and swings in data.

In actuality, the technique selected is determined by a number of variables, including the type of data, the labeled data available, the required degree of accuracy, and the available computer resources. In order to create reliable anomaly detection systems that can adjust to a variety of changing data contexts, hybrid approaches that combine several methodologies are frequently used.

Organizations can improve decision-making procedures, reduce risks, and guarantee the security and dependability of their data-driven operations by utilizing these several approaches to improve anomaly detection. The area of anomaly detection is still vital and active in the context of data science and artificial intelligence, even as techniques and technology continue to advance.

Real-World Applications

An extensive range of real-world applications rely heavily on anomaly detection, demonstrating the flexibility and significance of this technique in utilizing data science and AI/ML technologies. A common use case for anomaly detection is cybersecurity, where it is useful for spotting potentially dangerous activity and anomalies in networks. Anomalies like abrupt surges in data transfer or strange access attempts can be detected by observing network traffic patterns. This allows cybersecurity teams to take immediate action and stop possible breaches before they get worse.

Anomaly detection helps with patient monitoring and early disease identification in healthcare. Anomalies in vital signs or patient behavior can be used to identify crucial health events by studying medical data streams. For example, when a cardiac patient's monitoring data shows deviations from normal heart rate patterns, this might notify medical professionals to take immediate action, which may save lives.

Finance is another important area where anomaly identification is essential. Financial institutions use anomaly detection to find unusual trading trends, credit card usage anomalies, or fraudulent transactions. Anomalies, like unusually big transactions or transactions from unexpected places, can be quickly discovered by analyzing transaction histories and behavioral patterns. This helps to prevent financial losses and uphold customer trust.

Additionally, anomaly detection aids in maintaining operational effectiveness and product quality in manufacturing and industry. Anomalies suggestive of machinery failure or departures from ideal production parameters can be identified early on by keeping an eye on production procedures and sensor data from the equipment. By being proactive, this strategy lowers maintenance costs, decreases downtime, and boosts overall productivity.

Anomaly detection helps find unusual trends in environmental data, such as air quality measurements, weather patterns, or ecosystem changes, in the context of environmental monitoring and sustainability. In order to reduce potential effects on the environment and public health, these anomalies may indicate ecological shifts, climatic anomalies, or environmental risks. As a result, urgent action plans and policy changes may be necessary.

All things considered, anomaly detection greatly improves risk management, operational effectiveness, and proactive problem-solving in addition to improving decision-making processes in a variety of industries. The capabilities of anomaly detection are anticipated to develop further as AI and ML approaches progress, providing ever more nuanced insights and solutions to challenging real-world problems.

Conclusion

A vital part of data science and AI/ML applications is anomaly detection, which helps businesses proactively identify and reduce risks, boost decision-making processes, and increase operational efficiencies. Accurately and efficiently detecting abnormalities is becoming more and more important in today's data-driven world as technologies progress.

6

Artificial Intelligence in Data Science

6.1 FUNDAMENTALS OF ARTIFICIAL INTELLIGENCE

Artificial intelligence (AI) is a game-changing technology that can carry out operations that usually call for human intelligence. Reasoning, learning, problem-solving, perception, and language comprehension are among these tasks. Artificial intelligence (AI) can be broadly divided into two categories: general AI, which seeks to accomplish any intellectual work that a human can do, and narrow AI, which is created for specific purposes. Data science is one of the businesses that has been most significantly transformed by the incorporation of AI into numerous professions.

Components of Artificial Intelligence

The larger objective of artificial intelligence is to enable machines to carry out tasks that traditionally need human intelligence. Artificial intelligence is made up of a number of essential components. Among the main elements are Natural Language Processing (NLP), Deep Learning (DL), and Machine Learning (ML).

Machine Learning (ML)

The foundation of artificial intelligence is machine learning, which allows computers to learn from experience and get better without explicit programming. ML entails creating algorithms with the ability to recognize patterns and render judgments using data. Three primary categories of ML exist:

- **Supervised Learning:** This entails using a labeled dataset to train a model, where each training example has an output label associated with it. As it learns, the model can map inputs to the right output. Support vector machines (SVM), logistic regression, and linear regression are examples of common algorithms.

- **Unsupervised Learning:** In this scenario, data is provided to the model without clear instructions on how to use it. It must independently identify links and patterns in the data. Methods include association (like Apriori and Eclat) and clustering (like K-Means and Hierarchical Clustering).
- **Reinforcement Learning:** In this kind, an agent picks up knowledge through interacting with its surroundings and is rewarded or penalized for its activities. It seeks to maximize cumulative rewards over time. This is frequently utilized in robotics, gaming, and other contexts where making decisions is essential.

Deep Learning (DL)

The term "deep" refers to a particular subfield of machine learning that works with many-layered neural networks. Large datasets containing intricate, abstract patterns can be modeled by these deep neural networks. Thanks to its capacity to learn from raw data, DL has been especially successful in picture and speech recognition, eliminating the requirement for manual feature extraction. While recurrent neural networks (RNNs) function well with sequential input like text and audio, convolutional neural networks (CNNs) are frequently utilized for tasks involving images.

Natural Language Processing (NLP)

The interaction between computers and human (natural) languages is the main emphasis of natural language processing. It entails giving machines the ability to read, comprehend, and interpret human languages. NLP integrates DL, ML, and statistical models with computational linguistics. NLP is used in chatbots, sentiment analysis, speech recognition, and language translation. NLP techniques include a wide spectrum of approaches, from tokenization and basic text processing to more sophisticated models like transformers (e.g., BERT, GPT), which offer much enhanced language production and interpretation capabilities.

Computer Vision

Another crucial aspect of AI is computer vision, which entails giving robots the ability to comprehend and decide based on visual information from the outside environment. Tasks like object detection, image synthesis, and image categorization fall under this category. Deep learning models, in particular CNNs, are used in advanced computer vision techniques to achieve great performance and accuracy in the recognition and analysis of visual data.

Robotics

By combining AI with robotics, intelligent machines that can carry out activities fully or partially on their own are produced. In robotics, artificial intelligence (AI) consists of perception (using sensors to comprehend the world around you), decision-making (using algorithms to choose the optimal course of action), and actuation (carrying out tasks with the help of motors and actuators). Applications include robotic surgery, self-driving cars, and industrial automation.

Expert Systems

Expert systems are artificial intelligence (AI) algorithms that simulate human experts' decision-making processes. They address complicated issues in specialized fields including technical support, financial forecasting, and medical diagnostics using a set of rules and body of knowledge. These systems use inference and logic engines to generate answers based on pre-established rules and incoming data.

When combined, these elements enable AI systems to accomplish a great deal of work, such as identifying sounds and images, deciding for themselves, and communicating with people in a natural way. Comprehending these constituents is crucial for formulating and implementing artificial intelligence solutions in many sectors and uses cases.

Data Science Using AI and ML

Components of Artificial Intelligence

Machine Learning (ML):

The foundation of artificial intelligence is machine learning, which focuses on building systems that can recognize patterns in data, learn from them, and make judgments with little to no human input. As machine learning algorithms are exposed to more data, they are built to perform better over time. One of the main forms of machine learning is supervised learning, which entails training a model on a labeled datasetthat is, learning from input-output pairs. This includes methods such as support vector machines, logistic regression, and linear regression. Conversely, unsupervised learning works with unlabeled data and looks for hidden patterns without knowing the results in advance. Prominent examples of clustering techniques are K-means and hierarchical clustering. A more dynamic subset of machine learning is reinforcement learning, which trains models to make decisions by rewarding good behavior and punishing bad behavior. This technique is widely applied in gaming, navigation, and robotics.

Deep Learning (DL):

Neural networks having multiple layers are used in deep learning, a particular area of machine learninghence the name "deep." These networks can describe complicated, non-linear interactions in data because they are inspired by the structure and functions of the human brain. While Recurrent Neural Networks (RNNs) and their variants, such as Long Short-Term Memory (LSTM) networks, are particularly good at sequential data tasks like language modeling and time series forecasting, Convolutional Neural Networks (CNNs) are particularly good at image and video recognition tasks. Deep learning is a game-changer in computer vision, natural language processing, and speech recognition because of its remarkable capacity to automatically extract features from unprocessed input.

Natural Language Processing (NLP):

Through the use of natural language processing, computers are able to produce, comprehend, and interpret human language in a useful manner, bridging the gap between human and machine understanding. Large-scale natural language data processing and analysis are made possible by NLP, which employs computational linguistics and machine learning. Sentiment analysis, which assesses a document's emotional tone; machine translation, which translates text between languages; and chatbots, which can converse like humans, are important NLP activities. By offering more accurate language interpretation and generation capabilities, modern NLP modelssuch Transformer-based architectures like BERT and GPThave greatly advanced the field. These models power applications ranging from automated content creation to virtual assistants.

Computer Vision:

The branch of AI called computer vision gives robots the ability to comprehend and decide on the basis of visual data. It includes many different tasks like facial recognition, object detection, segmentation, and image classification. Convolutional neural networks (CNNs) are a technique used in computer vision. Because of its capacity to record spatial hierarchies in images, CNNs are very useful for interpreting visual data. Computer vision has several uses, such as surveillance systems for security, self-driving cars for navigation, and medical imaging for illness detection.

Robotics:

The interdisciplinary area of robotics uses artificial intelligence (AI) to create and construct robots that can carry out activities either fully or partially on their own. To create systems that can communicate with the real world, robotics combines computer science, electrical engineering, and mechanical engineering. Natural language processing for communication, reinforcement learning for decision-making, and computer vision for perception are examples of AI approaches in robotics. Applications for robotics include manufacturing, industrial automation, and healthcare, where robots help with surgery and rehabilitation.

Expert Systems:

Expert systems are artificial intelligence (AI) algorithms designed to mimic the decision-making and actions of a human or a company with in-depth expertise and experience in a given sector. These systems address certain issues, usually using a rule-based methodology, by utilizing an inference engine and a knowledge base of human experience. Expert systems are used to make high-quality decisions and recommendations based on large datasets in a variety of sectors, including financial services, medical diagnostics, and customer assistance.

By comprehending these fundamental elements, one may recognize the enormous potential and reach of artificial intelligence (AI) to revolutionize a number of industries through intelligent automation and decision-making.

Example: Model Performance Comparison

```python
import matplotlib.pyplot as plt
 Sample data
models = ['Logistic Regression', 'Decision Tree', 'Random Forest', 'SVM']
accuracy = [0.85, 0.82, 0.88, 0.86]
plt.bar(models, accuracy, color=['blue', 'green', 'red', 'purple'])
plt.xlabel('Model')
plt.ylabel('Accuracy')
plt.title('Model Performance Comparison')
plt.show()
```

Conclusion

The ability to analyze big datasets, find patterns, and make precise predictions has greatly increased with the incorporation of AI and ML in data science. Leveraging AI's full potential in tackling difficult challenges across multiple disciplines requires an understanding of its principles, including its diverse components and approaches.

6.2 AI TECHNIQUES AND ALGORITHMS

Data science has undergone a revolution thanks to artificial intelligence (AI) and machine learning (ML), which have made it possible to analyze enormous volumes of data and produce forecasts and insights that can be put into practice. The fundamental AI methods and algorithms that serve as the basis for data science applications are covered in detail in this chapter. We will study reinforcement learning, supervised learning, unsupervised learning, and important algorithms including decision trees, neural networks, and clustering methods.

1. Supervised Learning

An essential component of machine learning is supervised learning, in which an algorithm is trained using a labeled dataset. With this kind of learning, the training data is used to teach the model how to map input data to the appropriate output. The objective is to make accurate predictions on new, unseen data by generalizing from the patterns it has learned during training.

In supervised learning, the data set consists of input-output pairs, where each input is a vector of features and the output is the target variable. The learning process involves minimizing a loss function, which measures the difference between the predicted output and the actual output. This is achieved through optimization techniques such as gradient descent.

Key Types of Supervised Learning

1. **Regression:** Continuous values are predicted by regression methods. Predicting home values based on characteristics like location, size, and number of rooms is one example. A linear equation is used to represent the relationship between the input variables and the output in linear regression, a straightforward but effective regression technique. Non-linear relationships can be captured by more sophisticated regression techniques such as support vector regression and polynomial regression.

2. **Classification:** Classification algorithms categorize data into predetermined classifications by predicting category values. For example, identifying emails as spam or not, or making medical diagnoses using patient information. For classification tasks, algorithms like as logistic regression, decision trees, random forests, and support vector machines (SVM) are frequently employed. Neural networks, specifically deep learning models, have demonstrated remarkable efficacy in intricate categorization tasks such as speech and image recognition.

Process of Supervised Learning

1. **Data Collection:** Compile input-output pairs into a sizable, diversified, and representative dataset.
2. **Data Preprocessing:** Include missing value handling, feature normalization, and categorical variable encoding in this step of the data preparation process.
3. **Model Selection:** Based on the nature of the data and the issue (classification or regression), select a suitable model.
4. **Training:** Divide the dataset into sets for validation and training. Adjust the model's parameters to minimize the loss function as you train it on the training set.
5. **Evaluation:** Utilize metrics like as accuracy, precision, recall, F1 score for classification, and mean squared error (MSE) for regression to assess the model's performance on thevalidation set.
6. **Prediction:** Use the model to make predictions on fresh, untainted data after it performs well enough.

Applications for supervised learning are numerous and span many different industries. It is utilized in finance to forecast stock prices and score credit. It helps with disease diagnosis and individualized treatment programs in the healthcare industry. It supports targeted advertising and customer segmentation in marketing. Supervised learning, the cornerstone of many AI and ML systems, continues to propel progress across a wide range of domains by facilitating precise, data-driven decision-making.

2. Unsupervised Learning

Machine learning that works with unlabeled data is known as unsupervised learning. Unsupervised learning algorithms are made to look for innate structures or hidden patterns in the input data, as opposed to supervised learning, which trains the model using a dataset of input-output pairings. Because of this, unsupervised learning is especially useful for exploratory data analysis, in which the objective is to better comprehend the data, identify anomalies, or cluster related data points together without having access to the data labels beforehand.

Clustering is a fundamental technique in unsupervised learning that entails dividing data into discrete groups or clusters. K-Means is a well-liked clustering algorithm that seeks to reduce variance within each cluster. First, K centroids are randomly initialized. Next, each data point is iteratively allocated to the closest centroid, and the centroids are updated until convergence based on the average of the assigned points. This method is frequently applied in market segmentation, where companies can divide up their clientele into several groups according to their purchasing patterns, demographics, or other pertinent characteristics.

Principal Component Analysis (PCA) is a crucial technique in unsupervised learning that is employed for dimensionality reduction. Principal components, a new set of uncorrelated variables, are created from the high-dimensional original data by PCA. The amount of variance that each of these components extracts from the data determines its order. PCA minimizes the number of principle components while maintaining the majority of the data's variability, hence reducing the dimensionality of the data. This is especially helpful in situations where it's crucial to reduce the data size without significantly losing information, such image compression and noise reduction.

Association rule learning, which is frequently utilized for market basket research, is another type of unsupervised learning. This technique finds intriguing correlations or links between variables in huge datasets. For example, it may identify that consumers who purchase bread are also likely to purchase butter, allowing shops to arrange their products and promotions to best effect.

Unsupervised learning, in general, is an effective technique for revealing the underlying structure of data, offering insights that may not be visible through manual study. It is useful for a number of applications, such as financial analysis, natural language processing, and bioinformatics, where it is applied to the extraction of topics from text, the grouping of genes, and the identification of stock market patterns. Data scientists can make better decisions and comprehend complex datasets more fully by utilizing unsupervised learning.

3. Reinforcement Learning

A sort of machine learning called reinforcement learning (RL) teaches an agent to make decisions by interacting with its surroundings. Real-time learning (RL) is dynamic and interactive, in contrast to supervised learning, which trains the model on a fixed dataset. The agent can gradually learn the best techniques since it gets feedback in the form of incentives or penalties depending on the actions it performs.

The idea of trial and error lies at the heart of RL. The agent begins in the absence of any environmental knowledge and progressively gains it through experimentation and observation of different acts and their results. The agent must strike a balance between the urge to exploit known acts that provide large rewards and the need to explore novel actions to learn about their potential advantages. This exploration-exploitation trade-off is a crucial component of reinforcement learning.

Key Components of Reinforcement Learning

- **Agent:** The decision-making and action-taking entity.
- **Environment:** The external system that the agent communicates with and that reacts to its commands.
- **State:** An illustration of the environment's current state or configuration.
- **Action:** The range of actions or choices the agent is capable of making.
- **Reward:** The comments one gets from the surroundings after acting. It may take the form of a reward or a penalty.
- **Policy:** A plan of action that the agent employs in light of the situation at hand.
- **Value Function:** Assists the agent in forecasting possible future rewards by estimating the long-term return of states or state-action pairings.

Example: Training a Robot to Navigate a Maze

Think of a robot that is learning how to find its way through a maze to get to an objective. Every point within the maze represents a state, the robot is the agent, and the maze itself is the environment. The robot is able to move forward and turn left or right, among other movements. When the robot reaches the destination, it is rewarded positively; if it hits a wall or travels a longer route, it may be rewarded negatively.

Algorithmic Approaches in RL

- **Q-Learning:** This is a model-free technique that aims to learn the predicted utility of an action in a given state, or the quality (Q-value) of state-action pairings.
- **Deep Q-Networks (DQN):** To handle high-dimensional state spaces, as those in video games, this technology combines Q-learning with deep neural networks.
- **Policy Gradient Methods:** Suitable for continuous action spaces, these methods directly optimize the policy by computing gradients with regard to predicted rewards.

From playing challenging games like Go and chess to optimizing resource allocation in data centers, robotic control, and tailored recommendations, reinforcement learning has shown impressive effectiveness in a wide range of applications. Because of its capacity to pick up knowledge from interactions and develop over time, it's an effective tool for handling issues requiring strategic planning and flexible decision-making.

4. Neural Networks and Deep Learning

Neural networks are computational models modeled after the architecture and operations of the human brain. They are made up of interconnected layers of nodes, or neurons, that process incoming data and, in order to learn from it, modify their weights in response to the output error. During this process of learning, known as training, optimization techniques such as gradient descent are used to minimize the discrepancy between the actual and projected outputs. Neural networks are adaptable for a range of applications because they can mimic complicated, non-linear relationships in data.

Basic Structure of a Neural Network

Three primary types of layers are found in a typical neural network:

1. **Input Layer:** Gets the unprocessed input data.
2. **Hidden Layers:** Transparent layers that carry out calculations and identify characteristics in the data. There may be more than one hidden layer, each contributing a new degree of abstraction.
3. **Output Layer:** Generates the classification or final prediction.

Weighted connections bind every neuron in one layer to every other layer's neurons. During training, these weights are changed to reduce the prediction error. To add non-linearity to the neuron's output and allow the network to represent intricate patterns, activation functions like tanh, sigmoid, and ReLU (Rectified Linear Unit) are implemented.

Deep Learning

Deep learning is a kind of machine learning that makes use of deep neural networks, which are multi-layered neural networks. These networks are extremely efficient for tasks like picture and audio recognition, natural language processing, and more because of their depth, which enables them to simulate complex patterns and representations in big datasets.

Key Architectures in Deep Learning

1. Convolutional Neural Networks (CNNs): CNNs are designed specifically to interpret data structures that resemble grids, like pictures. At different levels of abstraction, they employ convolutional layers to recognize characteristics like edges, textures, and patterns. For image-related tasks like object detection, image segmentation, and facial recognition, this architecture works incredibly well.

- **Convolutional Layers:** To extract features from input data, use filters.
- **Pooling Layers:** Reduce computation by downsampling the spatial dimensions and concentrating on the most important aspects.
- **Completely Connected Layers:** Analyze the characteristics that were retrieved for tasks involving regression or classification.

2. Recurrent Neural Networks (RNNs): RNNs are appropriate for jobs involving time-series or natural language processing because they are made to handle sequential data. They are able to detect temporal connections because they keep track of the preceding inputs in the sequence.

- **Long Short-Term Memory (LSTM) Units:** An RNN type that helps the network learn long-term dependencies by mitigating the vanishing gradient issue.
- **Gated Recurrent Units (GRUs):** LSTMs simplified for faster training, yet they retain the ability to capture crucial temporal dependencies.

3. Transformers: Transformers have enabled effective parallel processing of sequence data, which has completely changed the field of natural language processing. They assess the relative relevance of various input sequence segments via processes known as self-attention mechanisms.

- **Attention Mechanism:** Allows the model to generate each output element by concentrating on pertinent portions of the input.
- **BERT (Translation-Based Bidirectional Encoder Representations):** A popular transformer model for comprehending a sentence's words in context both ways.

Deep learning models provide state-of-the-art performance across a range of areas, but their training demands substantial computer power and volumes of data. Their capacity to learn from unprocessed data with little feature engineering has advanced artificial intelligence and pushed the limits of what is possible for robots.

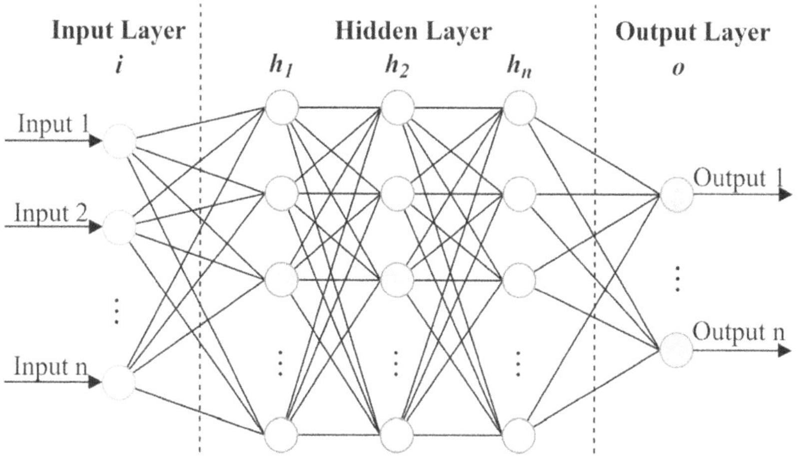

Table 3: Neural Network Layers Example

Layer Type	Number of Neurons
Input	784
Hidden	128
Output	10

This in-depth knowledge of deep learning and neural networks highlights how these technologies are revolutionizing data science and enabling cutting-edge applications in a wide range of industries.

Conclusion

The foundation of contemporary data science is made up of AI techniques and algorithms, which provide strong analysis and forecasting skills. Comprehending these methodologies is crucial for formulating efficacious data-driven resolutions throughout diverse domains.

6.3 AI IN PREDICTIVE MODELING

Predictive modeling is a statistical method that forecasts future events based on past data. In order to create precise and effective predictive models, this chapter examines how Artificial Intelligence (AI) can improve predictive modeling by utilizing Machine Learning (ML) techniques.

What is Predictive Modeling?

A fundamental component of data science and analytics is predictive modeling, which uses statistical methods and algorithms to forecast future occurrences or behaviors based on past data. In order to create predictions, this method entails building, testing, and verifying a model that can learn from historical data and apply that knowledge to newly discovered data.

The main objective is to develop a mathematical representation of the connections among different data points so that future trends can be accurately predicted.

Regression analysis, classification, clustering, and neural networks are only a few of the methods that make up predictive modeling; each is appropriate for a certain kind of prediction problem. For example, logistic regression can be used to predict binary outcomes like customer churn, while linear regression can be used to predict continuous outcomes like sales numbers. Predictive models have a direct impact on decision-making in a variety of industries, including marketing, finance, healthcare, and more, thus their accuracy and dependability are critical.

Modern predictive models offer a major advantage in strategic planning and operational efficiency by using vast datasets to find hidden patterns and connections that traditional methods might miss.

Key Components of Predictive Modeling Using AI

In order to create strong and accurate models that are able to make trustworthy predictions, predictive modeling with artificial intelligence (AI) requires a number of crucial processes. Hyperparameter tuning, model deployment and monitoring, model selection, training and evaluation, feature engineering, data collection and preprocessing, and model deployment are all included in these phases.

- **Data Collecting and Preprocessing:** This is the initial stage in which pertinent past data is obtained from many sources, including databases, APIs, and real-time sensors. To guarantee quality and consistency, the data frequently requires extensive preprocessing once it has been gathered. This entails addressing missing numbers, eliminating duplicates, and fixing any errors in order to clean up the data. Categorical data is converted into numerical representations using encoding techniques like one-hot encoding, and normalization and standards techniques are used to make sure the data is on a consistent scale.
- **Feature Engineering:** This is the process of selecting and extracting features. Finding the most pertinent variables that have the biggest influence on the predicted result is the process of feature selection. Numerous statistical tests and importance-based feature ranking algorithms can be used for this. In contrast, feature extraction aims to enhance the prediction capacity of the model by generating additional features from preexisting data. To capture temporal trends, this could involve creating interaction terms, polynomial characteristics, or data aggregation.
- **Model Selection:** Depending on the type of data and the nature of the problem, selecting the right AI model is essential. For example, logistic regression is utilized for binary classification tasks, while linear regression may be appropriate for predicting continuous outcomes. Neural networks, decision trees, random forests, and gradient boosting machines may be needed for more complicated tasks. Comparing various models according to their performance indicators and appropriateness for the given task is part of the selection process.
- **Training and Evaluation of Models:** Following model selection, the model is trained using the historical data. Usually, the data is divided into training and testing sets in order to assess the performance of the model. In order to reduce prediction errors, the model's parameters are adjusted as it learns from the training set of data. The model's performance is evaluated using evaluation metrics such mean squared error (MSE), recall, accuracy, and precision in addition to the F1-score. This stage makes sure the model is neither overfitting nor underfitting and that it generalizes adequately to new, unseen data.
- **Hyperparameter Tuning:** To improve the model's performance, its hyperparameters are optimized. Hyperparameters, which include learning rate, decision tree depth, and the number of

trees in a random forest, control the training process and model design. To find the ideal set of hyperparameter configurations that maximizes model performance, one can systematically investigate various configurations using techniques like Grid Search, Random Search, and Bayesian Optimization.

- **Model Deployment and Monitoring:** The model is put into a production setting where it can make predictions in real time after it has been trained and tuned. The model must be integrated with current systems and made capable of handling real-time data inputs before it can be deployed. Continuous monitoring after deployment is necessary to guarantee that the model's predictions hold true over time. Tracking performance indicators, identifying data drift, and retraining the model as necessary to accommodate evolving patterns and alterations in the underlying data are all part of this process.

These essential elements make predictive modeling with AI a potent tool that helps companies and organizations make data-driven decisions, foresee future occurrences, and gain a competitive edge.

Case Study: Predictive Modeling in Retail

We examine how a retail organization used AI-driven predictive modeling to solve the urgent problem of customer attrition in this case study. Retailers need to monitor customer churn, or the rate at which customers discontinue doing business with a company. Businesses must successfully predict and manage churn since high rates can have a substantial negative impact on sales and profitability.

Problem Statement

In order to proactively deploy retention techniques, the retail organization sought to identify consumers who were at risk of leaving. The corporation could target specific consumers with tailored offers and incentives in an effort to keep them around by estimating which ones were most likely to discontinue making purchases.

Data Collection

Gathering pertinent data was the process's first phase. The business gathered a sizable dataset that contained the following:

- **Customer Demographics:** Location, gender, age, and other private data.

- **Purchase History:** Thorough documentation of previous purchases, including quantity, cost, and kind of goods acquired.
- **Interactions with Customer Service:** Records of correspondence with customer service, comprising grievances, questions, and responses.

A comprehensive picture of client behavior and interactions with the business was given by this varied data set.

Feature Engineering

The organization conducted substantial feature engineering to improve the model's predictive power. Important attributes of the model were found to include:

- **Age:** Older consumers may behave differently when making purchases than younger ones.
- **Total Purchase Amount:** Higher overall purchase volume customers may have different turnover probabilities and a higher lifetime value.
- **Number of Complaints:** Recurrent grievances may be a sign of discontent, which raises the risk of attrition.

Other characteristics, such the time since the last purchase and the volume of customer support interactions, were also taken into account.

Model Selection and Training

The business decided to use a Random Forest Classifier, which is renowned for its resilience and capacity to manage big datasets with plenty of attributes, to forecast customer attrition. The model was trained on the training set after the data was divided into training and testing sets. Accuracy and the ROC-AUC score were employed as evaluation criteria, offering a balance between accurately identifying churners and non-churners.

The Random Forest model's resistance to overfitting and capacity to capture intricate feature relationships made it very useful.

Model Performance Evaluation

The effectiveness of the model was assessed using a range of measures. The ROC curve was utilized to evaluate the model's capacity to differentiate between non-churners and churners. It does this by plotting the true positive rate against the false positive rate.

Example Graph: ROC Curve:

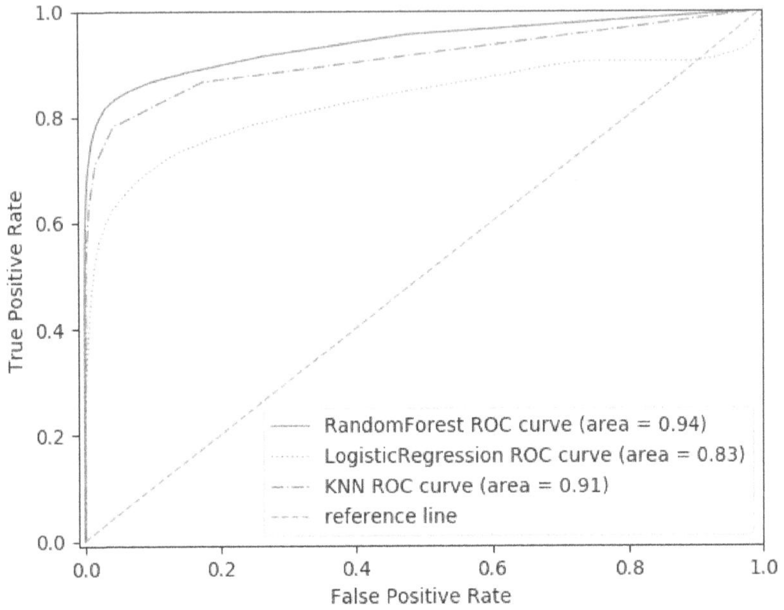

ROC Curve for Random Forest Classifier

Model Deployment

Once the model demonstrated acceptable performance on the test set, it was put into use in the real world. To give real-time projections of client attrition, the model was connected with the business's customer relationship management (CRM) system. This made it possible for the marketing team to pinpoint at-risk clients and provide them with tailored retention offers like exclusive deals or promotions.

Monitoring and Continuous Improvement

The model's performance was regularly tracked after deployment to make sure its forecasts held true over time. The business set up a feedback loop in which fresh data was used on a regular basis to retrain the model to reflect the most recent patterns and behaviors of the clientele.

Results and Impact

The predictive model's use significantly improved the business's retention tactics. Through precise identification of at-risk consumers, the business was able to lower its attrition rate by providing early and tailored interventions to these individuals. This proactive strategy increased customer happiness and loyalty in addition to aiding in client retention, which in turn increased sales and profitability for the business.

Finally, this case study shows how AI-driven predictive modeling may be used in the retail industry to reduce customer attrition. Businesses can obtain important insights into customer behavior and take proactive steps to keep their customer base by utilizing advanced machine learning techniques.

Conclusion

By handling huge information, automating procedures, and increasing accuracy, artificial intelligence greatly improves predictive modeling. Businesses may enhance outcomes, streamline operations, and make better decisions by utilizing AI in predictive modeling.

6.4 AI IN DECISION MAKING

The fields of artificial intelligence (AI) and machine learning (ML) are transforming decision-making in a number of ways. Large datasets, complex algorithms, and computing power are used by AI and ML to produce insights, forecasts, and automated judgments that are superior to those produced by conventional techniques. This chapter examines the advantages, difficulties, and potential applications of AI and ML in decision-making.

The Role of AI in Decision Making

Artificial intelligence (AI) brings automation, accuracy, and predictive power to decision-making processes that are often absent from traditional methods. Automation frees up human resources for more difficult activities by enabling AI systems to undertake repetitive and routine decisions, hence reducing human error. This is especially helpful for sectors like manufacturing, where AI can oversee quality control procedures and keep an eye on equipment maintenance requirements without requiring continual human intervention.

Another crucial benefit is precision, as AI systems are able to examine enormous information and find complex relationships and patterns that people might overlook. Making more accurate and well-informed decisions is facilitated by this capacity to swiftly and accurately absorb and interpret massive amounts of data. AI, for instance, can evaluate clinical data, research articles, and medical records in the healthcare industry to provide accurate diagnosis and treatment suggestions.

One innovative application of AI in decision-making is predictive analytics. AI models may predict future patterns and outcomes by utilizing historical data, which helps firms to foresee and get ready for possible opportunities or difficulties. For example, AI in finance can forecast market fluctuations, assisting investors in making more calculated choices. Similar to this, AI in supply chain management may predict changes in demand, enabling businesses to optimize inventory levels and cut expenses. Furthermore, personalization is a big advantage of AI, especially for customer-focused businesses like marketing and retail. In order to personalize interactions and recommendations and increase consumer happiness and loyalty, AI algorithms can examine individual preferences and behaviors.

AI has a wide range of applications in decision-making, including automation, accuracy, personalization, and predictive insights. These capabilities enable firms to make proactive, data-driven decisions that spur growth and innovation in addition to increasing efficiency and accuracy. AI technology is predicted to have an even greater influence on decision-making processes as it develops, providing a wider range of industries with increasingly complex and nuanced skills.

Components of AI in Decision Making

1. Data Collection and Preprocessing

Preprocessing and data gathering are essential components of any AI-driven decision-making system. Data collection from a variety of sources, including databases, sensors, social media, and transactional records, is part of this phase. The unprocessed data frequently include mistakes, duplication, and inconsistencies. In order to solve these problems, data cleaning eliminates or fixes erroneous data inputs. This is an important stage because the accuracy of the AI models is directly impacted by the quality of the data. Following cleaning, the data are transformed into an analysis-ready format using techniques including scaling, normalization, and encoding categorical variables. A strong foundation for further processes is laid by efficient preprocessing, which guarantees that the data given into AI models is accurate, complete, and formatted correctly.

2. Model Selection and Training

Selecting the right AI model is essential to obtaining precise and trustworthy decision-making. The particular issue being addressed, the type of data, and the intended result all play a role in the model selection process. For instance, deep learning models may be favored for complicated pattern identification in audio or image data, whereas decision trees may be chosen because to their interpretability in classification tasks. Following selection, the model is trained using historical data. Large datasets are fed into the model during this training phase, and iterative procedures are used to help the model discover patterns and relationships. Reducing the error between the expected and actual results is the aim. In order to increase accuracy and dependability, the model's performance is continuously improved by modifying parameters and enhancing the learning process.

3. Model Evaluation and Validation

To make sure the AI model works properly on both new, unseen data and training data, model validation and evaluation are crucial. In this step, the performance of the model is evaluated using a variety of measures, including accuracy, precision, recall, and F1 score. Overfitting is a prevalent problem that requires attention when a model performs well on training data but badly on validation data. The generalizability of the model is assessed with the aid of techniques such as cross-validation, in which the dataset is divided into several subsets and the model is trained and tested on various combinations of these subsets. The thorough testing procedure guarantees that the model can produce reliable forecasts in practical situations.

4. Deployment and Monitoring

Following validation, the AI model is implemented in a real-world setting to support decision-making in real time. The model must be integrated with current systems and tested for effective data processing and output generation before deployment may take place. To keep the model effective over time, performance must be continuously monitored. This involves monitoring key performance indicators (KPIs) and revising the model in response to the availability of fresh data or modifications in the environment. Frequent monitoring aids in detecting and resolving problems like data drift, which can impair the performance of the model and occur when the underlying data patterns alter. The accuracy and dependability of the model are maintained in dynamic contexts through ongoing refinement and retraining.

Applications of AI in Decision Making

1. Healthcare

AI has a significant impact on healthcare, changing patient care, treatment planning, and diagnosis. Artificial intelligence (AI) algorithms, particularly those that employ deep learning, may accurately identify diseases like tumors, fractures, and other anomalies by analyzing complicated medical data like MRI scans, X-rays, and histopathological pictures. In addition to imaging, AI helps forecast patient outcomes by examining electronic health records (EHRs) and finding trends that can point to potential health concerns in the future. AI is used to create personalized treatment regimens that match medicines to specific patient profiles, increasing efficacy and minimizing side effects. Chatbots and virtual health assistants driven by AI offer patients instant medical guidance and support, improving accessibility and lessening the workload for medical professionals.

2. Finance

AI transforms processes in the banking sector by providing sophisticated analytics and automation. Predictive models powered by artificial intelligence (AI) predict market trends and help traders and investors make wise decisions. By using machine learning to assess a person or business's creditworthiness more precisely than with conventional techniques, credit scoring models lower the risk of default. By continuously monitoring transactions and seeing odd trends that can point to fraudulent activity, artificial intelligence (AI) improves fraud detection. In banking, chatbots and virtual assistants improve customer experience and operational efficiency by processing routine questions, providing financial advice, and providing individualized customer service.

3. Supply Chain Management

Artificial Intelligence (AI) improves demand forecasting, inventory control, and logistics to optimize supply chain management. In order to forecast future demand, machine learning models examine past sales data, market patterns, and outside variables like weather and economic indicators. This allows companies to modify their inventory levels appropriately. Artificial intelligence (AI)-driven inventory management solutions minimize overstock and stockouts by determining the ideal stock levels. AI algorithms are used in logistics to improve delivery truck routes, reducing fuel usage and expediting delivery times. Predictive maintenance and real-time tracking of transportation machinery guarantee uninterrupted operations and minimize downtime.

4. Marketing

AI greatly improves marketing strategy by automating tasks and providing sophisticated data analytics. AI systems may create highly targeted marketing campaigns by segmenting clients based on their demographics, actions, and preferences by evaluating customer data. Collaborative filtering and other machine learning techniques are used to provide personalized suggestions that boost consumer engagement and conversion rates. Sentiment analysis tools gather information for marketing strategies by sifting through social media and other online platforms to see how the public feels about particular companies and items. Artificial intelligence (AI)-powered chatbots interact with consumers in real time, making product recommendations, responding to questions, and resolving problems to improve customer satisfaction and brand loyalty.

5. Manufacturing

Predictive maintenance systems powered by AI help manufacturers avoid equipment problems and save downtime. In order to prevent expensive failures, sensors gather data on machine performance, which AI systems then analyze to forecast when maintenance is required. AI also helps to enhance production processes by identifying inefficiencies and suggesting improvements based on data analysis from the manufacturing floor. AI-powered visual inspection systems in quality control are more accurate and consistent than human inspectors in identifying product flaws.

6. Retail

AI revolutionizes retail by boosting customer satisfaction, streamlining inventory control, and customizing the shopping experience. Sales data is analyzed by AI systems to forecast demand and effectively manage inventory levels. AI-driven recommendation engines in e-commerce make product recommendations based on user browsing history and preferences, which boosts consumer happiness and sales. Retailers handle orders, provide immediate customer service, and make tailored product recommendations with chatbots that are driven by AI.

7. Transportation

Through traffic management, driverless cars, and route optimization, artificial intelligence improves transportation. Traffic data is analyzed by AI algorithms to optimize routes, cutting down on fuel and travel time. Artificial intelligence (AI) systems in autonomous cars use sensor data to navigate and make decisions in real time, increasing efficiency and safety. Artificial intelligence is used by traffic management systems to monitor traffic flow and modify signals to ease congestion and enhance traffic flow.

8. Human Resources

AI automates hiring, employee engagement, and performance management, which simplifies human resources (HR). AI-driven applicant tracking systems evaluate resumes to find the most qualified applicants for available positions. Throughout the hiring process, chatbots converse with candidates, responding to their inquiries and offering updates. AI technologies assist HR managers in making data-driven decisions by analyzing employee data to find variables influencing performance and job happiness.

9. Agriculture

Through automated farming activities, weather pattern prediction, and optimal crop management, artificial intelligence (AI) increases agricultural productivity. Artificial intelligence (AI) systems use sensor and satellite image data to monitor crop health and suggest the best times to plant and harvest. Farmers can better plan their activities by using machine learning models that forecast weather conditions. AI-powered autonomous farming equipment increases productivity and lowers human costs by carrying out repetitive operations like planting, watering, and harvesting.

10. Education

AI improves student engagement, automates administrative work, and personalizes instruction in the classroom. AI-powered learning systems provide individualized learning experiences by tailoring content to each student's needs. Chatbots help students with their assignments, provide tutoring, and respond to inquiries. AI also streamlines administrative work, including scheduling and grading, freeing up teachers to concentrate more on instruction and student interaction.

Organizations may make better informed, effective, and efficient decisions by incorporating AI into these and other domains, which will spur innovation and industry growth.

Case Study: Predictive Maintenance in Manufacturing

A game-changing use of AI and ML in the industrial industry is predictive maintenance (PdM), which forecasts equipment problems ahead of time using data-driven insights. This method predicts possible problems by combining real-time sensor data, previous maintenance records, and sophisticated algorithms. This enables prompt maintenance scheduling and intervention. Minimizing unscheduled downtime, cutting maintenance expenses, and improving manufacturing processes' overall efficiency are the major goals.

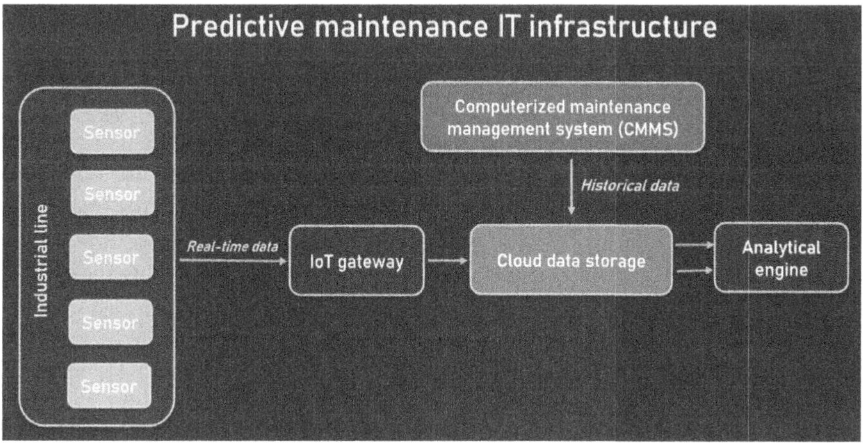

Data Collection and Analysis

A wide range of sensors are mounted on vital equipment in a typical PdM system to track variables including temperature, vibration, pressure, and acoustic signals. These sensors gather data continually, giving a stream of information regarding the operational state of the equipment in real time. In order to find patterns and abnormalities that predate equipment breakdowns, this data is then combined and processed using machine learning algorithms that have been trained on past data sets.

Machine Learning Models

Predictive maintenance can make use of a variety of machine learning models, such as:

- **Time Series Analysis:** Models that forecast values in the future by utilizing historical data trends.

- **Anomaly Detection:** Finding anomalies from standard operational parameters that could point to an impending malfunction.
- **Classification Models:** Utilizing input features to categorize operational states as either "normal" or "failure."

A manufacturing facility, for instance, could combine these models to keep an eye on the condition of its equipment. A time series model may predict a temperature spike that usually occurs before a motor fails, and an anomaly detection model could identify odd vibration patterns that point to bearing deterioration.

Implementation and Results

The AI models must be integrated into the manufacturing process in order to implement a PdM system. This involves putting in place criteria to notify maintenance teams, building dashboards to show the health of the equipment, and setting up data pipelines for real-time monitoring. The technology analyzes incoming data continually, giving maintenance staff predictive insights so they may take action before failures happen.

Benefits

Predictive maintenance has several advantages.

- **Reduced Downtime:** Maintenance can be planned during off-peak hours to minimize interference with production schedules by anticipating breakdowns.
- **Cost Savings:** Compared to emergency repairs, preventive measures are typically less expensive and help avoid the hefty costs related to unscheduled downtime.
- **Extended Equipment Lifespan:** By making sure that parts are repaired before they break, routine, data-driven maintenance can increase the usable life of equipment.
- **Safety Improvements:** Predictive maintenance lowers the possibility of mishaps and injuries brought on by unplanned equipment breakdowns.

Case Example: Automotive Manufacturing

Predictive maintenance was used to the robotic arms and conveyor systems of an assembly line in an automobile manufacturing facility. The system kept an eye on the state of the motors and bearings using thermal imaging and vibration sensors. Using machine learning models, this data was evaluated to forecast component failure dates, allowing maintenance to be scheduled during scheduled downtime.

Impressive outcomes included a 20% reduction in maintenance expenses, a 30% decrease in unscheduled downtime, and a notable increase in overall equipment effectiveness (OEE) at the plant. Additionally, the machinery's increased dependability enhanced the uniformity and quality of the production process, which raised customer satisfaction and decreased warranty claims.

Challenges and Future Directions:

Predictive maintenance has advantages, but it also has drawbacks. These include the high initial cost of sensors and data infrastructure, the difficulty of combining PdM systems with current IT and operational technologies, and the necessity for data management and interpretation expertise from qualified staff.

Future developments in AI and IoT are anticipated to improve predictive maintenance even more. Even quicker reaction times and more resilient systems will be possible with the incorporation of edge computing, which handles data locally as opposed to in a centralized cloud. Furthermore, as more complex and transparent AI models are created, forecast accuracy and dependability will increase, encouraging a wider acceptance of these technologies in the manufacturing sector.

Challenges in AI Decision Making

1. Data Privacy and Security

Sensitive personal data is frequently included in the enormous volumes of data needed to train AI algorithms. It is crucial to protect this data's privacy and security to avoid breaches and unwanted access. Organizations are required to abide by laws like the CCPA and GDPR, which specify stringent data protection procedures. This entails putting strong encryption methods into practice, finding safe ways to store data, and conducting frequent audits. Additionally, risks can be reduced while still allowing for the efficient deployment and training of AI by using differential privacy strategies and anonymizing data.

2. Bias and Fairness

The quality of AI models depends on the data used to train them. The AI model's decision-making is likely to be biased if the training data has biases in it. Unfair results may result from this in important domains including financing, recruiting, and law enforcement. A multifaceted approach is necessary to address bias, including fairness requirements in the model training process, bias detection techniques, and meticulous dataset curation. Maintaining fairness and equity in AI systems over time also requires constant monitoring and updating.

3. Interpretability

The interpretability of complicated models, particularly deep learning networks, is one of AI's major issues. These models frequently function as "black boxes," offering little information about how they make particular decisions. In industries like healthcare and banking, where knowing the reasoning behind choices is essential, this lack of openness can be problematic. In response, scientists are working on explainable AI (XAI) approaches that seek to increase the transparency of AI models. AI-driven decisions can be trusted and validated by stakeholders thanks to techniques like SHAP (SHapley Additive exPlanations) and LIME (Local Interpretable Model-agnostic Explanations), which aid in the interpretation of model outputs.

4. Scalability:

Technical and administrative difficulties arise when implementing AI solutions on a large scale. Robust infrastructure, ample processing resources, and effective data management techniques are necessary for large-scale implementation. To handle big datasets and intricate models, businesses need to invest in strong hardware, like GPUs and TPUs, and take advantage of cloud computing. Scalability also entails making sure AI models are capable of processing input in real-time and responding quickly. Additionally, to sustain AI systems' effectiveness over time and integrate them seamlessly into current processes, ongoing monitoring, upgrades, and optimization are required to accommodate changing data and usage patterns.

5. Ethical and Societal Impact:

Many ethical and social issues are brought up by the use of AI systems. These include the possibility of automation leading to the loss of jobs, the improper use of AI for social engineering and surveillance, and the wider effects of AI on human autonomy and judgment. A balanced strategy that includes creating moral standards, encouraging ethical AI usage, and interacting with a range of stakeholdersincluding ethicists, decision-makers, and the general publicis needed to address these issues. For AI to have a positive influence and build societal trust, governance structures that guarantee accountability and transparency in AI development and application must be established.

Conclusion

Decision-making procedures are being revolutionized by AI and ML because they offer precise, effective, and customized insights. The future of AI-driven decision-making will be shaped by continuing developments and ethical considerations, even in the face of continuous problems. Artificial Intelligence (AI) is poised to transform decision-making across multiple industries, resulting in increased effectiveness, reduced expenses, and improved outcomes.

6.5 ETHICAL CONSIDERATIONS IN AI

Ethical issues are vital in the field of Data Science, which uses AI and Machine Learning (ML), to make sure that technical breakthroughs are in line with social norms and values. This chapter examines some aspects of the ethical problems that AI systems raise as well as solutions.

Ethical Challenges in AI

AI ethics present a wide range of complex issues with broad ramifications for both technology and society. Bad faith in AI algorithms is one of the main issues. Large volumes of data are used by AI systems to identify patterns, but if the data is biased, the algorithms may reinforce and magnify such biases. Biased training data in facial recognition systems, for instance, might increase error rates for specific demographic groups, aggravating disparities in the workplace and in law enforcement, among other domains.

Furthermore, the massive collecting and utilization of personal data by AI systems gives rise to privacy concerns. Consent, transparency, and data protection become crucial issues when AI systems use sensitive data to make choices. In order to preserve public confidence in AI technology, it is imperative that individuals own autonomy over their data and are informed about its intended use.

Accountability and explainability is another important ethical dilemma. AI systems frequently act as "black boxes," making decisions that have an influence on people's lives without providing adequate justification. The inability of stakeholders to comprehend, contest, or rectify incorrect judgments made by AI systems may be impeded by this lack of transparency. Explainable AI (XAI) approaches must be used in order to reveal how AI systems make decisions and to hold them accountable for the results.

Moreover, the application of AI technology brings up more general ethical concerns of equity and fairness. Problems like algorithmic discrimination and the digital divide demonstrate how artificial intelligence (AI) has the potential to either exacerbate current inequities or be used to advance social justice and fairness. Throughout the AI system development lifecycle, inclusive methods, ethical design principles, and careful evaluation of data biases are necessary to address these difficulties.

Stakeholders researchers, legislators, and business executivesare calling for the establishment of ethical frameworks and regulatory actions in response to these ethical dilemmas. These frameworks are intended to serve as a guide for the ethical advancement and application of AI technologies, striking a balance between innovation and social values and guaranteeing that AI maximizes benefits and minimizes risks.

Identifying and proactively resolving these intricate difficulties is essential to navigate the ethical environment of artificial intelligence. We can exploit AI's potential to benefit society while reducing its hazards by encouraging openness, justice, and accountability in AI systems.

Mitigating Ethical Issues

In order to mitigate ethical difficulties in AI, complete techniques that support accountability, transparency, and justice throughout the lifecycle of AI systems are needed. The underlying ideas provided by ethical frameworks direct the creation, advancement, and application of AI systems. These frameworks ensure that AI applications do not reinforce or magnify biases seen in training data by placing an emphasis on human-centric ideals like justice, fairness, and inclusivity. Organizations can cultivate trust among users and stakeholders by giving priority to the ethical implications of their AI solutions by following to ethical principles.

Regulatory actions are essential for reducing ethical issues with AI. Laws and regulations governing the moral application of AI are being implemented by governments and regulatory agencies across the globe. AI systems are impacted by privacy and data protection regulations such as the California Consumer Privacy Act (CCPA) in the United States and the General Data Protection Regulation (GDPR) in the European Union. Aiming to provide clear guidelines for AI development and application, proposed laws like the EU's AI Act address concerns about responsibility, openness, and responsible application of AI technologies.

Moreover, by improving the interpretability of AI judgments, developments in explainable AI (XAI) techniques help to mitigate ethical problems. By allowing stakeholders to comprehend how AI algorithms get to particular conclusions, XAI techniques foster transparency and make it easier to spot and correct biases or mistakes.

All things considered, addressing ethical concerns in AI necessitates a multidimensional strategy that incorporates legal compliance, ethical frameworks, and technical advancements like explainable AI. Organizations may create AI systems that respect social norms and operate efficiently while also adhering to justice, accountability, and other ethical standards by giving ethical issues first priority. These initiatives are essential to building confidence and acceptance of AI technologies in a digital environment that is changing quickly.

Conclusion

To sum up, ethical issues must be incorporated into AI and ML processes in order to promote justice, trust, and social benefits. It is possible for stakeholders to responsibly promote AI technologies by addressing biases, guaranteeing privacy, and encouraging accountability.

6.6 CASE STUDIES OF AI APPLICATIONS IN DATA SCIENCE

The combination of Artificial Intelligence (AI) and Machine Learning (ML) in Data Science has completely changed how companies mine enormous databases for insights and make decisions. This chapter examines a number of interesting case studies where the use of AI applications has greatly improved data-driven strategies in a variety of industries.

Case Study 1: Predictive Analytics in Healthcare

Of course! A key use of artificial intelligence (AI) and machine learning (ML) in the healthcare industry is predictive analytics, which aims to transform patient care and treatment outcomes. Healthcare providers can forecast many health-related scenarios more accurately than with traditional approaches by using complex algorithms that leverage massive volumes of data from Electronic Health Records (EHRs), patient demographics, and medical histories.

Predicting patient outcomes is one of the main goals of predictive analytics in the medical field. In order to identify trends and forecast future health issues, supervised learning methods like Random Forests and Neural Networkswhich are trained on previous dataare used in this process. These models, for example, can forecast a patient's risk of contracting a specific illness based on their genetic makeup, lifestyle choices, and medical history.

Furthermore, by customizing interventions to meet the needs of each patient, predictive analytics helps to optimize treatment approaches. By analyzing data on treatment responses across similar patient cohorts, healthcare providers can personalize therapies for better outcomes. By cutting down on pointless treatments and hospital stays, this strategy not only increases operational efficiency but also improves patient care.

Predicting readmission rates is an important additional use. Predictive models can be used by hospitals to identify patients who are more likely to require a readmission, enabling preventative measures like patient education initiatives and follow-up care. This prevents unnecessary hospital stays, which lowers healthcare expenditures while simultaneously improving patient outcomes.

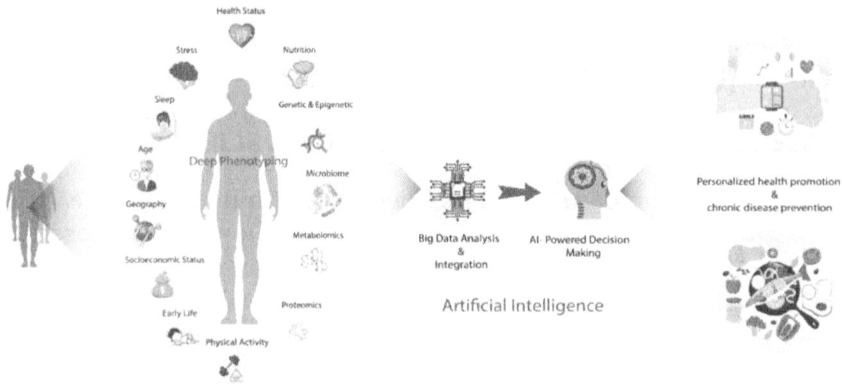

Predictive Analytics in Healthcare

Case Study 2: Financial Forecasting Using AI

Of course! AI-powered financial forecasting has become a vital tool for market players looking to gain an advantage in a turbulent and ever-more-complex environment. This case study serves as an example of how artificial intelligence (AI) and machine learning (ML) techniques are used to analyze large volumes of data, including current economic indicators and past market trends.

Methodology

AI is used in financial forecasting to find patterns and trends in historical data by utilizing complex algorithms like time-series forecasting models (like ARIMA and LSTM) and cutting-edge statistical methodologies. By capturing subtle linkages and dependencies that traditional approaches might miss, these models help to increase forecast accuracy.

Data Sources

Market prices, trading volumes, macroeconomic indicators, corporate financial statements, and even sentiment research from news stories and social media platforms are some examples of financial data sources. Due to the wide variety of data sources available, AI models are able to forecast using both quantitative measurements and qualitative insights.

Applications

There are numerous uses for AI in financial forecasting, including:

- **Stock Market Predictions:** By accounting for variables like past price fluctuations and market sentiment, AI models are able to predict stock values more accurately.
- **Risk Management:** By offering early alerts of possible market swings or abnormalities, AI helps in the assessment and management of financial risk.
- **Algorithmic Trading:** By executing transactions based on predetermined criteria and real-time data, automated trading techniques powered by AI algorithms can maximize investment decisions.

Benefits

Using AI in financial forecasting has a number of benefits.

- **Enhanced Accuracy:** AI models are capable of swiftly and accurately analyzing big datasets, spotting intricate patterns that human analysts might overlook.
- **Efficiency:** Financial professionals can concentrate on making strategic decisions instead of processing data when repetitive chores are automated.
- **Adaptability:** AI models are invaluable instruments in dynamic financial contexts because they can instantly assimilate new information and adjust to changing market conditions.

Challenges

Artificial intelligence (AI) financial forecasting has some drawbacks despite its potential:

- **Data Quality:** The relevance and quality of the data used for training and validation have a significant impact on the accuracy of AI models.
- **Interpretability:** Complex AI models may be challenging to understand, which raises questions regarding decision-making accountability and transparency.
- **Regulatory Compliance:** Adherence to regulatory frameworks is still a crucial factor, especially in highly regulated financial markets.

The use of AI in financial forecasting is a paradigm shift in the way investors and financial institutions assess and forecast market movements. Stakeholders in the quick-paced world of banking can obtain deeper insights, reduce risks, and seize opportunities by utilizing AI and ML. These technologies will likely have a greater influence on the financial sector as they develop, spurring innovation and changing conventional methods of risk and investment management.

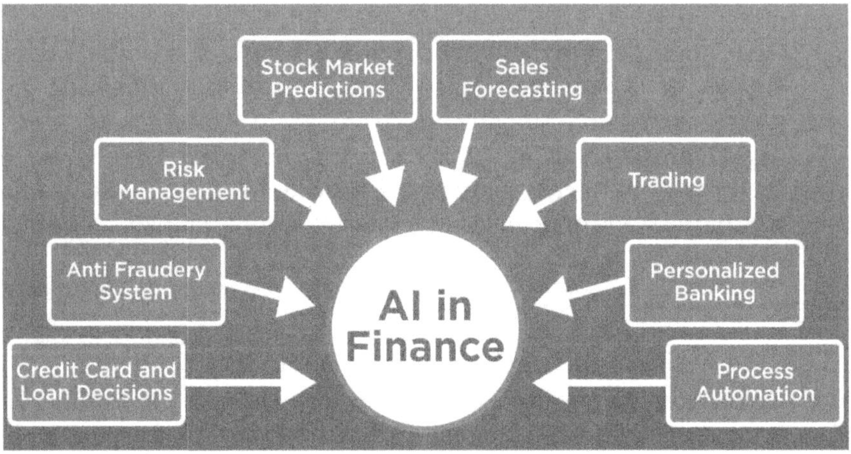

Case Study 3: Natural Language Processing (NLP) in Customer Service

By enabling businesses to automate interactions and improve user experiences through sophisticated language interpretation and creation techniques, Natural Language Processing (NLP) has completely transformed customer service. In this case study, natural language processing (NLP) technologies are utilized to effectively assess and address consumer inquiries and feedback, resulting in faster response times and increased customer satisfaction.

Data Utilization

Businesses use a tonne of textual data from a variety of sources, including customer evaluations, emails, chat transcripts, and posts on social media. NLP models are trained on this data in order to comprehend the subtleties of client language and sentiment.

Technological Advances

Sentiment analysis, entity recognition, and intent classification are just a few of the tasks that make use of state-of-the-art NLP models like BERT (Bidirectional Encoder Representations from Transformers) and GPT (Generative Pre-trained Transformer). With the help of these models, it is possible to accurately comprehend the intent and context of the consumer, enabling replies that are tailored to the situation at hand.

Implementation

Businesses incorporate natural language processing (NLP)-driven chatbots into their customer support systems to provide 24/7 assistance for common questions without the need for human participation. These chatbots are capable of responding instantly to a variety of questions, including those about products and troubleshooting, freeing up human agents to work on more complicated problems.

Benefits

There are several advantages to using NLP in customer service:

- **Improved Efficiency:** Autonomous reactions minimize wait times and boost promptness, resulting in elevated levels of client contentment.
- **Cost Savings:** Operational costs are decreased when human agents are used less frequently for regular tasks.
- **Scalability:** NLP-powered chatbots are able to manage several client engagements at once, smoothly scaling operations during busy times.

Challenges and Considerations

Despite its benefits, using NLP in customer service comes with certain drawbacks, like the need to maintain accuracy when interpreting a variety of languages and dialects, protect client data, and update models often to reflect changing customer preferences and behaviors.

NLP technologies have revolutionized customer service operations by allowing companies to deliver precise, fast, and customized interactions on a large scale. These technologies have the potential to significantly increase consumer satisfaction and engagement as they develop, giving businesses a competitive edge in the market.

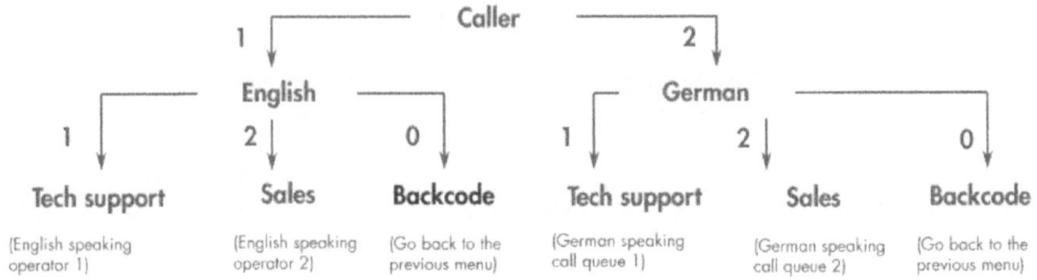

NLP in Customer Service

Case Study 4: Image Recognition in Autonomous Vehicles

In the context of autonomous cars, image recognition is essential to these vehicles' ability to sense and navigate their environment. Autonomous cars use a variety of sensors, including GPS, LIDAR, and cameras, to collect information about their environment in real time. Among these sensors, cameras with sophisticated image recognition software are essential for recognizing and understanding objects and situations while driving.

Methodology

Convolutional Neural Networks (CNNs) are the main method used in autonomous vehicle image recognition. When it comes to processing visual input, CNNs excel. They have demonstrated exceptional accuracy in tasks including object, lane, traffic sign, and pedestrian detection. Large datasets containing a variety of driving conditions and common items are used to train these networks.

Application

Essentially, autonomous cars use onboard cameras to continuously take and process images for image recognition. CNN models are then used to process these images in real-time, allowing for the detection and classification of items including other cars, pedestrians, bicycles, traffic lights, and obstructions. To guarantee safe and effective navigation, this information is essential for making snap judgments about steering, braking, and acceleration.

Challenges and Solutions

Problems and Solutions: Despite progress, there are still a number of issues with autonomous cars' image recognition systems. These include adjusting to changing lighting, bad weather, occlusions, and intricate urban settings. In order to overcome these obstacles, scientists are creating resilient algorithms that can manage these situations by strengthening the robustness of neural network models and implementing multi-sensor fusion approaches.

Results

Autonomous vehicles are now much safer and more dependable thanks to the use of image recognition technologies. Autonomous cars can traverse intricate situations by using accurate item identification and behavior prediction to make well-informed decisions. This feature not only increases passenger safety but also creates opportunities to minimize traffic accidents and maximize the effectiveness of transportation.

Future Directions

Forward-looking, current study endeavors to enhance the velocity and precision of image recognition algorithms, broadening the scope of identifying and comprehending increasingly complex facets of the driving milieu. Furthermore, it is anticipated that developments in AI-powered vision systems will improve autonomous vehicle adoption and performance in both urban and rural environments.

Image Recognition in Autonomous Vehicles

Image recognition is a key technology in the development of autonomous cars, enabling them to see, understand, and respond to their environment with a degree of accuracy and dependability that is necessary to secure broad acceptance and incorporation into regular transportation networks.

Conclusion

The case studies showcase the various uses of AI and ML in data science and their revolutionary influence on various sectors. As these technologies develop further, they present hitherto unseen chances for creativity and effectiveness in data-driven decision-making.

7

Practical Applications and Industry Use Cases

7.1 DATA SCIENCE IN HEALTHCARE

In the field of healthcare, data science enabled by machine learning (ML) and artificial intelligence (AI) has completely changed how we perceive and manage diseases. This chapter examines the revolutionary effects of data science on the healthcare industry, emphasizing important approaches, uses, and potential directions.

The Role of AI and ML in Healthcare

The amalgamation of artificial intelligence (AI) and machine learning (ML) in the healthcare sector signifies a significant progression that holds revolutionary potential. These innovations are revolutionizing not only diagnosis and therapy but also medication discovery, patient management, and large-scale data analysis.

AI systems are excellent at diagnosing medical imaging like MRIs, CT scans, and X-rays with never-before-seen accuracy in diagnostic medicine. Through the analysis of these photos, artificial intelligence (AI) systems may identify minute irregularities that could elude the most skilled human eyes, improving the accuracy and efficiency of diagnosis. This capacity guarantees early detection of diseases such as cancer, when early intervention greatly improves patient outcomes, in addition to expediting diagnosis.

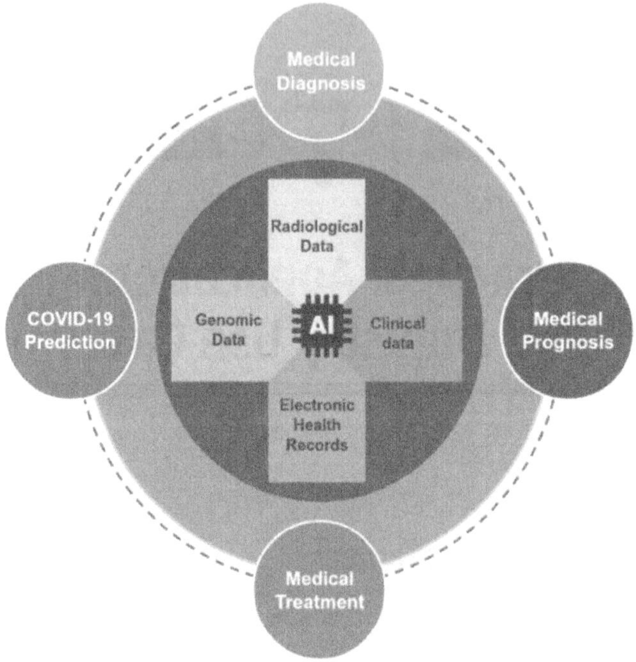

Furthermore, using extensive datasets to forecast patient outcomes is a critical function of AI-driven predictive analytics. In order to forecast risks for different disorders, machine learning models are able to evaluate enormous volumes of patient data, including genetic profiles, medical histories, and demographic data. This feature optimizes health outcomes and reduces needless procedures by enabling healthcare practitioners to customize treatment programs and preventive actions for each patient.

AI and ML enable the personalization of medicines based on genetic variants and other individual variables in the field of customized medicine. Since medications can be customized to a patient's specific biological composition, precision medicine presents hope for more effective treatments with fewer adverse effects.

By examining population-level data to find trends and patterns, artificial intelligence (AI) assists wider public health activities beyond the care of individual patients. This capacity is critical for public health policy formation, resource allocation optimization, and the prediction and control of infectious disease outbreaks.

Notwithstanding these developments, there are still difficulties in incorporating AI and ML into healthcare. Maintaining patient trust and adhering to laws like GDPR and HIPAA require ensuring data privacy and security. Furthermore, minimizing biases in algorithms to guarantee equitable treatment for various patient populations continues to be a crucial issue.

In the future, the advancement and use of AI and ML in healthcare hold the potential to significantly improve patient outcomes, advance medical practices, and spur innovations that could transform the way that healthcare is provided on a global scale. To fully utilize these technologies' potential to advance medicine as they develop, cooperation between researchers, technology developers, and healthcare professionals will be crucial.

Applications in Clinical Settings

The use of AI and ML in clinical practice has greatly improved patient care, diagnosis, and therapy planning, among other areas. The field of medical imaging has seen one of the biggest effects. Conventional techniques for analyzing medical pictures, such those from CT, MRI, and X-rays, frequently depend on human judgment and can be subjective. However, AI algorithms are very good at quickly and accurately evaluating vast amounts of imaging data, which helps radiologists find anomalies that they would miss or misinterpret. AI-driven image categorization systems, for example, can detect early indicators of diabetic retinopathy in retinal scans or point out minute abnormalities in mammograms.

Predictive analytics is another important application. Machine learning models are capable of forecasting the beginning, course, and possible consequences of diseases by utilizing past patient data, which includes demographics, medical histories, and lifestyle factors. These forecasts support preventive measures meant to avert difficulties in addition to helping medical professionals create individualized treatment regimens. Predictive models, for instance, can estimate the chance of readmission for patients with heart failure based on variables like age, comorbidities, and prior hospital admissions. This information helps healthcare teams to target interventions and lower readmission rates.

Another area where AI technologies are changing healthcare practices is natural language processing (NLP). Unstructured text data from clinical notes, electronic health records (EHRs), and medical literature is analyzed and interpreted using NLP algorithms. This feature makes it possible for healthcare professionals to swiftly obtain insightful information, which enhances decision-making and promotes better patient care plans. To help with disease surveillance and outbreak detection, natural language processing (NLP) has the ability to automatically extract relevant information from medical notes and update patient records or spot patterns in symptoms across patient populations.

Additionally, clinical decision support systems, which combine patient-specific data with best practices and medical knowledge libraries, are made possible by AI and ML. These systems give pertinent data, recommendations, and treatment alternatives based on patient profiles, assisting doctors in making evidence-based decisions. This capacity improves patient outcomes and fosters consistency in treatment practices in addition to increasing the effectiveness of healthcare delivery.

There are many different uses for data science that leverage AI and ML in clinical contexts, and these uses are still developing quickly. By increasing efficiency, accuracy, and patient outcomes, these technologies have the potential to completely transform the way healthcare is delivered. They can improve diagnostic accuracy in medical imaging, enable predictive analytics, and enhance clinical decision-making. There is yet hope for more advancements in population health management and customized medicine as long as research and development in this area continue.

Challenges and Ethical Considerations

An examination of the difficulties and moral issues related to data science in healthcare reveals a number of important points. A primary problem is privacy of data. Personal information contained in healthcare data is extremely sensitive and needs to be protected from breaches and unauthorized access. To preserve patient confidence and safeguard their privacy, strict adherence to laws like the Health Insurance Portability and Accountability Act (HIPAA) and the General Data Protection Regulation (GDPR) is necessary.

A noteworthy additional obstacle is algorithmic bias. Due to their heavy reliance on historical data, AI and ML models run the risk of unintentionally reinforcing existing biases in healthcare procedures. Algorithms may not appropriately reflect the healthcare needs of underrepresented demographic groups, for example, if their representation in training data is low, which could result in differences in diagnosis and treatment. To achieve fair healthcare results for all patient populations, addressing these biases calls for meticulous data gathering tactics, algorithmic transparency, and ongoing monitoring.

In addition, regulatory compliance is a recurring problem in the healthcare data science domain. To make sure that data handling procedures adhere to legal requirements, data scientists and healthcare professionals must negotiate a complicated web of rules and guidelines. This covers standards for data quality, interoperability, and the moral application of AI technologies in healthcare contexts in addition to data privacy laws.

The use of AI in healthcare presents ethical concerns around informed consent and patient autonomy. It is imperative that patients comprehend the implications and limitations of AI suggestions as these systems become more prevalent in medical decision-making. To keep patients' trust and make sure that choices reflect their preferences and values, it is crucial to be transparent about the workings of AI algorithms, any potential biases, and the role that human oversight plays.

Data science enabled by AI and ML has great potential to improve healthcare; nevertheless, these obstacles and ethical issues must be carefully considered. We can fully realize the potential of data-driven healthcare while maintaining ethical standards and advancing fair access to high-quality treatment for all people by resolving concerns about data privacy, algorithmic bias, regulatory compliance, and patient autonomy.

Future Directions

The field of data science in the healthcare industry is expected to experience significant progress in the future due to ongoing breakthroughs in artificial intelligence (AI) and machine learning (ML). Precision medicine is a popular trend that seeks to tailor medical procedures and therapies to each patient's unique genetic makeup, lifestyle, and environment. Through the utilization of extensive datasets such as patient histories, biomarkers, and genomic sequences, healthcare professionals are able to customize treatments to optimize effectiveness and reduce adverse reactions.

Furthermore, proactive disease management and epidemic prediction may be possible with the incorporation of AI into public health policies. Real-time population-wide data trend analysis using AI algorithms makes it possible to identify disease patterns early and respond quickly. This expertise is especially important for handling health emergencies around the world and allocating resources within healthcare systems as efficiently as possible.

Furthermore, the advancement of wearable technology and remote monitoring is improving the delivery of healthcare outside of conventional clinical settings. Healthcare providers can access real-time patient health insights from these devices, which continuously gather patient data such as vital signs and activity levels. AI-driven data analysis improves patient outcomes and lowers healthcare costs by enabling early health issue identification and prompt response.

The way AI and ML are used in healthcare in the future will be greatly influenced by ethical issues and legal frameworks. Building trust and promoting ethical use of these technologies requires protecting patient data privacy, reducing algorithmic biases, and abiding by strict regulatory requirements.

Data science has a great deal of promise to transform patient care in the future. This includes improved public health initiatives, remote monitoring, tailored medication, and predictive analytics. Collaboration between data scientists, policymakers, ethicists, and healthcare practitioners will be essential as these technologies advance in order to fully realize the benefits while properly handling obstacles.

Conclusion

The delivery of healthcare could be drastically altered by data science using AI and ML technologies to make it more effective, efficient, and personalized. The promise of data-driven healthcare is still very evident as we work through its complexities and difficulties: better patient outcomes and increased medical understanding.

7.2 DATA SCIENCE IN FINANCE

In the financial industry, where enormous volumes of data are produced every day from market transactions, customer contacts, and economic indicators, data science has become essential. Financial organizations may optimize investments, reduce risks, and improve customer experiences by utilizing AI and ML techniques.

Applications of AI and ML in Finance

Artificial Intelligence (AI) and Machine Learning (ML) have numerous and significant applications in the finance industry that are changing the way financial institutions function, make decisions, and engage with their clientele. Algorithmic trading is a prominent application of this technology. AI-driven algorithms quickly scan through vast amounts of market data to find trends and automatically execute trades based on pre-established parameters. These algorithms have the ability to maximize profits, reduce risks, and optimize trading strategiesall of which human traders could find difficult to discern. This increases overall profitability for financial organizations as well as trading efficiency.

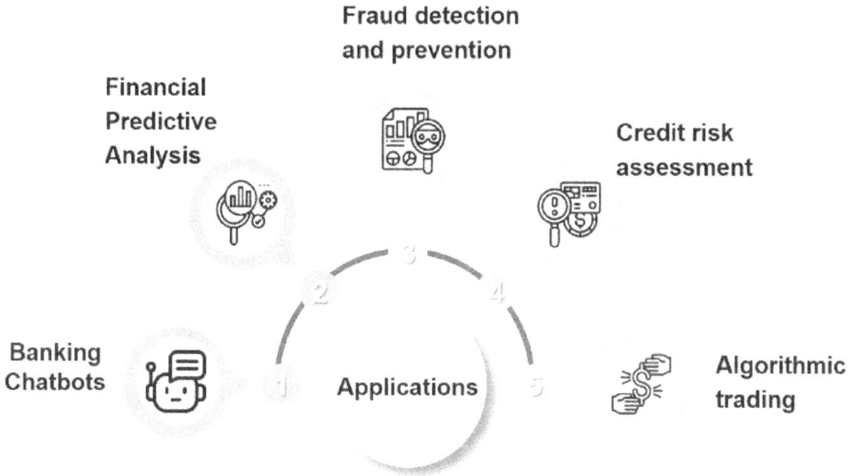

Risk Management is another important aspect. Machine learning models are skilled at identifying and controlling risks in a variety of financial contexts. For example, machine learning algorithms evaluate borrower data in credit risk assessment to forecast default risk, assisting banks in making better lending decisions. Additionally, AI algorithms are used in fraud detection to continuously monitor transactional data in order to spot potentially fraudulent patterns and suspicious activity. This proactive strategy improves security and trust in financial systems while also lowering financial losses.

Furthermore, AI and ML have completely changed Customer Analytics. Financial firms use these tools to examine the behavior, interests, and attitudes of their customers as shown by past transactions, interactions on social media, and other data sources. Banks may enhance customer satisfaction and retention rates by optimizing marketing efforts, personalizing services, and making relevant product recommendations based on a deeper understanding of consumer needs.

Apart from these uses, Portfolio Management also makes use of AI and ML. To build and optimize investment portfolios, machine learning algorithms can examine past data, market trends, and economic indicators. In the end, these models can maximize returns for investors by dynamically adjusting asset allocations based on shifting market conditions and risk preferences.

All things considered, the incorporation of AI and ML into the banking sector not only improves operational efficiency but also gives financial institutions the ability to innovate and remain competitive in a field that is changing quickly. The potential of these technologies to generate insights, reduce risks, and enhance financial decision-making procedures will only grow as they develop, bringing with them new prospects and developments for the sector as a whole.

Methodologies in Data Science

When it comes to applying data science methodologies to the finance industry, a few essential approaches and techniques are critical to changing the way financial organizations develop their services, evaluate data, and make choices.

The core of finance's data-driven decision-making process is Machine Learning Models. A variety of methods, including regression, classification, clustering, and deep learning, are included in these models. For example, regression models are widely used in finance to forecast continuous variables, like interest rates or stock prices, based on patterns in previous data. Classification models divide consumers into hazardous and creditworthy groups, which aids in credit score and risk assessment. Targeted marketing methods are made possible by the use of clustering algorithms, which help to segment clients based on patterns of behavior. Deep learning models are being used more and more for tasks like financial news sentiment analysis and market sentiment prediction using social media data because of their capacity to handle massive amounts of unstructured data.

Another important methodology in finance is Natural Language Processing (NLP), which makes it possible to extract insights from textual data sources including financial reports, social media messages, and news stories. NLP approaches are useful for summarizing large quantities of text into actionable insights, identifying important financial indicators and entities, and gauging market sentiment. Financial institutions may now monitor market movements, gauge investor mood, and make well-informed decisions based on textual data that was previously difficult to evaluate on a large scale by utilizing natural language processing (NLP).

For the purpose of modeling and forecasting financial data with temporal relationships, time series analysis is essential. Financial markets display seasonal patterns, cycles, and trends because they are fundamentally dynamic. Stock prices, interest rates, exchange rates, and other important financial measures are forecasted using time series analytic techniques including exponential smoothing, seasonality correction, and ARIMA (AutoRegressive Integrated Moving Average) models. These models are useful for more than just forecasting future trends; they may also be used to spot anomalies and comprehend the fundamental patterns that underlie financial data.

To optimize decision-making processes and model complicated financial scenarios, simulation and optimization techniques are applied. For example, Monte Carlo simulations are used to generate several probable future outcomes based on probabilistic assumptions, which are then used to estimate the risk of investment portfolios. Optimization algorithms, such as heuristic algorithms and linear programming, find the most effective way to allocate assets in a portfolio in order to meet predetermined financial goals while taking risk tolerance and liquidity needs into account.

Emerging technologies like blockchain and Distributed Ledger Technology (DLT) are transforming fields including smart contracts, digital currencies, and decentralized finance (DeFi). Blockchain technology reduces the need for middlemen and increases efficiency in financial transactions by offering transparency, security, and immutability. Smart contracts enable faster and more secure transactions by automating the execution of contractual agreements based on predetermined circumstances.

A wide range of approaches and technologies are used in data science approaches applied to finance, all of which are vital in utilizing data to spur innovation, enhance decision-making, and reduce risks in the financial industry. These approaches hold the potential to completely transform the financial industry in the future by providing more individualized services, more predictive capacities, and increased operational efficiencies as they develop and combine with AI and ML breakthroughs.

Case Studies and Success Stories

Predictive Analytics in Stock Market Forecasting

Predictive analytics used to estimate stock values is one interesting example study. With the use of sophisticated machine learning algorithms and previous market data, financial analysts are now able to forecast future price movements more accurately. Strategic investment decisions, for example, can be informed by algorithms trained on large datasets because they can spot patterns and trends that human analysts would miss. By foreseeing market swings, these predictive models not only maximize portfolio management but also reduce risks.

Fraud Detection and Prevention

Machine learning models are used for financial transaction fraud detection and prevention in another noteworthy application. Through real-time analysis of transactional data, these algorithms are able to identify aberrant patterns that may point to fraudulent activity, such as atypical spending habits or unapproved access attempts. By assuring safe and dependable transaction processes, this proactive strategy not only protects financial institutions from potential losses but also builds client trust.

Customer Segmentation and Personalization

Financial institutions can more effectively segment their clientele and tailor their offerings by utilizing AI-powered customer insights. Through the analysis of customer behavior patterns, preferences, and transaction histories, these algorithms are able to customize product offerings and marketing campaigns to match specific demands. This focused strategy raises overall profitability and increases client retention rates in addition to increasing customer satisfaction.

Risk Management and Compliance

In the financial industry, machine learning algorithms are essential to risk management and regulatory compliance. These models evaluate and reduce risks related to loan approvals, investment strategies, and regulatory changes by examining large datasets on credit ratings, market volatility, and economic indicators. This proactive approach to risk management optimizes financial decision-making processes and guarantees compliance with regulatory obligations.

Conclusion

The fusion of data science, AI, and ML is changing the financial environment, offering more profound insights, facilitating better decision-making, and boosting operational effectiveness. Data scientists play an increasingly important role in financial institutions as technologies advance, helping to use data-driven strategies for competitive advantage and sustainable growth.

7.3 DATA SCIENCE IN RETAIL AND E-COMMERCE

Recent advances in data science, artificial intelligence (AI), and machine learning (ML) have brought about a fundamental revolution in the retail and e-commerce sectors. This chapter examines how these technologies are transforming how companies in the retail and e-commerce sectors run, make decisions, and interact with consumers.

Role of Data Science in Retail and E-commerce

Beyond typical analytics, data science plays a huge role in retail and e-commerce. It includes a complex method for deciphering and applying data to inform strategic choices and improve operational effectiveness. The ability to leverage the massive volumes of data generated by transactions, supply chain activities, and external market factors is at the heart of this revolution.

Retailers and e-commerce platforms can gain a detailed understanding of customer behavior using data science, which makes segmentation and customisation techniques more effective. Businesses can develop customized marketing campaigns and product suggestions by examining demographic data, purchasing trends, browser history, and even sentiment analysis from social media. This raises conversion rates and client retention in addition to improving customer happiness.

Furthermore, data science is essential to inventory management and demand forecasting. In order to precisely forecast future demand, AI and ML systems examine past sales data in addition to external factors like seasonality, economic indices, and even weather patterns. Retailers may increase overall operational efficiency and profitability by optimizing inventory levels, minimizing stockouts, and reducing overstock situations with the use of this predictive capability.

Data science plays a key role in customer-centric applications as well as the optimization of pricing strategies via dynamic pricing algorithms. Based on consumer demand signals, rival pricing, and market conditions, these algorithms modify prices in real-time. Retailers can maintain their competitiveness in a dynamic market by maximizing revenue and profit margins through the implementation of dynamic pricing.

Moreover, data science is revolutionizing security protocols and fraud detection in the retail and e-commerce industries. Real-time machine learning models examine transactional data to find abnormalities and patterns suggestive of fraud. This proactive strategy not only reduces monetary losses but also builds credibility and trust with clients.

Data science driven by AI and ML is transforming e-commerce and retail by facilitating data-driven decision-making in a variety of business operations domains. Data science has many uses that are constantly expanding, ranging from supply chain optimization and fraud protection to customer interaction and targeted marketing. In today's digital economy, adopting these technologies is crucial for companies looking to maintain their competitive edge and provide exceptional customer service.

Case Studies and Practical Applications

Dynamic Pricing

Real-time pricing strategy optimization through data science methodologies is demonstrated by dynamic pricing. Retailers employ artificial intelligence (AI) algorithms to monitor competition pricing, past sales data, market conditions, and even customer behavior in order to dynamically modify prices. For instance, algorithms might automatically raise or drop prices to maximize revenue and profit margins during periods of high demand or in response to changes in competition prices. By providing fair market prices, this responsive pricing strategy not only increases competitiveness but also improves customer perception.

Fraud Detection

Fraud detection is a crucial use of AI and ML in e-commerce. Large volumes of transactional data are analyzed by algorithms to spot trends that point to fraudulent activity, like strange purchasing behavior, repeated unsuccessful payment attempts, or inconsistent shipping addresses. Businesses can prevent financial losses from fraudulent transactions and preserve client trust by identifying irregularities in real-time. In order to increase detection accuracy and adjust to changing fraud strategies, advanced machine learning models are always learning from fresh data, which improves overall security measures.

Personalized Recommendation Systems

In order to improve the online purchasing experience for customers, recommendation algorithms are essential. To give tailored product recommendations, AI-powered algorithms examine demographic data, past purchase history, browsing patterns, and even social media connections. These systems make recommendations for products based on each customer's interests and previous interactions using collaborative filtering, content-based filtering, and hybrid techniques. Businesses can boost customer happiness, cross-selling opportunities, conversion rates, and customer satisfaction by providing pertinent ideas; these factors will eventually lead to revenue development.

Supply Chain Optimization

Retailers may improve supply chain operations by using data science to get insights from AI and predictive analytics. Through an examination of past sales data, inventory levels, weather trends, and transportation logistics, companies can enhance their ability to predict demand and streamline inventory management. Predictive models facilitate last-mile delivery procedures, optimize warehouse operations, and help locate any bottlenecks in the supply chain. This proactive strategy guarantees that items are available when and where customers need them, while also cutting costs and improving operational efficiency.

Customer Segmentation and Personalization

Data science is used by segmentation and personalization methods to separate customers into discrete groups according to their preferences, behavior, and demographics. Retailers may customize product offerings, marketing campaigns, and promotions to each segment's unique requirements and interests by having a thorough grasp of these groups. Real-time customer data analysis is done by AI algorithms to provide personalized experiences like content recommendations, tailored discounts, and focused email campaigns. This strategy boosts lifetime customer value, promotes brand loyalty, and encourages greater customer interaction.

Conclusion

The retail and e-commerce industries are changing as a result of data science, which is made possible by AI and ML. It helps companies make data-driven decisions, increase operational effectiveness, and provide individualized customer experiences. Adopting these improvements as technology develops will be crucial to maintaining competitiveness in an increasingly digital world.

7.4 DATA SCIENCE IN MANUFACTURING

Processes, efficiency, and quality control have been completely transformed in the field of modern manufacturing through the combination of Data Science, Artificial Intelligence (AI), and Machine Learning (ML). This chapter examines the ways in which these technologies can be used to forecast maintenance requirements, improve overall productivity, and optimize operations.

Role of Data Science in Manufacturing

Data science is essential to the modern manufacturing scene because it uses cutting-edge methods like artificial intelligence (AI) and machine learning (ML) to mine massive amounts of data for useful insights. This data, which records every aspect of the manufacturing process in real-time, comes from a range of sources, including sensors, IoT devices, and industrial gear.

Predictive maintenance is among the core domains in which data science is particularly strong. AI algorithms are able to predict possible equipment breakdowns ahead of time by combining historical data analysis with real-time sensor readings. By taking a proactive stance, unplanned downtime is reduced, maintenance plans are optimized, and operating expenses are eventually decreased. To increase productivity, manufacturers might proactively arrange maintenance interventions, such as component replacements or scheduled repairs during planned downtime.

Furthermore, by providing real-time manufacturing process monitoring and analysis, data science improves quality control. By identifying anomalies and departures from defined quality requirements, machine learning algorithms can identify possible flaws early in the manufacturing cycle. This capacity allows for ongoing development by locating the sources of errors and maximizing production parameters, in addition to guaranteeing that goods fulfill strict quality standards.

Data science enhances supply chain management by optimizing logistics and inventory levels. Artificial intelligence (AI)-powered analytics predict demand patterns using past data and market trends, preventing unnecessary inventory buildup and guaranteeing that materials and components are available when needed. This effectiveness lowers waste, shortens lead times, and improves the supply chain's general flexibility and ability to react quickly to changes in the market.

Furthermore, data science plays a role in strategic decision-making in addition to operational efficiency. AI models analyze data from the manufacturing ecosystem as a whole, including consumer reviews and industry trends, to offer insightful recommendations for new product development and market placement. Based on predictive analytics, manufacturers can customize their products, increasing consumer happiness and giving them a competitive edge in the market.

The incorporation of Data Science with AI and ML holds the potential to open up new avenues for productivity, creativity, and expansion as the manufacturing sector continues to embrace digital transformation. But issues like cybersecurity, data integration, and the requirement for qualified workers continue to be important factors. Tackle these obstacles head-on if you want to fully utilize data science to propel manufacturing forward in the future.

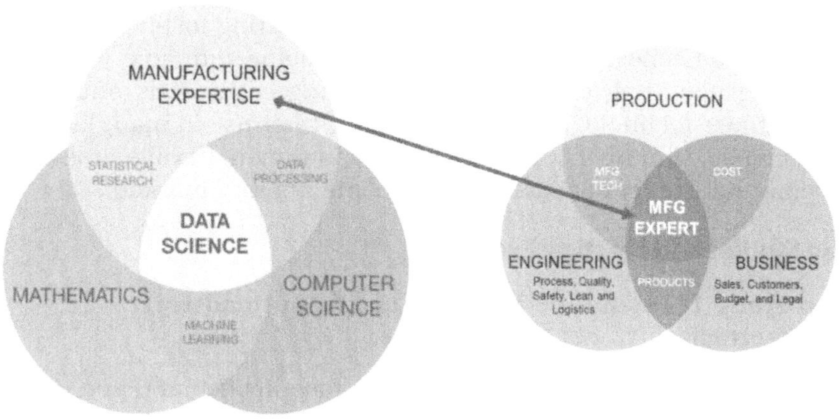

Applications of AI and ML in Manufacturing

The utilization of Artificial Intelligence (AI) and Machine Learning (ML) in the industrial sector is essential for augmenting productivity, elevating the caliber of products, and streamlining operational procedures throughout the entire production cycle. Predictive maintenance is one of the key uses, in which AI systems examine past maintenance logs and real-time sensor data to forecast equipment faults before they happen. This proactive strategy guarantees unbroken production cycles, lowers maintenance costs, and minimizes downtime.

Furthermore, quality control makes heavy use of AI and ML. Large-scale data analysis from production processes can be used by machine learning models to quickly and accurately identify abnormalities and product flaws. This capacity leads to continuous process improvement and less waste by helping manufacturers to find the core causes of problems in addition to improving the quality of their products.

AI-driven analytics are essential for supply chain optimization since they help with inventory level management, demand forecasting, and logistics optimization. Manufacturers can increase supply chain efficiency by optimizing material flow, cutting lead times, and saving storage costs by utilizing AI algorithms.

Additionally, by spotting patterns and trends in production data that human analysis might miss, AI and ML help with process optimization. These insights assist producers in optimizing energy use, adjusting production settings, and raising overall operational effectiveness. For instance, AI models are used in complex manufacturing contexts such as semiconductor fabrication to analyze large datasets from manufacturing processes and maximize wafer production yields.

The application of AI and ML in manufacturing fosters innovation and competitiveness in a continually changing industry while also improving operating efficiencies and cutting costs. It is anticipated that as these technologies develop further, their use in manufacturing will increase, leading to smarter factories and more flexible production systems that can satisfy the needs of contemporary markets.

Case Studies and Practical Examples:

Case Study 1: Predictive Maintenance in Automotive Manufacturing

Production line uptime is essential to meeting demand and cutting costs in the automotive industry. The use of AI and ML algorithms to support predictive maintenance is essential to guaranteeing that machinery and equipment run well and don't break down unexpectedly. Manufacturers are able to forecast when parts are likely to break by examining data from prior maintenance records and sensors installed in equipment. By scheduling repair during planned downtime, this proactive method minimizes unanticipated disruptions and maximizes overall equipment effectiveness (OEE). Predictive maintenance models, for example, were used by a large automaker to reduce annual maintenance expenses by 30% while simultaneously reducing downtime by 20%.

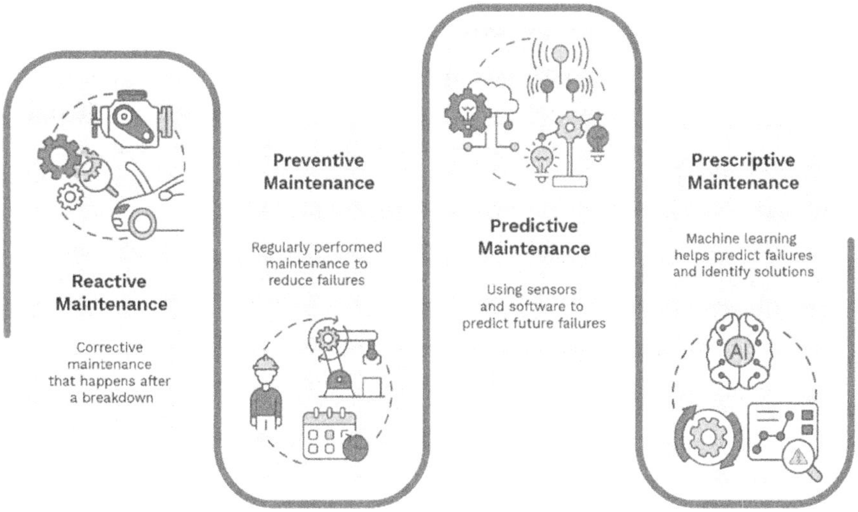

Case Study 2: Quality Improvement in Electronics Manufacturing

Maintaining a high standard of product quality in the electronics manufacturing industry is critical to customer happiness and brand reputation. Large datasets of manufacturing parameters and metrics related to product quality are analyzed in real time using machine learning algorithms. These models may spot any flaws early in the production process by identifying trends and abnormalities, which enables quick corrective action. For instance, a well-known electronics firm used image recognition algorithms to check circuit boards for flaws like component misplacements or soldering errors. This automated inspection greatly decreased scrap rates and rework expenses while simultaneously increasing defect detection rates by 25%.

Practical Example: Supply Chain Optimization

Another area in manufacturing where AI and ML are having a big impact is supply chain operations optimization. Manufacturers may increase the accuracy of demand forecasting, expedite logistics, and manage inventory levels by utilizing machine learning algorithms and predictive analytics. One multinational consumer goods company, for example, combined their supply chain management system with AI-driven demand forecasting algorithms. They were able to maintain excellent service levels and cut surplus inventory by 15% thanks to this connection, which resulted in significant cost savings and increased customer satisfaction.

Practical Example: Energy Efficiency in Manufacturing

One significant cost component in manufacturing activities is energy usage. In order to find potential for increasing energy efficiency, artificial intelligence (AI) algorithms can examine data on energy usage via sensors and smart meters. Manufacturers can attain substantial savings in energy consumption and operational expenses by means of equipment scheduling optimization, real-time energy demand fluctuations adjustment of production processes, and implementation of predictive energy management systems. For instance, the implementation of AI-based energy management systems at a steel manufacturing facility resulted in an annual 10% reduction in energy consumption through predictive maintenance of energy-intensive equipment and production schedule optimization based on real-time energy pricing.

Challenges and Future Directions

Even though Data Science, AI, and ML have significantly improved manufacturing, there are still a number of obstacles to overcome and room for growth.

Data Integration and Quality

The integration of disparate data sources is one of the main obstacles to the application of AI and ML in manufacturing. Large volumes of data are produced in manufacturing settings by a variety of sources, including sensors, machinery, and ERP systems. It is essential to integrate and harmonize this data in order to create precise AI models and derive insightful conclusions. Furthermore, accurate decision-making and predictive analytics depend on consistent and high-quality data across various systems and processes.

Cybersecurity Concerns

Cybersecurity becomes a major worry as manufacturing processes grow more networked through IoT devices and cloud-based systems. It is critical to defend intellectual property and sensitive production data against online attacks. Strong cybersecurity measures are necessary for manufacturers to protect their operations and uphold confidence with partners and consumers. These measures include encryption techniques, access controls, and ongoing monitoring.

Workforce Upskilling and Adoption

The proficient use of AI and ML technologies necessitates a personnel with the necessary skills to comprehend, operate, and oversee these sophisticated systems. A lot of manufacturing jobs are changing, and these jobs now call for new programming, data analysis, and AI model deployment skill sets. To fully utilize data science and artificial intelligence (AI) in manufacturing environments, it is imperative to upskill current staff members and draw in fresh people with these areas of expertise.

Ethical and Regulatory Considerations

Transparency, accountability, and bias reduction become critical ethical considerations as AI and ML systems make increasingly sophisticated judgments in manufacturing processes. To guarantee responsible and sustainable use of these technologies, manufacturers must navigate legal frameworks pertaining to data protection, algorithmic fairness, and ethical AI deployment.

Future Directions

Future developments in data science in manufacturing seem promising in terms of additional innovation and optimization. Technological developments in digital twins, autonomous systems, and AI-driven robotics have the potential to completely transform manufacturing capacities. These technologies make it possible for manufacturing processes to be adaptable, meaning they can change quickly in response to shifting operational and market situations.

Collaborative Ecosystems and Industry 4.0

Future development will be fueled by the idea of Industry 4.0, which is defined by the integration of digital technologies into every facet of industry. Manufacturers, technology companies, and academic institutions work together to create collaborative ecosystems that stimulate innovation and hasten the adoption of AI and ML solutions. To push the boundaries of intelligent manufacturing systems forward, interdisciplinary cooperation and knowledge exchange are crucial.

Even if data science, artificial intelligence, and machine learning present revolutionary possibilities for the industrial sector, it will be critical to solve issues like data integration, cybersecurity, labor upskilling, and ethical concerns. Future manufacturing processes may be more robust, effective, and competitive if these technologies are adopted with a strategic focus on innovation and cooperation.

Conclusion

Manufacturing is changing as a result of data science, which is fueled by AI and ML. It promotes innovation, increases operational effectiveness, and makes decisions wiser. It is anticipated that as technologies advance, their influence on production procedures will increase, opening the door to an increasingly linked and efficient industrial environment.

7.5 DATA SCIENCE IN SOCIAL MEDIA AND MARKETING

Social media platforms are becoming essential spaces for brand promotion, consumer insights, and engagement in the field of modern marketing. This chapter examines how data science, machine learning (ML), and artificial intelligence (AI) interact with social media marketing. By utilizing these technologies, marketers may gain unprecedented insights into customer behavior, enhance their campaigns, and customize user experiences.

Role of Data Science in Social Media Marketing

Data science plays a critical role in social media marketing, utilizing cutting-edge tools like machine learning (ML) and artificial intelligence (AI) to optimize marketing strategies and change the way organizations interact with customers. Fundamentally, data science gives marketers the ability to mine enormous volumes of social media data for insightful information that helps them make decisions at every level of the marketing funnel.

Audience segmentation and targeting is one important factor. Marketers can examine user demographics, behaviors, and interests derived from social media interactions using advanced algorithms. Thanks to this in-depth knowledge, audiences may be precisely segmented into significant clusters, allowing for customized marketing campaigns based on the interests of individual customers. Through the identification of these categories, marketers may successfully target their audience with highly targeted content and adverts, leading to increased engagement and conversion rates.

Content personalization is another important application. Marketers may now dynamically modify content delivery based on user interactions and preferences seen on social media platforms thanks to data science. Brands can optimize the relevance and effect of their messaging by customizing content in real-time through the use of AI-driven recommendation systems and predictive analytics. In addition to improving user experience, this tailored strategy strengthens bonds between companies and customers, which eventually promotes brand advocacy and loyalty.

Additionally, sentiment analysis is essential for maintaining customer connections and brand reputation on social media. Data scientists can monitor and analyze public opinion toward a brand or product in real-time by utilizing natural language processing (NLP) tools. With this skill, marketers may take advantage of good comments, proactively handle crises, and quickly recognize and address growing difficulties. Brands may avoid reputational issues and preserve a positive image among their target audience by keeping an eye on sentiment patterns.

Case Studies and Examples

1. Sentiment Analysis on Twitter

Sentiment analysis is a potent tool for real-time understanding of how the public feels about certain companies, goods, or events. Marketers can classify tweets into good, negative, and neutral categories according to their emotional tone by applying natural language processing (NLP) algorithms. Sentiment analysis, for example, can be used to measure first reactions and pinpoint areas of praise or potential problems before a product launch. This study aids in both maintaining a positive brand image and making timely adjustments to marketing initiatives.

Example: Consider a corporation that is introducing a new model of smartphone. Sentiment analysis of tweets mentioning the product shows that there was an upsurge in favorable sentiment during the revealing event, which was followed by continuous conversations and comments. Sentiment trends are shown over time in the graph (Figure 1), with peaks and valleys corresponding with important marketing initiatives or outside events.

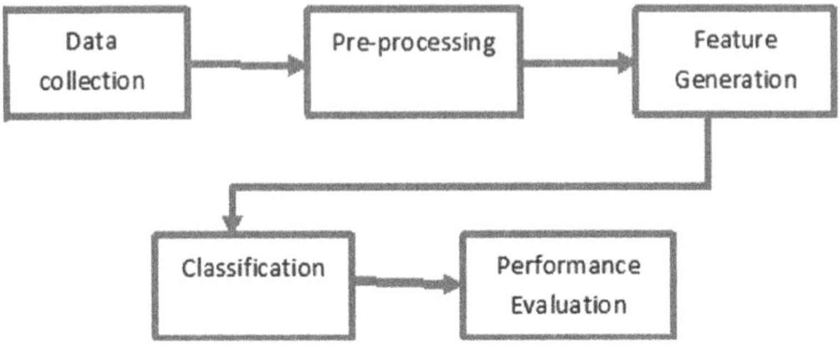

Sentiment Analysis Method

2. Customer Segmentation on Facebook

In order to target particular audience segments with marketing initiatives, customer segmentation is essential. Marketers can cluster users based on shared attributes like demographics, interests, and historical actions by using machine learning algorithms like clustering. By delivering content in a personalized and targeted manner, this segmentation greatly increases engagement and conversion rates.

Example: Think about a fashion retailer who segments its clientele with Facebook Insights. Clustering algorithms do this by examining user interactions, likes, shares, and comments on postings, which help to identify different customer groups. Figure 2 shows how various demographics interact with the brand on Facebook; each cluster corresponds to a distinct set of interests and actions. With this fine-grained insight, marketers can create promotions and content that are more efficiently suited to each segment.

Practical Applications and Benefits

The following instances highlight the useful uses of data science in social media marketing:

- **Real-time Decision Making:** Sentiment analysis allows marketers to respond quickly to fluctuations in public opinion, resolving issues or highlighting favorable comments right away.
- **Personalized Marketing:** By delivering tailored offers and information, customer segmentation enables marketers to build stronger bonds and boost consumer loyalty.
- **Optimized Campaigns:** By predicting user behavior and optimizing ad placements, machine learning algorithms make

sure marketing funds are spent wisely to maximize return on investment.

In an increasingly competitive digital marketplace, businesses may improve their marketing tactics and forge closer relationships with their audience by utilizing these data-driven insights. The incorporation of AI and ML into social media marketing will enhance campaign efficacy and targetability as these technologies develop further.

This enlarged section offers a closer look at how data science approaches improve social media and marketing decision-making and strategy creation, highlighting the observable advantages using particular case studies and examples.

Applications of Machine Learning in Social Media

Applications of machine learning (ML) in social media go much beyond simple statistics and have a significant impact on how advertisers interact with consumers and refine their campaigns. Predictive analytics is a well-known application in which machine learning algorithms examine past data to detect patterns and anticipate customer behavior. This feature enables marketers to make data-driven choices on campaign tactics, product launches, and content production.

Furthermore, by using user data to customize ad placements, machine learning (ML) facilitates sophisticated ad targeting. For every advertisement, algorithms evaluate user behavior, interests, and interactions to determine which audience groups are most relevant. By reducing the amount of money spent on unrelated audiences, this tailored strategy not only increases marketing efficacy but also improves return on investment (ROI).

Additionally, sentiment analysisa crucial aspect of social media monitoringis greatly aided by machine learning algorithms. These algorithms are able to instantly analyze and classify user sentiments regarding brands or products by utilizing natural language processing (NLP). This feature enables marketers to take advantage of favorable sentiment trends, manage brand reputation, and respond quickly to customer feedback.

Additionally, chatbots with machine learning capabilities are revolutionizing social media customer support. These AI-powered chatbots make use of machine learning (ML) models to comprehend and provide highly accurate and personalized responses to client requests. Chatbots automate repetitive tasks and offer immediate support, improving user experience and guaranteeing 24/7 customer care.

To put it simply, the use of machine learning to social media gives marketers access to accurate targeting tools, actionable insights, and improved customer interaction tactics. These technologies will only become more sophisticated in their application in social media marketing as they develop, spurring efficiency and innovation in digital marketing strategies.

Conclusion

By providing unmatched insights into customer behavior and preferences, combining data science with AI and ML skills transforms social media marketing. This chapter has used examples and applications from real-world situations to illustrate the transformative power of these technologies. Data science is becoming an essential component of contemporary marketing strategy as social media and the methods and resources available to marketers both continue to develop.

7.6 FUTURE TRENDS IN DATA SCIENCE

The future of the quickly developing fields of data science is being shaped by ongoing developments in machine learning (ML) and artificial intelligence (AI). This chapter examines new developments that, in the years to come, will completely change the way data science is practiced.

1. Deep Learning and Neural Networks

Key developments in Data Science include Deep Learning and Neural Networks, which use artificial intelligence to accomplish amazing feats in pattern identification, decision-making, and predictive modeling. Fundamentally, Deep Learning uses interconnected layers of algorithms called neural networks to simulate how the human brain processes information. These networks have the ability to autonomously learn hierarchical data representations, extracting complex information that may be missed by more conventional machine learning techniques.

Deep Learning's exceptional accuracy at processing large volumes of unstructured data, including text, audio, and images, is one of its main advantages. This skill has sparked innovations in a number of fields, such as speech recognition, natural language processing, and computer vision. Convolutional neural networks (CNNs), for example, have revolutionized image classification tasks that were previously thought to be difficult. CNNs are capable of accurately detecting and classifying objects in images with human-level precision.

Furthermore, Deep Learning's adaptability goes beyond static jobs to dynamic contexts where judgments need to be made instantly based on ever-changing input streams. Because of their superiority in processing sequential data, recurrent neural networks (RNNs) and their variations, like long short-term memory (LSTM) networks, are essential for tasks like sentiment analysis, language translation, and time series forecasting.

Neural network topologies are becoming more complicated and large in size as computer power and Deep Learning frameworks continue to progress. With the help of methods like transfer learning, which involves optimizing previously trained models for certain tasks, practitioners may now use cutting-edge AI capabilities more widely and produce remarkable outcomes with a smaller amount of data and processing power.

2. Explainable AI (XAI)

Explainable AI (XAI) aims to solve the crucial requirements of interpretability and transparency in AI systems, especially in situations where decisions have an effect on people or society as a whole. Understanding how AI models make judgments is becoming more and more crucial as these models get more sophisticated and are incorporated into a wider range of industries, including criminal justice, healthcare, and finance.

Deep neural networks and other conventional machine learning models are frequently regarded as "black boxes," with their inner workings being obscure and challenging to understand. Concerns of bias, justice, and the capacity to review AI system judgments are raised by this lack of transparency. By offering insights into the decision-making process of models, explainable AI solutions seek to address these issues by improving the models' understandability and accountability to stakeholders.

In AI, explainability can be achieved in a number of ways. Making explanations for the predictions you make, emphasizing the features or other factors that affected the model's output, is one popular technique. Model-agnostic approaches (e.g., LIME and SHAP) and saliency maps, together with feature significance analysis and other techniques, assist in identifying dependencies and correlations in the data that inform model choices.

In addition, XAI makes it easier for humans and AI systems to collaborate by offering validation of model outputs and domain-specific insights. In fields like financial risk assessment or medical diagnostics, where human judgment and expertise are vital, this kind of cooperation is imperative.

In order to maintain justice, build trust, and comply with regulations, explainable AI practices will be essential as AI develops and becomes more deeply integrated into society. XAI increases the interpretability and transparency of AI systems, which boosts their acceptability and usefulness in a variety of contexts and sectors in addition to increasing their dependability.

3. Federated Learning

Federated Learning is a novel technique to machine learning that leverages the pooled wisdom from decentralized data sources while addressing privacy concerns. Since centralized data aggregation is necessary for traditional machine learning models, there are serious privacy and security concerns, particularly when handling sensitive data.

Federated Learning addresses these issues by enabling the cooperative training of a shared machine learning model without the need for raw data exchange between numerous edge devices (such as servers, smartphones, and Internet of Things sensors). This is how it usually operates:

1. **Decentralized Training:** Federated Learning maintains data localized on individual devices or servers rather than transferring it to a central server. Based on its local data, each device computes model updates separately.
2. **Aggregated Learning:** These local modifications (model parameters) are safely and privately aggregated on a regular basis. No device's data is exposed thanks to strategies like differential privacy and secure aggregation.
3. **Iterative Improvement:** As more devices contribute their updates, the combined model is subsequently enhanced iteratively. This process keeps going until the model's accuracy is at a level that is acceptable.

Federated Learning Offers Several Advantages

Privacy Preservation: By keeping data on local devices, you lower the chance of unauthorized access or data breaches.

- **Scalability:** It makes it possible to scale machine learning systems to numerous devices without centralizing data, which may be unsafe or impractical.
- **Edge Computing Efficiency:** Federated Learning minimizes latency and bandwidth usage by executing computations locally, which qualifies it for real-time applications in Internet of Things and edge computing scenarios.

Federated Learning finds applications in a variety of fields, including industrial IoT (optimizing manufacturing processes without revealing proprietary data), personalized recommendation systems (protecting user data privacy), and healthcare (where patient data privacy is crucial).

Federated Learning is a noteworthy development in machine learning methodologies that corresponds with the increasing significance of data privacy and the developing potential of edge computing. Federated Learning is positioned to be a key component in allowing safe and effective AI applications across a variety of fields as technology advances.

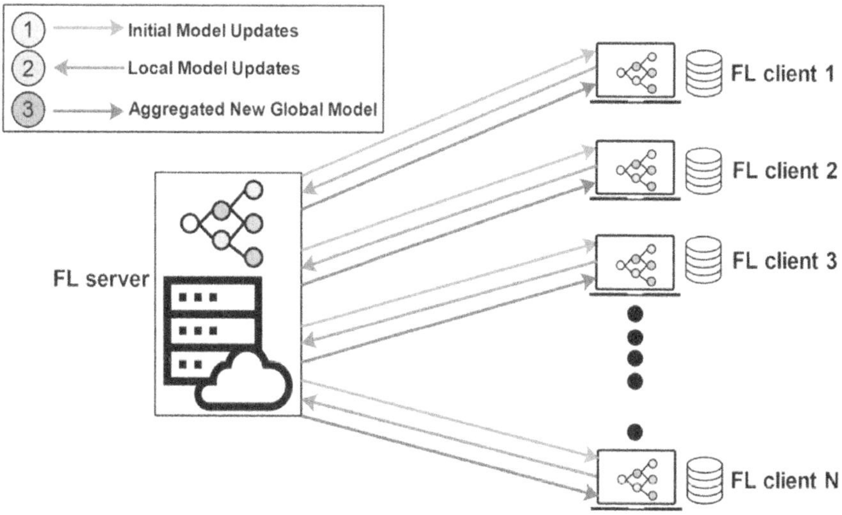

Federated Learning Process

4. Automated Machine Learning (AutoML)

Within the subject of Data Science, Automated Machine Learning (AutoML) is a revolutionary technique that seeks to automate and simplify the intricate process of applying Machine Learning (ML) to real-world situations. In the past, developing and implementing machine learning models required a high level of proficiency in feature engineering, model selection, data preprocessing, and hyperparameter tweaking. By automating these processes, autoML aims to democratize this process and increase ML's accessibility for people and organizations lacking in-depth ML knowledge.

The key components of AutoML include:

1. **Automatic Preprocessing of Data:** This include managing missing values, scaling features, encoding categorical variables, and carrying out any additional required data transformations. These processes are automated by autoML technologies to guarantee that data is ready for model training.
2. **Engineering Features:** Enhancing the performance of the model requires careful feature engineering and selection. AutoML algorithms have the ability to automatically detect pertinent characteristics, generate additional features, and choose the subset of features that most enhances the model's predictive ability.
3. **Model Selection:** AutoML frameworks assess several machine learning algorithms and determine which one performs best by using predetermined measures (such as accuracy, precision, and recall). This procedure takes into account the dataset's properties and seeks to automatically identify the best model.
4. **Hyperparameter Optimization:** A model's performance is greatly affected by the tuning of hyperparameters (such as learning rate and regularization strength). The process of finding the ideal hyperparameters is automated by autoML, usually through the use of grid search or Bayesian optimization approaches.
5. **Pipeline Optimization:** In addition to automating specific activities, autoML improves the entire machine learning pipeline, which includes model selection, hyperparameter tuning, feature engineering, and data preprocessing. The scalability and time-to-deployment of ML models are enhanced by this end-to-end automation.

The time and resources needed to develop ML solutions can be decreased with AutoML, freeing up domain experts to concentrate more on business decision-making and result interpretation than on technical implementation. Additionally, AutoML facilitates incremental improvements in model performance by enabling rapid prototyping and experimentation.

Despite its benefits, AutoML is not a one-size-fits-all solution and may have drawbacks based on the problem's complexity and the level of domain expertise needed. However, it represents a big step toward democratizing access to ML capabilities and fostering creativity across industries with its ongoing advances and incorporation into multiple ML platforms.

5. Augmented Analytics

In the field of data science, augmented analytics is a revolutionary method that uses machine learning and artificial intelligence (AI) to improve on conventional analytics procedures. In contrast to traditional analytics, which frequently necessitates a large amount of manual labor and domain knowledge in order to extract insights from data, augmented analytics uses sophisticated algorithms and techniques to automate and enhance these procedures.

Natural language processing (NLP) is one of the main elements of augmented analytics. With the use of natural language processing (NLP), consumers may communicate with data in everyday language, ask meaningful questions, and get useful, actionable answers. For non-technical users, this feature greatly reduces the entry barrier, enabling anyone to examine data and draw conclusions without requiring in-depth technical knowledge.

Additionally, automated insights generation is incorporated into augmented analytics. Large-scale datasets are analyzed by machine learning algorithms to find hidden patterns, trends, and anomalies that human analysts might not see right away. Augmented analytics speeds up decision-making and helps businesses react quickly to shifting market conditions or new possibilities by automating the process of gaining insights.

Additionally, the accuracy and dependability of analytics outputs are improved by the integration of AI and ML algorithms. These algorithms can find correlations and prediction linkages that older methods would miss since they can handle large, complicated data sets with high-dimensional properties. Businesses may more confidently and precisely predict future trends, customer behavior, and operational consequences thanks to this predictive capabilities.

Practically speaking, augmented analytics systems are revolutionizing a wide range of industries, including manufacturing, retail, healthcare, and finance. Organizations may use data-driven insights to uncover new revenue streams, enhance resource allocation, and streamline processes by utilizing AI and ML.

Enhanced analytics signifies a paradigm shift in the way businesses use data to spur creativity and decision-making. Augmented analytics gives companies the ability to maximize the value from their data assets and get a competitive edge in today's data-driven market by fusing human experience with AI-powered automation.

6. Edge AI and IoT Integration

A significant development in the field of data science, the integration of Edge AI with the Internet of Things (IoT) offers disruptive possibilities for real-time data processing and decision-making. Large volumes of data are typically gathered by IoT devices from sensors and endpoints, and then sent to centralized cloud servers for processing. Although efficient, this method's data transfer and storage can result in latency problems, bandwidth limitations, and privacy issues.

By enabling data processing directly on IoT devices or at the network's edge, nearer to the data generation location, Edge AI solves these problems. Without depending on cloud connectivity, quick insights and decisions can be made thanks to this localized processing capacity. Without constant communication to a centralized server, Edge AI, for instance, can evaluate sensor data in real-time in industrial Internet of things applications to identify anomalies, forecast equipment failures, and maximize operational efficiency.

Additionally, Edge AI minimizes the exposure of sensitive data, improving data security and privacy. To lower the danger of data breaches, only pertinent insights or aggregated data summaries may be provided to central computers rather than raw data transmitted over networks.

In terms of technology, Edge AI is implementing machine learning models that are lightweight and tailored for edge devices. To guarantee effective operation within the limitations of IoT hardware, model compression and quantization techniques are frequently used. With limited computational resources, these models can carry out tasks like natural language processing, picture identification, and predictive analytics directly on edge devices.

The convergence of Edge AI with IoT creates new opportunities in a number of areas, such as smart cities, healthcare, transportation, and agriculture. Through the implementation of intelligent decision-making at the edge, enterprises can enhance the dependability of Internet of Things applications, save operational expenses, and expedite reaction times.

A paradigm shift in data science is represented by edge AI and IoT integration, which provides decentralized intelligence that improves scalability, security, and efficiency in data-driven applications. These technologies are anticipated to play a pivotal position in propelling innovation and molding the forthcoming of intelligent systems and connected gadgets as they advance.

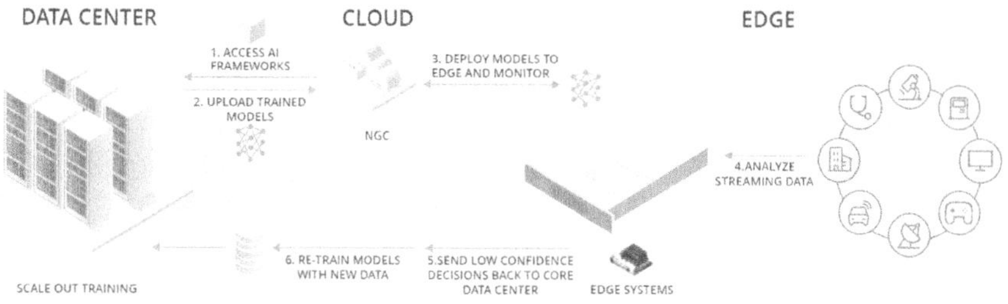

Edge AI

The development of AI and ML technologies will impact data science in the future. These trends will influence how businesses use data to spur innovation and obtain a competitive edge as they develop further.

Conclusion

Summary of Key Learnings

We have investigated basic ideas, sophisticated methods, and useful applications in our exploration of the field of data science utilizing AI and ML. These tools enable us to extract knowledge and make defensible decisions from data. This chapter provides a thorough synopsis of our main discoveries, distilling the spirit of our investigation.

Key Topics Covered

1. **Introduction to Data Science:** We investigated the fundamental ideas and techniques of data science that are necessary to derive significant insights from data. Understanding the entire data lifecyclefrom collection and cleaning to transformation and analysiswas part of this. In order to guarantee dependable analytical results, we underlined the need of data quality and integrity and discussed methods like data wrangling and preprocessing. We also looked at the iterative nature of the data science process and the function of domain expertise in posing data-driven queries.

2. **Machine Learning Foundations:** A major component of our journey was machine learning, which included both theoretical foundations and real-world implementations. We discussed supervised learning approaches, in which algorithms, such decision trees for classification tasks and linear regression for regression tasks, learn from labeled data to provide predictions. In addition, techniques for clustering and dimensionality reduction such as principal component analysis (PCA) and k-means clustering were investigated as unsupervised learning methods. Additionally, reinforcement learning was presented, emphasizing its use in instructing agents on how to make judgments in a series of changing circumstances.
3. **Artificial Intelligence Applications:** Our research on artificial intelligence covered a wide range of fields, demonstrating how it is transforming many different businesses. We looked at computer vision applications, which include object identification and image classification, and natural language processing (NLP) applications, which include sentiment analysis and text production. Furthermore, the application of AI to robotics and autonomous systems was discussed, highlighting developments in motion planning, perception, and control algorithms.
4. **Advanced Data Analysis Techniques:** The focus was on advanced data analysis techniques, which emphasized the significance of statistical inference and effective visualization. We used data visualization tools such as seaborn and matplotlib to show how visual representations improve comprehension of the data and provide insights. Our investigation relied heavily on statistical techniques like feature engineering and hypothesis testing, which offered strict frameworks for evaluating theories and refining prediction models.
5. **Big Data and Cloud Computing:** Our approach to data processing and storage has changed with the advent of Big Data and Cloud Computing. We investigated cloud computing platforms such as AWS and Google Cloud, taking advantage of their capabilities and scalability to handle big information and carry out intricate calculations. The introduction of frameworks like Hadoop and Spark highlighted their function in distributed computing and made it possible to handle and analyze data at scale in real time.

Practical activities and real-world case studies were included with every lesson to ensure that students understood the principles and could apply them in a variety of situations. By grasping these fundamental and sophisticated ideas, we prepared ourselves to take on challenging data science problems and use AI and ML to spur innovation and well-informed decision-making across a range of industries.

Summary of Achievements

We have hit important benchmarks in our investigation of Data Science with AI and ML, which have strengthened our comprehension and utilization of these revolutionary technologies.

First of all, we have honed a strong Python programming skill set that is specifically useful for data analysis and machine learning. We were able to successfully handle data, use different algorithms, and create prediction models thanks to this fundamental skill set. We improved our understanding of topics like data preparation, feature engineering, and model evaluation by applying these techniques to actual datasets through practical projects and assignments.

In addition, our trip developed critical thinking skills necessary for data-driven decision making. We gained knowledge on how to assess the benefits and drawbacks of various machine learning models, decipher their results, and iteratively improve our strategies in light of actual data and statistical insights. Our investigation of sophisticated data analysis approaches, such as statistical procedures like regression analysis and hypothesis testing, and data visualization using programs like matplotlib and seaborn, enhanced this analytical rigor.

In our educational process, ethical issues were also crucial. We had in-depth conversations about the appropriate application of AI and ML technologies, including topics like algorithmic bias, data privacy, and the wider societal effects of automated decision-making systems. This ethical consciousness emphasized our dedication to the responsible and moral application of these technologies, guaranteeing that our discoveries and advancements benefit society.

Our successes in Data Science with AI and ML are a reflection of both our technical proficiency and our deeper comprehension of the ramifications and potential uses of these technologies. Equipped with this understanding, we are ready to take on new data science issues in the future, promote innovation in our industries, and maintain the moral principles that protect the objectivity and integrity of our work. These accomplishments demonstrate our commitment and development in this exciting and quickly changing industry.

Future Directions

Let's examine data science's potential uses of AI and ML in more detail:

- Future developments in data science and artificial intelligence are expected to bring about a number of revolutionary changes. Explainable AI (XAI) is one important field of research and development that aims to increase the transparency and comprehensibility of AI models. The capacity to comprehend and have faith in the results of AI systems is becoming more and more important as they are included into decision-making procedures in a variety of businesses. The discipline is moving toward more accountable and trustworthy AI solutions with the help of techniques like algorithmic transparency, feature importance analysis, and model visualization.
- Federated learning is another exciting direction in machine learning. It is a decentralized method where models are jointly trained across several devices or data sources without exchanging raw data. This paradigm allows for the collective improvement of AI models while addressing privacy issues by maintaining the localization of sensitive data. Federated learning is especially important in industries with strict data privacy laws, such as healthcare, banking, and telecommunications, where cooperation is crucial for improving models.
- In addition, the ethical implications of AI are becoming more and more prominent. Ensuring Fairness, Accountability, and Transparency (FAT) in AI systems is crucial as AI technologies become more widespread. Concerns including reducing bias in datasets and algorithms, guaranteeing inclusivity in AI applications, and creating guidelines for responsible AI deployment are all included in the category of ethical considerations. Ethical AI development techniques are being made possible by programs like AI ethics boards and standards like the IEEE's Ethically Aligned Design.
- Finally, AI-driven automation is revolutionizing industries through process optimization, cost reduction, and innovation acceleration. AI-driven automation is optimizing workflows and helping businesses to make better use of data. Examples of this include automated chatbots for customer care and predictive maintenance in the manufacturing sector.

- Advances in automating processes, federated learning, ethical considerations, and explainability will characterize the future of data science employing AI and ML. Organizations may fully utilize AI to promote innovation, transparency, and ethical integrity in their data-driven activities by adopting these trends appropriately. By utilizing data intelligently, these initiatives not only foresee future issues but also set the groundwork for long-term prosperity and societal benefits.

Conclusion

We now possess the skills and knowledge necessary to successfully negotiate the complexity of today's data-driven environments thanks to our investigation of data science employing AI and ML. We can continue to have a significant impact on the field and create substantial outcomes by carefully utilizing these insights.

Integration of AI and ML in Data Science

The combination of machine learning (ML) with artificial intelligence (AI) is a major development in the field of data science. This chapter examines the ways in which these technologies interact to improve decision-making processes in a variety of fields by drawing insightful conclusions from data.

AI and ML: Foundations and Definitions

In the context of data science, let's take a closer look at the principles and concepts of machine learning (ML) and artificial intelligence (AI).

The vast subject of computer science known as Artificial Intelligence (AI) is devoted to building devices and systems that are capable of carrying out tasks that normally call for human intelligence. These activities include decision-making, identifying patterns in data, comprehending natural language, and even picking up knowledge from experience. AI is divided into two primary categories:

1. **Narrow AI:** This kind of AI is made to carry out a single task or a limited set of tasks. Facial recognition software, language translation utilities, and streaming platform recommendation algorithms are a few examples.
2. **General AI:** Also referred to as strong AI or human-level AI, this term describes AI systems that are generally capable of displaying cognitive capacities similar to those of humans. They are able to comprehend, acquire, and apply information across a broad range of tasks.

AI techniques commonly employed in Data Science include:

- **Natural Language Processing (NLP):** Provides computers with the ability to comprehend, translate, and produce human language. Applications include chatbots, language translation, and sentiment analysis on social media.
- **Computer Vision:** Utilizing algorithms, this field processes and analyzes visual data from the outside environment to facilitate activities like autonomous driving, object identification, and picture recognition.
- **Robotics:** Utilizing AI, this field enables applications in space exploration, manufacturing, and healthcare by controlling the movements and interactions of robots with their environment.

Machine Learning (ML) is a branch of artificial intelligence that focuses on creating algorithms that let computers learn from and make judgments based on data. Three general kinds can be distinguished among ML algorithms:

1. **Supervised Learning:** Using labeled data, a model is trained so that the algorithm learns how to map input data to the appropriate output. Applications including picture categorization, spam detection, and sales forecasting are frequently used.
2. **Unsupervised Learning:** This method trains the model to find patterns and relationships on unlabeled data. Unsupervised learning applications include market basket analysis, anomaly detection, and clustering techniques.
3. **Reinforcement Learning:** In this paradigm, agents are trained to choose actions in a way that maximizes cumulative reward in a given environment. Applications include robotic control, autonomous driving, and game play (e.g., AlphaGo).

Machine Learning techniques are integral to Data Science processes such as:

1. **Feature Engineering:** Choosing and modifying variables (features) to increase the precision and effectiveness of the model.
2. **Model Training and Evaluation:** Using historical data, models are iteratively optimized to produce precise predictions or classifications.
3. **Deployment and Monitoring:** Introducing trained models into operational settings and keeping an ongoing eye on their efficacy and performance.

Through the integration of AI and ML, data science firms can automate decision-making procedures, find hidden patterns that might spur innovation and competitive advantage, and extract insightful information from massive volumes of data. Data-driven decision-making will continue to be shaped by these technologies as they develop, having an increasing impact on a variety of industries like marketing, manufacturing, healthcare, and finance.

Comprehending these fundamental ideas is essential for properly utilizing AI and ML in the Data Science domain, allowing experts to fully utilize these revolutionary technologies.

Integration in Data Science Workflow

In the context of data science, let's take a closer look at the principles and concepts of machine learning (ML) and artificial intelligence (AI).

The vast subject of computer science known as Artificial Intelligence (AI) is devoted to building devices and systems that are capable of carrying out tasks that normally call for human intelligence. These activities include decision-making, identifying patterns in data, comprehending natural language, and even picking up knowledge from experience. AI is divided into two primary categories:

1. **Narrow AI:** This kind of AI is made to carry out a single task or a limited set of tasks. Facial recognition software, language translation utilities, and streaming platform recommendation algorithms are a few examples.
2. **General AI:** Also referred to as strong AI or human-level AI, this term describes AI systems that are generally capable of displaying cognitive capacities similar to those of humans. They are able to comprehend, acquire, and apply information across a broad range of tasks.

Applications of AI and ML in Data Science

Numerous fields, each reaping the benefits of these cutting-edge technology, use AI and ML applications in data science. AI and ML, for example, are transforming diagnostics in the healthcare industry by analyzing medical pictures to find anomalies and forecast patient outcomes. This improves treatment planning and individualized medication in addition to hastening diagnosis. Artificial intelligence (AI) algorithms are used in banking to sort through enormous volumes of transactional data and spot trends that point to fraud, protecting financial organizations and their customers. Additionally, recommendation systems driven by AI in marketing evaluate client behavior and preferences to provide tailored recommendations that increase customer happiness and engagement.

AI and ML are used by the manufacturing sector for predictive maintenance, in which sensors gather information on the operation of machinery and algorithms forecast malfunctions before they happen to reduce downtime and maximize output. These uses highlight how AI and ML may revolutionize operations, enhance decision-making, and spur innovation in a variety of industries. As these technologies develop further, their incorporation with data science offers even more breakthroughs, opening up new avenues for research and development in domains like driverless cars and climate modeling, among others.

Conclusion

Data science's incorporation of AI and ML revolutionizes sectors and improves decision-making skills by turning raw data into meaningful insights. The applications of these technologies will grow as they develop, presenting fresh chances and difficulties in the area of data-driven innovation.

Future Directions and Emerging Technologies

Data science is being revolutionized by the sciences of artificial intelligence (AI) and machine learning (ML), which provide new techniques for evaluating enormous datasets and producing insights that can be put to use. This chapter examines the potential paths forward and cutting-edge ML and AI technologies that could further revolutionize data science.

1. Advances in AI and ML Algorithms

Significant advancements in AI and ML algorithms have been made recently, expanding the realm of data science possibilities. The most significant developments have been in deep learning, reinforcement learning, and transfer learning, each of which has made a distinct contribution to the discipline.

- **Deep Learning:** Utilizing intricate neural networks with numerous layers, deep learning is at the forefront of AI innovation and enables comprehensive modeling of high-dimensional data. This method has shown great success in natural language processing, picture and speech recognition, and even in gaming contexts. Notable turning points include the creation of recurrent neural networks (RNNs) for sequential data and convolutional neural networks (CNNs) for image processing. In the future, scientists will concentrate on developing more effective network topologies, such transformers, which have transformed language models and improved performance while lowering computing costs.

- **Reinforcement Learning:** Another field that is developing quickly is reinforcement learning (RL). In reinforcement learning (RL), agents are trained to make a series of decisions by rewarding desired results and punishing undesired ones. This learning paradigm has been effectively used to both strategic games like chess and go, as well as autonomous systems like robotic control and self-driving cars. It is anticipated that future RL research would explore more dynamic, complicated situations, improving the agent's capacity for long-term planning and last-minute adjustments.
- **Transfer Learning:** This revolutionary technique greatly reduces the need for large labeled datasets by enabling pre-trained models to be modified for new applications. This method is especially useful in fields where data is expensive or hard to come by. To achieve excellent performance with minimal data, a model that was trained on a large dataset of general pictures might be adjusted for particular medical imaging tasks. It is anticipated that developments in transfer learning will concentrate on enhancing the efficacy and efficiency of this process of adaptation, permitting more widespread use in a variety of domains.

All things considered, these developments in AI and ML algorithms are improving data science's capabilities and opening up advanced analysis tools to a larger range of applications. The potential for artificial intelligence (AI) and machine learning (ML) to tackle complicated problems and advance technology remains enormous as long as these frameworks are refined and innovated within.

2. Integration with Big Data Technologies

The handling and processing of enormous datasets is being completely transformed by the combination of big data technologies with AI and ML. This synergy makes it possible to extract important insights from massive data sets, which is crucial in today's data-driven environment. Important big data technologies like Apache Spark and Hadoop offer the foundation required for distributed and scalable data processing. Large datasets can be stored over several nodes using Hadoop's distributed file system (HDFS), which ensures fault tolerance and high availability. However, Spark's in-memory computing capabilities greatly accelerate data processing processes, which makes it perfect for machine learning iterative algorithms.

Furthermore, the development of cloud-based data platforms, including Google Cloud Platform, Microsoft Azure, and Amazon Web Services (AWS), has made powerful computing resources and storage options more accessible to a wider range of users. These platforms let businesses scale their AI and ML workloads without making significant investments in physical infrastructure since they offer managed services for data input, processing, and analysis.

An additional crucial component of this connectivity is real-time analytics. Through the utilization of real-time processing frameworks like Apache Flink and streaming data platforms like Apache Kafka, enterprises may quickly react to changing circumstances and obtain insights by doing analytics on the fly. This feature is especially important for applications where rapid data-driven decisions are critical, such fraud detection, network security, and dynamic pricing.

In addition, edge computing is becoming a key tool in big data integration with AI and ML. Edge computing lowers latency and bandwidth consumption by locating computation and data storage closer to the data source. This is crucial for Internet of Things (IoT) applications, self-driving cars, and smart cities, where large volumes of data must be processed in real time at the network's edge.

In general, more effective, scalable, and real-time data processing and analysis are being made possible by the integration of AI and ML with big data technologies, enabling organizations to get deeper insights and make better decisions.

3. Ethical and Responsible AI

Making sure AI and ML technologies are used ethically and responsibly is crucial as they grow more and more integrated into our daily lives. Fairness, accountability, transparency, and the effects of AI systems on society are only a few of the many factors that are included in the broad category of ethical AI. Mitigating bias in AI models is a major difficulty that might result from algorithmic flaws or biased training data. Artificial intelligence (AI) bias can result in unfair decisions, especially in delicate fields like recruiting, financing, and law enforcement. By using more diverse datasets and developing algorithms that take fairness into account, researchers are developing techniques to identify and minimize bias.

Another crucial component of ethical AI is data privacy. The increasing volume of personal data being gathered and processed makes it imperative to protect people's privacy. Models may learn from data without disclosing sensitive information because to techniques like federated learning and differential privacy, which are compliant with more stringent international data protection laws like GDPR.

In order to guarantee that AI systems be utilized responsibly, frameworks and policies for AI governance must be established. This entails establishing moral standards, carrying out effect analyses, and assembling interdisciplinary teams to supervise the creation and application of AI. AI ethics boards are being established by organizations more frequently in order to direct their AI strategy and guarantee adherence to moral guidelines.

Moreover, explainability and transparency are essential for fostering confidence in AI systems. It is necessary to create interpretable models and provide detailed documentation of AI processes in order for users and stakeholders to comprehend how AI choices are made. The goal of explainable AI (XAI) research is to improve human comprehension of complex models.

Finally, it is necessary to discuss how AI will affect society, including how it will affect jobs and economic inequality. AI has the potential to destabilize the economy by dislodging jobs as it automates more work. In order to train workers for new roles in an AI-driven economy, initiatives for workforce transition and education must be developed.

A holistic strategy that addresses social implications, privacy protection, strong governance, bias mitigation, and openness is necessary for ethical and responsible AI. We can make sure that AI technologies are created and applied in ways that benefit society as a whole by giving these factors priority.

4. Emerging Applications of AI and ML

AI and ML are advancing into a wide range of fields, transforming sectors and spurring innovation in ways that were unthinkable a few years ago.

- **Healthcare:** Through improvements in diagnostics, individualized treatment plans, and predictive analytics, AI and ML are revolutionizing patient care in the healthcare industry. When compared to conventional ways, AI-powered diagnostic technologies can diagnose illnesses like cancers or fractures earlier and with greater reliability by analyzing medical images with high accuracy. Utilizing machine learning algorithms, personalized medicine adjusts medications based on each patient's unique genetic profile, increasing effectiveness and decreasing side effects. By using predictive analytics, healthcare practitioners may foresee patient outcomes and hospital resource requirements, which improves patient care and operational efficiency. AI may eventually help with drug discovery by employing algorithms to identify which chemicals are most likely to be effective, which would speed up the creation of new therapies.

- **Finance:** AI is being used by the financial industry for a number of purposes, including algorithmic trading and fraud detection. Large volumes of market data are analyzed in real-time by AI-driven trading algorithms, which enable trades to be executed at speeds and accuracy that are unmatched by humans. Machine learning models sort through transaction data in fraud detection to find suspicious activity, minimizing false positives and improving fraud prevention. AI is also helping risk management, as sophisticated models offer scenario evaluations and risk assessments that are more precise. Financial modeling could undergo even more change because to cutting-edge technologies like quantum computing, which could make it possible to solve intricate optimization issues that are today unsolvable by conventional computers.
- **Agriculture:** AI is being used in precision agriculture to increase farming sustainability and efficiency. Artificial intelligence (AI) systems monitor crop health, soil conditions, and weather patterns by analyzing data from sensors, satellites, and drones. Farmers can optimize pest management, fertilization, and irrigation with this data-driven method, increasing yields while using less resources. AI-guided autonomous tractors and harvesting robots are completing jobs precisely and effectively, saving labor expenses and boosting output. We may anticipate more intelligent system integration in agriculture as AI technology develops, promoting sustainable farming methods and food security.
- **Retail:** AI and ML are transforming the customer experience and operational effectiveness in the retail industry. ML algorithms-powered personalized recommendations improve consumer engagement by making product recommendations based on unique tastes and behavior. AI is optimizing inventory management by forecasting demand patterns and controlling stock levels to cut down on waste and boost availability. AI-powered solutions in logistics improve delivery routes, saving money on transportation and speeding up delivery times. In addition, AI-powered chatbots and virtual assistants are offering

round-the-clock customer support, managing questions and problems with an increasing level of complexity and human-like communication.

- **Transportation:** Artificial intelligence is advancing the transportation sector significantly, especially in the areas of driverless cars and intelligent traffic control. With AI algorithms installed, self-driving cars are able to identify impediments, navigate through challenging situations, and make split-second judgments that protect the safety of its occupants. Utilizing artificial intelligence (AI), smart traffic management systems evaluate traffic patterns and modify signal timings to ease congestion and enhance traffic flow. These developments aim to decrease emissions, shorten travel times, and improve road safety. More effective ride-sharing services and public transportation systems are also being made possible by the use of AI into transportation infrastructure.
- **Manufacturing:** Industry 4.0, or the fourth industrial revolution, is being driven by AI and ML. Automated systems and robots with AI capabilities are accurately and efficiently doing dangerous and repetitive activities. Machine learning (ML) enables predictive maintenance, which reduces maintenance costs and downtime by tracking the health of machines and anticipating problems before they arise. AI-powered QC systems check goods for flaws, guaranteeing excellence and cutting down on waste. With the increasing automation and intelligence of manufacturing processes, we can anticipate lower prices, more productivity, and better quality products.
- **Education:** AI is enhancing administrative effectiveness and personalizing learning experiences in the field of education. Intelligent tutoring systems provide individualized education and feedback by adjusting to each student's unique learning style and pace. AI-driven analytics monitor student progress and pinpoint areas for development, assisting educators in providing focused interventions. Automating administrative processes like scheduling and grading allows teachers to concentrate on instruction. With the use of virtual reality and natural language processing, artificial intelligence in education could lead to more dynamic and immersive learning environments in the future.

As technology and creativity continue to push the frontiers of what is possible across a variety of industries, these new uses of AI and ML are just the beginning.

5. Quantum Computing

By utilizing the ideas of quantum mechanics to process information in ways that classical computers are unable to, quantum computing offers a revolutionary departure from previous paradigms in computing. Because of the phenomena of superposition, quantum bits, also known as qubits, can exist concurrently in several states, in contrast to classical bits, which indicate either a 0 or a 1. This greatly increases the computing capability of quantum computers for specific tasks by enabling them to execute numerous calculations in parallel.

- **QML, or Quantum Machine Learning:** There is a lot of potential for improving machine learning algorithms with quantum computing. Quantum algorithms have the ability to enhance pattern recognition skills, optimize complicated systems, and speed up data processing. Support vector machines and clustering algorithms, for example, might handle high-dimensional data more effectively in the quantum realm than in the conventional one.
- **Quantum Optimization:** Quantum computing has enormous potential to solve optimization problems, which are fundamental to many disciplines such as engineering, finance, and logistics. Using big, complicated datasets, quantum annealing and other quantum optimization techniques can find optimal or nearly optimal solutions to challenging optimization problems considerably more quickly.
- **Quantum Simulation:** Simulating quantum systems is one of the most interesting uses for quantum computing. This is especially true for disciplines like chemistry and material science, where a grasp of atomic and molecular interactions is essential. It would be hard to accurately represent chemical reactions, pharmacological interactions, and novel materials using classical computers; yet, quantum simulations can shed light on these topics.
- **Quantum Cryptography:** The field of cryptography is significantly impacted by quantum computing. Quantum cryptography presents a challenge to traditional encryption techniques but also provides new avenues for safe communication. Theoretically unbreakable encryption is made possible by quantum key distribution (QKD), guaranteeing the safe transfer of sensitive data.
- **Challenges and Future Prospects:** Despite its promise, quantum computing is still in its infancy and faces several

technological obstacles. The two main challenges are error correction and keeping qubits in a stable state (coherence). Ongoing study and development, though, are quickly expanding the sector. Businesses such as Google, IBM, and startups are making progress in creating quantum processors that have higher qubit counts and better error rates.

As quantum technology develops, data science will probably see revolutionary breakthroughs that make it possible to solve issues that were previously unsolvable and spur innovation across a range of sectors. By pushing the limits of what is computationally possible, the combination of quantum computing with AI and ML will create new opportunities.

Conclusion

Data science employing AI and ML has a very bright future thanks to ongoing algorithmic improvements, huge data integration, ethical considerations, and new applications. These sectors will open up new avenues for impact on society and innovation as they develop.

Made in the USA
Monee, IL
04 November 2026

67384730R00148